The Sexual Outlaw
A DOCUMENTARY

Other Books by John Rechy

CITY OF NIGHT

NUMBERS

THIS DAY'S DEATH

THE VAMPIRES

THE FOURTH ANGEL

The Sexual Outlaw

A DOCUMENTARY

BY JOHN RECHY

A Non-Fiction Account, with
Commentaries, of Three Days and Nights
In the Sexual Underground

GROVE PRESS, INC.

NEW YORK

ISBN: 0-394-41343-1
Grove Press ISBN: 0-8021-0131-3

Library of Congress Catalog Card Number: 76-54487

First Edition 1977
Second Printing 1977

Manufactured in the United States of America

Distributed by Random House, Inc., New York

GROVE PRESS, INC., 196 West Houston Street, New York, N.Y. 10014

For all
the anonymous
outlaws.

And for the memory of my mother.

ACKNOWLEDGMENTS

WITHOUT IN ANY way indicating that they agree or disagree with any or all of the points of view expressed in this book, I would like to thank the following:

Evelyn Hooker, for having waged "the fight" years ago, when it was truly dangerous to do so.

The publishers of *One Magazine,* the organizers of The Mattachine Society, and all the other courageous "old fighters" (now often sadly ignored) of the advance guard—and the "new fighters" of Stonewall.

The National Endowment for the Arts, for their grant during, but not specifically for, the writing of this book.

Glenna Luschei, for her encouragement and for years-long friendship.

Albert L. Gordon, for his strong opinions, which often conflicted with mine but always elicited constructive consideration.

Bill Regan, for sharing his definite points of view.

Barry Copilow, and many others, for important data, and trust.

Don Allen, editor of my first four books, for his belief in me throughout the years.

Floriano Vecchi, for so much friendship, and affection.

Melodie Johnson, for her invaluable opinions—and a sustaining, uniquely warm friendship.

And Marsha Kinder, for her encouragement and creative criticism—and for a very special loving friendship.

CONTENTS

FOREWORD

Like the incidents narrated in this book, the locales included are real. However, with the exception of impossible-to-disguise locations, the names of some streets, places, and areas of the sexhunt have been changed. Their descriptions remain as they exist.

Since the sexual underground explored in this book is a floating one, it is possible that a few of the places included here will have stopped being "active" by the time of publication. Already the Santa Monica pier has been demolished. Yet for each place that is torn down or busted, similar ones will instantly appear.

In presenting a true spectrum of the promiscuous experience, I have at times altered the sequence of events. For example, the incidents described on pages 223–226 happened in 1973, but I have placed them in the present of this book; and some contacts occurring in another weekend, or on a weekday, are included here, and replace others.

The speeches and some of the answers in the interview sections have been expanded from their original versions.

This book is set in Los Angeles, but it might as easily be set in any other large American city. Each has its comparable sexual underground. Smaller cities have their own modifications.

J.R.

"Living an experience, a particular fate, is accepting it fully. . . . It is not a matter of explaining and solving, but of experiencing and describing."
—ALBERT CAMUS,
The Myth of Sisyphus

"And still deeper the meaning of that story of Narcissus, who because he could not grasp the tormenting, mild image he saw in the fountain, plunged into it and was drowned. But that same image, we ourselves see. . . . It is the image of the ungraspable phantom of life; and this is the key to it all."
—HERMAN MELVILLE,
Moby Dick

Friday

11:07 A.M.   *The Apartment. The Gym.*

HE PREPARES his body for the hunt. A dancer at the bar. A boxer in the ring. Prepares ritualistically for the next three days of outlaw sex. The arena will be streets, parks, alleys, tunnels, garages, movie arcades, bathhouses, beaches, movie backrows, tree-sheltered avenues, late-night orgy rooms, dark yards.

The city is Los Angeles.

Beyond the window of his apartment, yellow-green palmtrees stand aloofly. Later they will watch distantly as he prowls through the floating sexual underground.

He is stripped to sweat-faded cutoffs. His pectorals are already pumped from repetitions of dumbbell presses on a bench, inclined, flat, then declined; engorged further by dumbbell flyes extending the chest muscles into the sweeping spread below the collar. His "lats"—congested from set after set of chin-ups—slow, fast, wide-grip, medium-grip, weights strapped about his waist for added resistance that will allow him to do only half-chins as the muscles protest—flare from armpits to mid-torso. His legs are rigid from squats held tense at half-point.

Round, full, his arms are hard, hard from sets of curls, the dumbbell an appendage of strength and power in his hands. The horseshoe indention at his triceps is engraved sharply by repetitions of barbell extensions.

Now the barbell—chrome, red-collared—rests at his feet. Dark weights are balanced harmoniously on each side of the bar. He bends over, jerking the bar widely in one move to his shoulders, and barely pausing, lifts it over his head and lowers it behind his neck. The deltoid muscles waken in welcome shock. One repetition, another, and another. Eight. Nine. Ten. He reverses the motions, places the bar at his feet. Breathing deeply, he moves away from the bar for thirty seconds only. Sweat coats his body like oil and stains the cutoffs at his groin. Deliberately he avoids the mirror on the wall. That crucial encounter comes only at the last.

He does another set of standing presses with the loaded barbell, heavier now with added dark round plates. Seven sets in all, decreasing repetitions, adding weight each set.

He lies on the bench, declined, his feet strapped at the ankles with a belt at the upper end. He raises his torso only a few precious inches, hands at his back, crunching the abdominal muscles until the ridges ache. Seventy-five repetitions. His stomach demands to stop. Twenty-five more. Muscles strain against the flesh. Twenty-five more.

He jumps off the bench. He's panting, his body is electric.

He looks down at the loaded barbell. He will attempt one more press. He adds plates to each side. He raises the bar to his shoulders, begins to lift it over his head. Muscles protesting, the weight pauses midway. His will insists. He challenges the moment's stasis.

Breathing orgasmically, he exhales and with a thrust of his hips he raises the bar over his head.

Now in its mysterious rite of destruction and construction, the body is rushing fresh blood to pulsing muscles, making them stronger and bigger, preparing them for the next, heavier onslaught, the next steel workout. Tomorrow his muscles will be larger than today.

He stands before the mirror. His cock strains against the sweat-bleached cutoffs.

1:04 P.M. *Santa Monica. The Beach.*

He parked his car in the lot near the crumbling pier. Here, tribal crowds thin into exile territory. Near a squat, short restroom, men on towels watch new arrivals to the beach.

As he walks on the hot sand, he carries a beach mat and a thermos full of protein to feed his muscles throughout the day. He's wearing his workout trunks over a very brief bikini which snaps at the sides. His already copper tan is rendered deeper by a film of oil. From behind blue-tinted sunglasses, he surveys those gathered here, intercepts looks—but he moves along the sand toward the ocean. Like the day and the sky, the ocean is blue and magical.

At the edge of the beach, huge, rough rocks separate this portion from another. He climbs over them, toward the fire-gutted skeleton of a pier. Decaying boards slant toward the sand. The beach extends in a lapping tongue; men lie singly in that parabola of sand—the more committed in brief bikinis, or almost naked—genitals sheltered only by bunched trunks.

Locating his beach mat, Jim strips to the white bikini; he pushes it up even farther on his thighs. He drinks from the thermos of protein. Now he stretches on the sand, eyes closed, aware of prowling figures rehearsing for the balletic cruising already commencing mutely under the shadowy pier.

Not yet. For him, not yet.

Jim—he calls himself that sometimes, sometimes Jerry, sometimes John—removes the bikini, lies boldly naked on the sand. Because of a mixture of Anglo and Latin bloods, his skin quickly converts the sun's rays into tan; the tan turns his eyes bluer; long-lashed eyes which almost compromise the rugged good looks of his face, framed by dark hair. The sun licks the sweat from his body.

As he lies passive to the sun's indifferent love, he imagines how his body looks to others: naked, tanned, hairs gleaming, muscles sequined with sweat on oil. . . .

He wakes abruptly. A youngman is squatting next to him, hand sliding along Jim's muscled body toward the hardening cock.

A few yards away, an old fisherman, his wife huddled on the shore like ragged flotsam beside him, throws his line into the restive ocean.

2:25 P.M. *The Pier.*

Jim twisted his body away from the youngman's spidery touch. Not yet. He wanted more sun; he lay longer like a sacrificial warrior surrendering to it.

Now he's ready. He drinks again from the thermos. He puts on the sweat-faded cutoffs, leaving the bikini, his sunglasses, the thermos, and the beach mat in a secluded place. He looks at the gutted pier.

Years ago it supported a carnival street, brazen in its garish tackiness, a discord of colors and "architecture" warring furiously. Tattoo parlors with butterflies, hearts, nude women; arcades lighting up neon pinball mazes; imitation-foreign restaurants with patchwork faces. Then came the rock groups and their followers, the flowers in their hair soon to wilt; summer radicals drove out old sailors and derelicts. Inevitably the dinosauric demolition machines came crushing everything into dust. The shells of buildings remained, as if the pier had been bombed. Then came fire. And another fire. The pier became a blackened skeleton. Below it, a subterranean world thrived among falling posts and dank sand.

A gladiator, Jim stares at the arena under the pier. The sunlight stops sharply at the mouth of the rotting wooden cavern. An invisible boundary observed by the light. Beyond the twilight opening, the mouth darkens deeply.

As he moves into the periphery of the dusky cavern, he's aware of his bare feet touching the hot sand. He pauses, to feel the texture of the grains of crushed white earth. At first there is the heat of the sand, where the sun has scorched for hours. Just at the moment that he would have moved to break the sensation of heat, his feet sink below the surface. He looks down. Among the pale grains, some gleam in glassy pinpoints. The sand forms mounds. As his feet move barely, feeling the surface heat again but not as intense, the sand forms new curves, almost pinnacles. Rushing grains slide down to fill new hollows. He sees shapes of vague geometry. He looks a few feet away and sees a series of ripples in the sand. A choppy breeze chose this one area to carve. Only a few inches away, the beach is moist where the retreating tide clung farthest. There, the sand looks brown. He sees the undecipherable message the scratchy footprints of a bird have left. He walks toward the moist parabola. Only his toes touch the moist section. His heels remain on the hot dry beach. He's aware—but the perception is not as clear as he anticipated—of the dual sensation. He stands there for moments. Then he buries his feet deliberately in the moisture. He feels the cool grains of sand sliding, surrounding. He takes a few more steps and looks back at his footprints molded parallel to the scratchings of the bird. He inhales the odor of water and sand and seaweeds and the moisture clinging to the sunless rotting pier. He presses one foot, to etch a deeper footprint on the wet sand. Then he moves on.

Under the pier, the sand is moist. He passes from day to twilight to night in moments. In this darkness only violence or sex can happen. An experienced hunter, Jim knows that although he sees no one yet in the murky mist—and his eyes are adjusting quickly—soon, very soon, figures will emerge. Shadows within shadows.

For moments, he stands in the twilit area; exhibiting his body, making sure, as always, that he is clearly seen.

Look. There's a black solitary outline in the depths of the pier. Jim moves farther into the shadowed world. The sand, untouched by the sun, becomes wetter. His eyes adjust totally.

Beyond, the tide rises. *Swoosh!* Swoosh. *Swoosh!* Swoosh. Sounds echoing in the dark. Through slits left exposed by boards fallen in diagonal patterns on the sand, shafts of light penetrate like cold knives.

Jim moves fully into exile country. Just as he knew, there are many other outlaws here. At least six shadows materialize into bodies as they glide closer like hypnotized birds. Against a pole, two men are pasted to each other. Muted sighs and moans blend with the lapping sound of the ocean beyond.

Knowing that a loose circle of ghostly figures is focusing on him as he stands in a pocket of dim light, Jim pulls out his cock as if to piss. Quickly, a tall slender young outlaw holds Jim's cock. Almost as quickly, a short, tightly sculpted, goodlooking youngman, completely naked, trunks in his hand, is licking Jim's sweaty chest. The moist tongue slides down Jim's stomach, encloses the cock still held by the tall one. For seconds only, Jim inches farther into the dim-lit cave within the darker cave, so that his gleaming body being adored will be visible like a pornographic photograph.

Moving back into the shadows, Jim reaches down and grasps the blood-flushed cock of the youngman sucking him. It feels like an extension of his own. Now both Jim and the naked youngman stand, cocks pressed together in one thick shaft, which the tall one sucks.

Other shadows cluster, watching, forming other intimate groups nearby. The tall youngman licks Jim's balls, the tongue explores his buttocks. Swiftly turning his body around, torso bending forward, back to Jim, the naked youngman parts his own buttocks, inviting Jim's full cock to enter the waiting asshole. With his finger, Jim feels the tiny knot of flesh, locating the entry for his cock. The tall man thrusts his tongue into the crack of Jim's buttocks. The naked youngman reaches back, guiding Jim's cock into the saliva-moistened ass.

But now Jim's not sure he wants to fuck. A switch has been touched, loosing an electric sexuality; he does not want to end the scene with orgasm—not yet; his flexing muscles are riding on the kinetic motion of the earlier workout; he will require much more than these moments' sextime.

But the firm round ass grinds, insisting. Jim lets his erect cock touch the puckered point of entry, and then slide up against the crack, mixed sweat lubricating cock, ass, pubic hair. The tall youngman slides on the sand between Jim's arched legs and licks his balls. With one hand Jim grasps the slender waist of the naked youngman, with the other he holds the other's round cock about to burst.

Clustered throughout under the crumbling boards in the water-decayed cavern, other outlaw torsos shine darkly in the mottled light. The sound of sucking, of sliding flesh. Sighs. Sounds of orgasm float through the darkness.

Two more outlines have materialized about Jim—he feels more mouths. His mind explodes with outlaw images:

men and men and men, forbidden contacts, free, time crushed, intimate forbidden strangers.

Sensations increase, a tongue slides over his balls, another on his ass, his cock still only simulating entry into the anxious asshole. And now his lips are on those of a beautiful youngman suddenly beside him, and in one swift thrust Jim's cock enters the grinding ass, and his hand holds the squirting cock of the naked youngman he's fucking.

Male and male and male, hard limbs, hard cocks, hard muscles, hard stomachs, strong bodies, male and male.

Jim is close to coming. His hand is sticky with the cum of the naked youngman he's still fucking, and he rubs the moist cum on the face of the tall man licking his balls, and Jim and the beautiful youngman continue to kiss.

Not yet!

Jim breaks away from the bodies.

Again in the shaft of light, he adjusts his trunks. Carefully avoiding the broken boards, the rusted nails, he moves toward the sun. Into the bright beach.

He blinks.

He returns to his beach mat, again he drinks from the thermos of protein.

Removing his trunks, he walks naked into the ocean's tide, letting the water wash his body.

The old fisherman and his ragged wife continue obliviously staring toward the horizon vanishing in the rising mist.

Clothes adjusted now—the warm sun evaporating the moisture on his body—blue-tinged sunglasses covering his eyes again, beach mat rolled, thermos under one arm, Jim looks at the dark shell of crumbling pier. Nothing seems to move there, no sound comes from it.

A youngman emerges from out of the scorched darkness. He and Jim glance at each other in recognition. Is that the youngman he fucked or the one he kissed?

They walk away in opposite directions.

VOICE OVER: *Promiscuous Rage*

I SPEAK TO a mixed group of gay and straight people:

The promiscuous homosexual is a sexual revolutionary. Each moment of his outlaw existence he confronts repressive laws, repressive "morality." Parks, alleys, subway tunnels, garages, streets—these are the battlefields.

To the sexhunt he brings a sense of choreography, ritual, and mystery—sex-cruising with an electrified instinct that sends and receives messages of orgy at any moment, any place.

Who are these outlaws?

Single men, married men; youngmen, older ones; black, white; your brothers, your fathers; students, teachers, bodybuilders, doctors, construction workers, coaches, writers, cowboys, truck drivers, motorcyclists, dancers, weightlifters, actors, painters, athletes, politicians, businessmen, lawyers, cops.

What creates the sexual outlaw?

Rage.

None more easily prosecuted—even so-called liberals condone his persecution—his is the only minority against whose existence there are laws. Labeled a seducer of unwilling partners, he knows that "homosexual rape" is rape of homosexuals by heterosexuals. Branded a child molester, he knows heterosexual molestation far, far exceeds that of homosexual. And he knows that what police chiefs proclaim "rampant violent gay crime" is crime by straight gay-haters against homosexuals.

A man emerges staggering out of the brush in a park, his face smashed in blood. Yelling "Queer! Queer!" four thugs kicked and beat him with sticks. The cops are called. Not one shows up.

But tell them two men are fucking, and they'll storm the area in minutes.

Easy, often set-up homosexual arrests may be callously used to cover up statistically the staggering number of unsolved murders, robberies, rapes. An arrest—often arbitrary (you were there)—brings instant punishment, even when you're finally proved "not guilty": handcuffing, incarceration, insults, the outrageous fees of attorneys, bail, the slaughtering anxiety of court appearances, and your life waits. Widespread entrapment—creating the "crime" it insists it wants to curb—gives cops a destructive means of purging latent devils. Cops in vice trials clumsily lie, knowing that sex convictions will be brought in on the flimsiest evidence. Threatened by prison, homosexuals will bargain to plead guilty to uncommitted charges.

Buddy-locked in steamy squad-car intimacy, cops cruising gay areas turn up their speakers to screech: "Cocksuckers!"

Homosexuals in jails are threatened with castration and shock as "cures." Official routine beatings and roundups of gays by cops encourage murderous lunatics to prowl cruising areas with guns, broken bottles, rocks, police clubs.

Jack Paar on television and Liza Minnelli in a magazine joke about "fags."

Ancestral rage. Death by sword or other torture decreed for homosexuals by ecclesiastical courts. Burnings at the stake into the nineteenth century.

"I'd rather go out with a fag than a boring man any day," says Marisa Berenson in Newsweek.

Rage.

Handcuffs, incarceration, courts, bankruptcy—all because of the mere accusation of a gay act, actual or only solicited.

Life and prison sentences are still a reality for homosexuals. Men convicted in California of merely asking to make it with another adult male must register as "sex offenders" for the rest of their lives; they are through in many professions and in all requiring state licensing. "Lewd conduct" convictions, also requiring sex-offender registration, have been brought in on assertions that two men were kissing, dancing together, even holding hands.

Suicides.

"Sex offenders" may be brought in for questioning by the police at any time in connection with real sex crimes, no matter how remote in nature to the basis of the original arrest.

Indiscriminately wrecked lives. Lost jobs, broken families. Constant fear. Rage.

A priest tries to organize a "Homosexuals Anonymous." *Thou may want to, but thou shalt not actually fuck or suck.* It results immediately in a suicide attempt.

Two adult males are followed by cops to a completely secluded dark area. After minutes, the cops flash lights into the car, pull the men out, beat them. Convicted of sodomy, the two are sentenced to eight years in prison. The Supreme Court refuses them a hearing.

Cowardly punks crushed tightly in hot cars, hot knees touching hot knees in hateful intimacy, throw rocks, bottles, and refuse at cars in cruising areas. "Fags!" they scream, echoing the cops and looking forward to the night they will bring guns with them.

Rage at law as criminal, doctors as perpetrators of sick myths. Religion as killer. Rage at the selective use of Biblical scripture to condone hatred.

The only main minority never to receive even token acknowledgment on a major-party platform is the homosexual minority. Even the vague phrase "sexual preference" has been knocked out.

"You are polluted and filthy," reads a pamphlet circu-

*lated at gay gatherings by "Jesus people." "You will not be
gay in hell, but tormented far worse than in this life."*

"Homosexual acts are inherently immoral, abnormal,
perverted, disgraceful, degenerate, degrading, and criminal," screeches an "Information Paper" issued by a Los
Angeles Deputy Chief of Police for wide police and
"constituent" circulation.

The victim of a mugging becomes the criminal if he's
gay. An easily claimed homosexual advance is an acceptable defense for murder: "I beat the queer because he tried
to make me, sir."

*"KILL FAGS!"—words scratched on walls of Hollywood
toilets.*

In this context the sexual outlaw flourishes. The pressures produce him, create his defiance. Knowing that each
second his freedom may be ripped away arbitrarily, he lives
fully at the brink. Promiscuity is his righteous form of
revolution.

No stricture—legal, medical, religious—will ever stop
him. It will only harden his defiance. Neither sinful,
criminal, nor sick—he knows that to try to force him not to
be a homosexual *is* sinful, criminal, and sick—and as
impossible as forcing a heterosexual not to be a
heterosexual.

Why is the homosexual hated? Since he is not a child
molester nor a seducer of the unwilling, how does he
threaten the straight world?

He weakens the "moral fabric"? Did Michelangelo? Da
Vinci? Socrates? Did Proust? Did Shakespeare with the
sonnets? Did Tchaikovsky?

Do we threaten survival of the species? We provide a
stopgap against a dangerously burgeoning population.

What is the real reason for the hatred?

I pause in my talk to this mixed group. Soon I'll go on to
define what I believe is the real "gay threat." Now I look at
the audience, and to the homosexuals here I want to say:

"You have an untested insurrectionary power that can
bring down their straight world. Use it—take the war
openly into the streets. As long as they continue to kill us,

fuck and suck on every corner! Question their hypocritical, murderous, uptight world."

But I don't say that. Why?

Because promiscuity, like the priesthood, requires total commitment and sacrifice.

3:48 P.M. *The Restroom by the Pier.*

JIM STANDS PISSING at the urinal, aware of a man sitting in the open stall at the end of the row. A youngman is lingering before the metallic mirror. Finished, Jim turns, his trunks still open, allowing his cock to remain exposed before the man in the stall. The man licks his lips in signal. The youngman at the mirror advances.

Jim moves into the stall and puts his cock in the waiting mouth.

The other watches.

Jim pulls away, adjusting his clothes hurriedly as they hear footsteps entering the restroom.

The silent identification is given in a glance by the new presence, a goodlooking bodybuilder. Jim's hand drops lightly before his own groin; the man who just entered touches it. The youngman who stood at the mirror has moved into the stall with the other. Aware that they may be interrupted at any moment, Jim and the other move into a vacant stall. Open mouths kiss, hands touch trunk-straining groins. The two bodies thrust against each other, oblivious to all danger. Mouths devour tongues; hands pull down trunks, touch hard muscles. Jim feels the other's warm cum on his stomach, and his own cock stretches, bursts, pours out the withheld thick white liquid onto the other's smeared cock.

A hostile presence enters the restroom. He is totally unaware of the sex-charged currents.

The outlaws separate.

Outside, Jim feels a sad joy.

The sun and the beach are white now. Sea birds on the sand are clustered in rows facing the ocean.

Jim has spoken not a word to anyone today. Not one.

MONTAGE: *The City*

LATE ONE SUNDAY a fire swept acres of forested canyons, threatening the outskirts of the city. At first it was only a cloud on the horizon, like the fog that invades the beaches. But this time the cloud came from inland. It thickened. The lacy white darkened, tinged with gray. It floated across the city toward the ocean as if to connect with the smog. At night the air hung heavy with ashy clouds.

The next morning the sun came out hot, a luminous orange as if everything were on fire without flames. An eerie phosphorescence covered Los Angeles. As the afternoon sun attempted powerfully to penetrate the clouds of smoke, the city turned fiercer orange. On the sidewalks, through the patches of palmtree shadows, the glow created pools of frozen fire.

As the residents fled dark with ashes, the ravaging flames devoured hilly acres.

In the city, you stepped out and tasted the ashes, felt them on your face. The odor of fire singed your senses. Behind smoky clouds, the sun was an incandescent balloon.

When the fire was over, the residents returned doggedly to rebuild their homes in the exact areas scorched, and they braced for the rains, recalling the months-long storm in the sixties when an avalanche of mud swallowed the rebuilt houses.

In Southern California.

Shaped on the map like a coffin—center of prettydeath, flowers already here for the burial, or miraculous recovery. Death or purification. By fire, water, quivering earth.

Shaped too on the map like a twisted handmirror—world center of narcissism. The silver, colored movies, the golden weather, the white beaches from Zuma to Laguna invite the glorious burnt bodies to perform a ritual of exhibitionism under the adoring sun.

And until the impotent citizens rose in wrath to ban it, a nude beach beyond sand and craggy rocks nestled under steep cliffs. Nude men. Nude women. (The male outlaws climbed the rocks farther on, to dangerous secluded caves just barely above the roaring tide threatening to enter. Against the rocks bodies meshed with bodies under the promiscuous sun.)

City of lost angels.

Death, narcissism, and fire.

Health cults and criminal smog. Sick cops and saintly sinners. Beach and forest. Paradise and hell.

Hot Santa Ana winds pant into the city.

The city that thrives on disaster. A huge street painting at the corner of Santa Monica and Butler depicts its collapse—truncated freeways, ocean flooding the desert. Daily, radio stations document freeway disasters: truck jackknifed, car overturned, pedestrian wandering on freeway. . . . The reports have the rhythm of a song, and the unspoken refrain is: *Survive!*

Life is lived at least seven degrees—to choose a number—more fully here than elsewhere. Los Angeles is a metaphor for the future. It will happen here first, the best and the worst.

After all, isn't this the last frontier?—here that all the expectations bunched tightly and seeded—when there was no more land to push into. Here that the country ends, its energy now electrified by intimations of disaster. Beyond—is suicide, where the country plunges into the waiting ocean.

Survive!

Fire swallows, the earth rumbles, mudslides crush. Homes collapse like toys. But new houses and lives are rebuilt on the brink. SLIDE AREA—signs along the awesome coast boast proudly. Jagged cliffs challenge along the ocean:

Survive!

SCIENTISTS PREDICT MASSIVE EARTHQUAKE IN L.A. WITHIN YEAR, the newspaper proclaims. You incorporate the knowledge and live life *eight* degrees more fully now.

At the corner of Highland and Franklin, when Hollywood traffic is a crush of metal and chrome in the sweating sun, skinny shirtless boys take turns standing on their heads on a crumbling stone wall—exhibitionistically breaking records before the involuntarily captive audience.

Survive!

If the earth shrugs and thrusts this glorious city into the ocean, the rest of the country will follow, with hurricanes, tornadoes, fires, tidal waves, and killer winds.

5:12 P.M. *Hollywood Boulevard.*

HE PARKS ON A side street. He's wearing Levi's and cowboy boots, no shirt. Sunglasses. Though his muscles have lost their pump from the morning's workout, they are beginning to ache deliciously, a signal of the body's rite of resurrection.

Traffic jammed, Hollywood Boulevard is at its trashiest under a stoned white sun. This street—a tattered crazy old woman, sweet at times, dangerous at times—is clashing rows of tawdry clothes shops, smelly quick-food counters, mangy arcades, patchy stores, movie theaters. Beyond the tops of frayed buildings, palmtrees look away disdainfully.

Periodically, campaigns will be mounted to clean up the boulevard. Merchants will call for a return to its former elegance. Yet no one can remember when Hollywood Boulevard, unworthy symbol of glamor, *was* elegant. Even stars' names nobly engraved in bronze into the sidewalks have turned gray and sullen. Castouts from the American myth glorified by films have taken over like locusts. Without even noticing it, the outcasts step on the names of the great stars. This is the exiles' turf now, fought for in blood skirmishes with merchants, cops, citizens' groups. The outcasts endure on the carnival street.

Jim walks shirtless along it. Even when the weather is

cool, he wears little—partly discipline of his body, partly proud exhibitionism. He nods to other outlaws. Other malehustlers. Though on the beach he cruised only for excitement, on the boulevard—and on Selma, the tacky side street he will soon move into—he will hustle for money; then he will most often pretend to be "straight"—uncomfortably rationalizing the subterfuge by reminding himself that those attracted to him will usually—though certainly not always—want him to be that, like the others of his breed.

They stand now, his breed, in clusters outside the Gold Cup Coffee Shop, the Pioneer Chicken. Youngmen—younger certainly than he, he knows, though he doesn't show his age—who recognize him easily as one of them and feeling the bond of exiles nod and say, What's goin on? Masculine men with shifting eyes, watching for clients and cops.

Jim may pause for a few words, but not for long; he's an outsider among outsiders.

At Highland and Hollywood, the queens, awesome, defiant Amazons, are assuming their stations. The white queens are bleached and pale, the black ones shiny and purple. Extravagant in short skirts, bouffant hairdos, luminous unreal mouths and eyes. The transsexuals are haughty in their new credentials.

"Ummmm-*ummmmm*," a black queen approves Jim's bare muscles as he moves toward Selma.

Men in cars, off work for the weekend, are circling the streets for male prostitutes.

5:39 P.M. *Selma.*

A semi-residential district just one block south of the boulevard, the area of Selma at first seems unlikely as a main area for malehustling: Old squeaky houses have been broken up into rooms populated by old ladies and gentlemen who keep birds, maybe parrots. A shocked Baptist church, white and pure, glowers at the hustlers who use its steps and pillars to display their bodies for sale, occasionally strumming guitars until the cops come by. A large parking lot sits dully behind the Catholic church—all grand steeples and mute mystery—on Sunset Boulevard. A small deserted playground is locked behind meshed wire. Car-repair garages, crumbling closed hamburger stands patched with torn cardboard, more parking lots—this, at first, is Selma. But soon after, it's male prostitutes standing singly or in groups along the street, at corners, before rooming houses providing ready access for paid contacts.

Jim walks along this familiar street.

"What's happenin?" A blond hustler who like himself has survived many streets, many cities, many nights asked Jim that question.

"Not much—with you?" Jim answers. He pauses; the two stand eyeing the prospective clients cruising the blocks.

For long, the two, Jim and this blond man, were hostilely aware of each other—a hostility conveyed by the fact that they would cross the street to avoid direct encounter. Why? Mutual recognition. Although Jim is dark, the other blond, both are husky, and each is much classier, yes, than the younger, much younger, boys and men who flash and sputter in their gaudy—beautiful—youth; who will not survive, no—the streets devouring them and replacing them with fresher bodies, each day; who will remember the times when they glimpsed other worlds, glimpses made possible only by their young bodies and only for interludes.

But Jim and this blond hustler have other than that, a certain street elegance which speaks of rare street survival. Yes; and that was what formed the mute hostility, now mute bond, the unstated secrets each knew intuitively about the other's survival: You're older than you look. You love the streets even when they fight you—and you go on, with style. You're smarter than you act, and you're not so tough. And we both know— ... But that remains unexchanged.

"Making it, making it," the blond hustler answers. He's wearing a tanktop which shows off broad shoulders.

Jim expands his. They laugh briefly, glancing at each other and away.

After many nights avoiding direct encounter, they

spoke; a night when each decided not to cross the street in avoidance. In a sense they startled each other into speaking, and the blond one said, "What's happenin?" and Jim answered, "Not much—with you?" "Making it, making it." And so it became a litany, a rote message of survival, repeated each encounter afterwards, except that they would alternate in asking the first question, assuming a mutuality. Today it was the blond man's turn.

They split. Jim walks on. A man drives up behind him, stops, motions him over. Jim is suspicious, the man stopped too quickly—hardly had a chance to see him. "Looking to make some money?" he asks Jim. Convinced the man is a vice cop—and he's driving a suspicious Plymouth—Jim walks right up to the window. The driver leans over. Jim says, "Fuck off!" Looking back, prepared to warn him, he sees that the blond hustler too is avoiding the same man.

Despite its dangers, Jim loves this street. Despite— . . . He remembers with what anxiety he returned to it after years away. He blocks that memory.

Another car has slowed down. But Jim doesn't encourage him either;—he's got to be extra cautious. He's on probation.

FLASHBACK: *Selma. A Year and a Half Ago.*

He hadn't even seen the man. It was a Friday, like tonight. He had just been driven back to the street by a man he had just made money from. He hadn't noticed the car parked by the lot behind the Catholic church until the driver blew his horn at him. Jim glanced at him. The man waved him over. Jim crossed the street, stood on the sidewalk near the car. The man, slightly out of shape, veering toward premature middle-age, opened the passenger door. "Get in?"

Jim did.

"I got some bucks burning a hole in my pocket," the man said.

"I could use them," Jim said.

"I know an alley we can go to—haven't got much time."

"Uh, first let's get straight how much and what for," Jim

said. "I, uh, don't do anything." He was not at all attracted
to this man; Jim would merely allow him to blow him.

"Okay with me," the man said. "I just dig your body.
How's twenty bucks for a few minutes on a dark street?"
When Jim agreed, the man started the car, drove on, turned
the corner, stopped at the intersection at Sunset Boulevard.
Two hands thrust suddenly from the sidewalk through the
open window pulled Jim roughly back by the shoulders.

"Vice officers!—you're under arrest," both men said.

Jim was handcuffed, taken to the Hollywood station,
booked for prostitution, fingerprinted, frisked intimately
about the groin. That night other street hustlers greeted
each other noisily in jail throughout the night. Jim was
bailed out by a friend. That same night—dark morning—he
was back hustling on Selma.

5:55 P.M. *Selma.*

He's on probation now—for about six more months.
What angers Jim most is that in his arrest report—to cover
up the illegal entrapment—the cop said Jim had approached him and asked for sexmoney; it angers him
fiercely even to remember, because such an approach
would violate his rigid style.

A man has been circling the block, eyeing him, looking
back, pausing, returning. After another U-turn, the man
stops. Jim sees a large, blond, well-dressed man. Jim walks
very slowly toward the open window.

"You look good enough to eat," the man calls out.
"Where you headed?"

"Nowhere—just hanging out."

"Want to get in and talk?"

Jim doesn't. He wants to study the man further. If he
even gets in the car, and the man's a cop, he'll have
violated a condition of his probation.

"You've got a gorgeous body, worth paying for," the
man says.

Jim loves to hear his body praised. He stretches it.

"Can we get together?" the man asks. "Say, you're not a
cop, are you?"

Jim laughs. "Fuck no—are you?"

"Of course not." As verification, he allows his hand to dangle out the window and touch Jim's groin lightly. "Let's go to my place."

"I don't do anything," Jim says.

"I don't want you to," the man says.

6:17 P.M.   *Laurel Canyon. Someone's Home.*

"Actually I'm a very well-known writer. I've written several books."

The man's home is all brown leather and plastic; glass windows for walls. Trees protect it all. Drawings and photographs decorate the bedroom.

"Yes," the large blond man continues, "I'm told I'm a very talented writer. So you see, I have my . . . intellect, and you, well, you have your body—that's your talent. We both have something beautiful."

Jim lies naked on the man's bed. The man sits beside him fully dressed.

"Of course I'd like to have a body like yours," the man goes on—defensively, Jim knows, because he desires Jim and will pay to have him and Jim does not desire him, "but not if it meant—well—that I'd be not as . . . creative—smart—as—well— . . . People with beautiful bodies aren't very— . . . They— . . ."

Jim listens with secret amusement. And indeed he believes in the construction of his body as equal art form. Determined hours of thrusting and pushing iron. The result, the muscular body, is put on display; his prize will be to be desired.

His naked brown body is stark on the white sheets. Jim feels the man's adoring tongue over his flesh.

Afterwards, the man wants to arrange to see him again. But Jim will not commit himself. Paying him twenty dollars, the man tells Jim: "I want to give you more than we agreed—but I don't have any more cash with me. I'll give you a check. What's your name?"

"It's— . . . Skip the check," Jim says.

VOICE OVER: *Interview 1*

A WRITER FOR a literary magazine calls me up about an interview. I'm wary. I ask him to send me some of the interviews he's done. They're good, and with writers I know. When he calls up again, I agree. My place or his? His.

I arrive at the building. Two-story Spanish-style apartments, gardens with bleeding flowers kept neat by—of course—an oriental gardener: like a forties movie. Barbara Stanwyck might answer the doorbell. Now I realize I've been here before. With the interviewer's neighbor? it amuses me to think. Maybe with his roommate. That would be— . . . Or— . . . ! No, impossible.

Yes. The man who opens the door is a man I've been with, anonymously, right in this apartment. Instantly we recognize each other. Identities and splintered memories spiral. The first time, neither had known who the other was. Then—I was a silent street figure. Now—here I am a writer, and there he is the interviewer! Finally, I laugh. "Oh, no!"

"Oh, yes," he says.

"Hey, man— . . ." I begin to lapse into street jargon. Then I say, "At least you won't have to ask me if my work is autobiographical."

We start the interview slowly, adjusting to the fusing realities. He asks me mild questions—about Los Angeles (I

say it is perhaps the most exciting city in the world), about
New York (I tell him that when I left there, I thought, My
God, I'm still alive!).

Still slowly, but edging along, he asks me: "Don't you
think that now all the blatant sexuality has made Los
Angeles less sexy?"

I answer: "No. For me the ideal sexiness, finally, is a
loose one, not a hidden one. Some people think a tantalizing sexuality is more intriguing. I love going around
without a shirt."

I go on to evoke a symbol of repression. I tell him I was
on a private beach recently with some very gorgeous
people, males and females, tanned, exposed, beautiful,
bikinied bodies. Suddenly a figure appeared, a small,
wrinkled dinosaur of a man; he was wearing a shirt, shorts,
shoes, body hidden almost totally to the brash sun. A
woman was with him, and a bodyguard followed behind.
The eyes of the sagging-skinned man met ours, invisible
guns pointed at us. Ronald Reagan, his wife, and bodyguard
passed on.

Now the interviewer asks me how old I was when *City
of Night* was published.

I try to be cool, but a monster figure of the gay world
has been evoked—age. "That would be a way of figuring out
how old I am now, and I'm very sensitive about telling my
age."

A bad moment. He asks my opinion of the gay
liberation movement.

"It's done a lot of good, and I am for it." But I add
mentally: When it isn't being used as ultimate cop-out, as it
is now, increasingly.

The interviewer moves into the mined area of
relationships.

Well, I have made mild flirtations in that area, and I
might still try. I tell the interviewer: "A brilliant psychiatrist friend of mine upheld that what is so alienating about
homosexual relationships is that they begin with the
intimacy of sex instead of proceeding toward it. To get a
relationship going, you have to work back. Perhaps this is
the reason so few homosexual relationships last."

(Reading that portion of the interview now, two or so

years later, I'm disappointed with myself for that answer. By implication, I elevated relationships over promiscuity. I will have to think about that more.)

Suddenly the interviewer shocks me: "Why are you so reticent about your age?"

I stumble badly: "...extremely narcissistic ... appearance ... bodybuilding ... muscles.... My body is important, I love my body...." I pull away: "I never tell strangers that I'm a writer." I'm telling him what he already knows, and I'm putting him down subtly. "On the street, I'm another person."

He smiles. He knows. "There's also a certain suggestion of violence in your street appearance," he recalls. "I assume that's intentional?"

The bad moment passes. Our identities adjust again to the present. "I've been told that often. There are times when I use it deliberately. People are attracted to it, and the narcissism in me loves the adoration. But there are times when, with someone, I think it's going to be sweet. Suddenly, though, what the other person wants is the fulfillment of the promise, even unconsciously sent out, of toughness. Sometimes I'm with someone and I get a hint of his humanity—and I would like to pursue that more. But I know that if I drop the street role, that will destroy his fantasies about me. In a way it's a trap: What often attracts people to me on the streets is what often isolates me."

"You presumably make a living by writing, so why do you still go out hustling the streets?" he asks me bluntly.

"Listen, I shouldn't answer that question," I surprise myself by saying. But I do. Yet when he sends me the typescript of the interview, I surprise myself again. Feeling slightly unfaithful to the streets I love, I substitute the following evasive answer: "Hustling is linked to narcissism, and being paid is proof that one is very strongly desired and desirable."

We move into the area of promiscuity. I define my "numbers" trip—sex with one after another after another. I estimate I've been with over 7000 people, but I know it's more. I chose the "7" because it's my lucky number. Thousands of sex encounters are not rare in the gay world.

Now the saboteur in me interrupts: "But I don't mind telling you, sometimes I feel despair about the promiscuity scene." In fascination, I hear the saboteur go on: "It has nothing to do with morality; all I know is that sometimes after I've been with dozens of people, I just want— . . ."

To die.

The part of me true to the streets wrestles with the strong saboteur: We're still so influenced by the straight world's crap. Tell someone recurrently that he's a sinner, sick, and a criminal—and how do you escape totally?

The interviewer asks me: "Is your entire sexual scene one of not responding to other people?"

I answer: "My primary scene, yes."

But I should say: Not totally. When I hustle, yes; when I'm into "numbers," mostly. But there are other times of mutual exchange, yes. Yes; and I do cherish those times.

There's a pause. I speak about the need to do away with *all* laws against consenting sex acts.

"But if sex in the streets became legal," he voices the familiar argument, "don't you think that when the danger disappeared, so would most of the excitement?"

If so, then cops and judges and closeted police chiefs should be the first to talk it up! I answer: "It would merely result in another kind of joy, an unthreatened excitement." I think now of the remark by an ex-vice cop turned writer, who in an interview voiced the stupid cliché of bigoted psychologists and sex-threatened cops that the main element in gay public sex is "the chance to be caught, the chance to be punished." Wrong, wrong, ignorant bullshit. Public sex is revolution, courageous, righteous, defiant revolution.

He asks: "Does your 'numbers' trip help you avoid the realization that time is passing?"

Again. I answer nervously: "Of course." I don't tell him what I'm remembering, the initial terror I experienced on returning to Selma after years away. I go on: "In my book *Numbers* there's a place where Johnny Rio thinks that if he keeps going sexually, time and death can't reach him."

(I began—literally—to write *Numbers* as I drove out of Los Angeles back to El Paso, with my mother—who had stayed with my sister—holding a writing pad on the console and me steering with one hand, writing with the other, veering off the road now and then, and my mother warning gently, "Be careful, my son." . . . I had returned to the sexual arena of Los Angeles after years of relative seclusion in El Paso, preparing my body with weights—and the arena soon centered in Griffith Park, that Eiffel Tower of the sexual underground. I went there every day, counting sexual contacts, the frenzy increasing to make up for "lost time"—which, of course, is never done; and years later I would spookily return to break "Johnny Rio's"—my character's, based on my own—"record" in that park. That book was written in three months with a compulsion as fierce as that which had propelled the sexual hunt in the park.)

I should have told the interviewer that perhaps I feel totally alive only when I'm working out with weights, when I'm having sex, and when I'm writing a book.

The interviewer asks, "Where does a sexual life like yours lead?"

The outlaw hunt, the precarious balance, dangers, excitement, the joy, freedom, defiance, the aloneness (the times when I can *taste* aloneness like ashes in my mouth), all that—and the acute sense of being in touch every single moment with *life*.

I answer: "I'll just go on becoming better—or, if things get grim, there's always suicide."

Too grim. I say:

"I think it's important to make an attractive death, and that's where the concept of suicide comes in. One's autobiography as novel. My life is so intertwined with my writing that I almost live it as if it were a novel. When do you end a novel? At its most dramatic moment. Your life, if you make it a work of art, should end at exactly the right moment. Like a novel. So I simply conceive of things going on and on until I don't want them to any more. Then they can be stopped." Still too grim. I laugh again. "Finally, that's the only freedom you have . . . the freedom to die."

7:01 P.M. *Selma. The Hustling Bar. Selma.*

Rendered glorious by the deadly smog, the setting sun burns brilliant red. Palmtrees cut long shadows as Jim walks along Selma. The blond hustler is gone. Many other hustlers are out in the warm evening.

"MOVE ON! THIS IS A NO–LOITERING AREA! YOU ARE SUBJECT TO ARREST IN FIVE MINUTES!"

The harsh voice coming suddenly from the bullhorn of the cruising cop car jars the early night. The car following slowly, the malehustlers saunter away. But they'll return in a few minutes.

Jim will last out the cops. He'll go to the hustling bar a few blocks away, until the street cools.

A yellow-lighted bar—two rooms, a pool table in one, a dirty umbrella of smoke encloses it. Later tonight this bar will be jammed with drifting, sometimes dangerous, young-men, slightly older than most on the streets. In the back room a few—it's too early yet—shoot pool, displaying tight bodies in slow motion. A man offers Jim a drink, but he doesn't want that slow commitment, not now, not when the outlaw stirrings are already demanding a night drenched in sex.

On his way out, he's stopped by a tough-looking lean youngish man wearing an eye patch. Jim recognizes him as a male pimp who runs a motel; different types of available men mill in the lobby late at night. "I could use a guy like you," he tells Jim. "Safer this way—and more bread." Jim takes the man's card, a printed card. Safer. He knows he won't call.

On the street the cops are gone for now, and the outlaws are back.

8:05 P.M. *Dellwith.*

He ate at a restaurant; meat, rare, and vegetables and salad and milk. He imagines the nutrients coursing to feed his muscles.

Now he drives along the grand old houses of Los Feliz Boulevard, elegant Hollywood; palmtrees are haughtier at the foot of once-fabulous estates hiding in the hills. The sun floats eerily low for orange moments.

He drives into Dellwith, a section of Griffith Park. A brook feeds lush trees and burning-bloomed flowers.

Into the park. A restroom hides among quiet trees. Beyond it, small forests of brush shelter paths into the soft hills. Many cars are parked on the sides of the dirt road. Jim can see men floating in the darkening greenery.

A youngman approaches him. "Wanna come home with me?"

He's not that attractive, and Jim wants more than one person now. "Uh—I just got here."

"I'd go in the bushes with you," the youngman understands. He blurts out the hateful memory: "But I'm scared. I was almost busted here a couple of weeks ago. We were in the bushes, and two vice cops yelled Freeze! I ran away, I stumbled, I thought I'd broken my ankle, I couldn't move. I just lay there hiding in the bushes for hours, till it got real dark, and then I crawled to my car."

Rage rising orgasmically, Jim walks into the dangerous area. A man sits hunched on a rock. Jim stands before him, letting the man blow him openly. Jim's rage ebbs. Nearby, pressed darkly against the trunk of a tree, hugging it tightly, pants to his ankles, a man is being fucked by another. The man against the tree invites Jim to join. But the thought of the earlier youngman's painful flight, the hiding for hours, persists. Past men cruising, Jim walks back to his car.

9:08 P.M. *Downtown Los Angeles.*
Moodily he decides to drive to downtown Los Angeles, in search of ghosts.

Wilshire. LaFayette Park. Often on late warm nights he would lie on the concrete ledge in back of the closed branch library, surrendering to a daring mouth. . . . Westlake. He pauses in his car, remembering. Ducks clustering coldly on a small island on the lake made strange sounds while silent outlaws gathered in alcoves or in a grotto under a gently flowing fountain, water splashing bodies lightly. . . . Oh, and the theater across the street—the enormous balcony where Jim was "wounded" one late night. He stood on the steps, his cock in someone's mouth. Footsteps! He pulled up his zipper, it caught the skin of his cock. Panicking, he pulled down, and the zipper bit the skin again. He bears the tiny wound of battle, an almost indiscernible scar, like the ghost of a butterfly.

Hunters have long abandoned this area to the jealous cops and the senior citizens waiting sadly to die.

Jim drives on.

Downtown Los Angeles. Hope Street, where he lived years ago.

Pershing Square. Preachers bellowed sure damnation, always for tomorrow. Malehustlers sat in the benign sun. Queens dared to appear in make-up. Torn down, the square rebuilt. The outlaws fled. To Hollywood Boulevard.

Jim parks his car on Spring Street. He drinks from the thermos of protein. He puts on a brown leather vest. No shirt; his chest gleams brown.

Tattered hopelessly, Main Street is a gray area smothering in grime. Afloat in dope and the odor of cheap fried chicken. Harry's Bar. Smoky yellow. Years ago, the main hustling turf. Now the hustlers here are older, meaner, heavily tattooed. Deeply, deeply exiled. Fussy old men wipe their bar glasses secretly, eyeing the rough hustlers. Jim doesn't stay long.

To Wally's Bar. Once it was the wildest; clients, queens,

hustlers coming together to drink in an often-festive mood. Euphoria tinged with hysteria.

Now rough black, Chicano, and white transvestites and transsexuals reek of vile perfume and violence. Black pimps and tattooed convict lovers. Violent hustlers.

"Hey, muscle baby, you oughtta be in the movies!" a towering giant of a queen tells Jim. "Porno movies, honey!"

Not a hostile statement, no, it is an acknowledgment that he doesn't look defeated, like the others; his is not a wasted body. Jim feels trapped in the tightly coiled violence of this snakepit of exile.

A stoned white queen—six-inch platforms, foot-high bouffant wig, stars pasted on siliconed breasts—suddenly pulls a knife on a black queen with purple lips. The glittering stars scatter onto the filthy floor.

Has memory transformed reality? Was it always like this? A casbah of the dazed dead?

Jim drives back to Hollywood.

10:32 P.M. *Greenstone Park.*

You drive in a curve and you park in an arc a few feet below a slope of well-tended grass. Across the road is a concrete alcove. Beyond it and another grassy slope a stone ledge separates this part from a treed down-sloping hill. To the other side of the alcove, the path curves through thick dark trees for a distance of perhaps a block.

At the lot, Jim pauses by his car. He knows the dangers.

Remembers the night the darkness lit up as if by a wrathful white sun. Sexhunters froze in the light-slaughtered night. The strange glare came from a demonic cop helicopter hovering over the park. It spewed its vengeful light while vice cops on the path rushed at the outlaws. Jim plunged down the slope of trees to the safety of the street.

And then there are the recurrent nights when gay-haters terrorize the paths, with knives, stones, broken bottles.

Still, the park flourishes.

There is always a mistiness here, you'll notice, created in part by the feeble mothy lights from antique lamps, and

by the fans of lacy trees filtering it, a mistiness emphasized
by a hypnotized silence broken only by the sound of feet on
moist, crushed leaves, or by sex sounds. Or violence.

FLASHBACK: *Greenstone Park. A Year Ago.*

It was past 2:00 in the morning. Thick mist draped the
cruising shadows along the paths that night. Figures
squeezed like clinging limbs against dark tree trunks.

Crack!

The unmistakable sound of a bullet tore the silence and
the fog. A gasp. A body fell on dried leaves. Squish.

Crack!

Another shot. Again the muted sound of wet leaves,
scattered by grasping, dying hands. Another gasp, softer,
the sound of spitting blood. A figure staggered onto the
concrete alcove and fell back dead. The other still moaned.

The murderer—the outlaws had rushed along the path
to see his car speeding away—entered the courtroom with
his smiling girlfriend.

MIXED MEDIA 1

POLICE REFUSE TO ARREST

Stabbing Suspect Seen Again,
Escapes Again

". . . a prime suspect in [the] stabbing of a . . . 15-year-old boy . . . at the headquarters of the Radical Gay Christians . . . was spotted . . . preaching through a bullhorn at a [rock] concert [and] condemning . . . homosexuals, and all anti-Establishment people and praising Jesus, the Bible, and the police. . . . Police refused to arrest him [despite being informed] that there was a felony warrant out for his arrest."

—*The Advocate,*
account of incident occurring
November 25, 1975, in Los Angeles

"Middle America's visceral distaste for sexual deviation is not . . . easily put down. . . . In New York City, the City Council seems about to vote [a civil-rights bill for homosexuals] down. In Missouri, a bill has been introduced that would require all homosexuals to register with the state. . . . In Boulder, Colorado, a university town with a reputation for easy-going liberalism, voters rejected by a 2-to-1 margin an ordinance that would have forbidden job discrimination against homosexuals. . . .

"[In the fight in New York City] the Uniformed Fire Officers, in a $10,000 ad campaign, charged that it 'would force an employer to hire a pervert . . . expose our children to the influence of sodomites . . . destroy the teamwork of the fire department . . . permit sodomites, perverts, and deviates to live and work where they choose.' The archdiocese newspaper *Catholic News* called homosexuality 'a menace to family life. . . .' "

—*Newsweek,*
May 20, 1975

CHURCHES REVIEW ATTITUDE ON 'GAYS'

". . . The American Lutheran Church drew some fire recently when it was learned that a $2,000 grant was made to the gay caucus in its ranks. . . . 'For a major board of one of the country's major denominations to identify through its budget with an organization promoting blatant transgression of the revealed word of God is a sign of a sinking back to the level of official immorality. . . .' "

—*Los Angeles Times,*
July 7, 1975

"A last and particularly important finding [based on a study of the effects of liberalized laws in certain states], given the present concern for crime control, was that 50% of the police reported that decriminalizing private homosexual behavior had allowed them to spend more time on serious crime. . . ."

—*Los Angeles Times,* Op-Ed Page,
October 16, 1975

INTELLIGENCE UNIT RULES
ELUDE POLICE PANELISTS

". . . The current 1975–76 PDID [Public Disorder Intelligence Division, a Los Angeles police division which

gathers information on 'dissident' groups and individuals]
budget of $3.26 million pays for 91 sworn personnel and 15
civilians. This is nearly double the number of sworn
personnel—52—assigned to robbery–homicide and com-
pares with 44 assigned to burglary–auto theft, 63 to bunco–
forgery, 144 to administrative narcotics, and 72 to administrative vice."

> —*Los Angeles Times,*
> December 28, 1975

BURGLARIES ON RISE, D.A. SAYS

"Substantial increases in burglaries during the last ten
years in both the city and county of Los Angeles were
reported. . . . In the city, the volume of burglaries climbed
from 50,771 in 1965 to 67,799 in 1975. Last year 22.1%
were solved."

> —*Los Angeles Times,*
> December 5, 1975

HOMICIDES LEAD
3.6% JUMP IN
L.A. CRIME RATE

". . . Homicides in Los Angeles rose to 619—the first
time murders had topped 600 for a year. The figure
presented an increase of 17.5% over 1974 figures."

> —*Los Angeles Times,*
> January 7, 1976

"The Los Angeles City Attorney's . . . office now
handles up to 500 gay-bar arrests a year, and many of them
. . . involve offenses no more serious than patrons holding
hands or dancing together."

> —*Los Angeles Times,* Editorial,
> April 24, 1974

ELDERLY WOMAN RAPED, ROBBED

"An elderly woman was raped and robbed in her West
Hollywood apartment, police said. It was the 37th such

incident in Los Angeles' West Side since police began their search for the so-called West Side Rapist in November, 1974."

—*Los Angeles Times,*
May 10, 1976

"We used to have to stake out in [a certain public] restroom—a lovely job, you can imagine. Talk about where have all the flowers gone, let me tell you. So we would have to make arrests down there, and one gay painted a sign on the wall—an arrow—and it said: 'Vice Cops Watch Here.' And it pointed up to a screen on the wall where, indeed, we would be concealed.... The L.A.P.D. has always maniacally prosecuted vice and victimless crimes far beyond what they have to do.... Well, the police will beat up anybody.... Let me tell you about reality.... If a guy [arrested] hits you, being a human being ... you hit him back, only you don't hit him back once, you hit him back three times or four or five or however many it takes to get the rage out of your system, because you're a human being.... He knocks one tooth out, you knock all his teeth out.... Just life. So when a gay says: 'Cops beat us up. The cop beat me up.' Well, the fact of the matter is, I've nothing to brag about, but I was a vice cop and I probably arrested 300 or 400 gays in my life."

—Ex-cop turned writer,
speaking on beatings, vice arrests, and
being a "human being."
New West Magazine,
July 19, 1976

AN INSTANT CURE

"...when the board [of trustees of the American Psychiatric Association] voted last December to cease classifying homosexuality as a 'mental disorder,' ... opponents of the ruling circulated petitions, issued angry statements, and forced the APA into an unprecedented action: ... for the first time in [its] 129-year history, a board decision is being put to a vote."

—*Time,*
April 1, 1974

"... Probably the most recent information in the matter [of child molestation] is [a] report by the State Department of Mental Hygiene, 'Another Look at Sex Offenders in California.'

"That study of 887 pedophiles (persons favoring children as partners) at Atascadero State Hospital—65% of them from Los Angeles County—revealed that 75% were heterosexual, while only 20% were [exclusively] homosexual."

—Los Angeles Times,
October 28, 1973

"Historical evidence has shown that homosexuals are prone to violence and other forms of criminal conduct, most notably ... molestation of adolescents and children."
—Testimony of a Los Angeles policeman during hearings to review the penal code,
—Los Angeles Times,
March 25, 1974

LAPD SEX SCANDAL

MORALS PROBE REVOLVES AROUND POLICE, GIRL SCOUTS

"A number of Los Angeles police are under investigation for alleged sexual misconduct with members of the Hollywood Division's girl explorer scouts ... a youth auxiliary group for girls 14 and up...."

—Valley News,
August 24, 1976

SOUTH PASADENA OFFICER CHARGED IN SEX CASE

"A 10-year South Pasadena police department veteran was arraigned ... on charges resulting from an alleged sexual encounter with a 15-year-old ... girl."

—Los Angeles Times,
October 15, 1976

NEW SEX CASE AT TWO
POLICE DIVISIONS PROBED

"New allegations of sexual misconduct involving some of its officers are being investigated by the Los Angeles Police Department, the agency said in a cryptic statement.... Department rumors have circulated for weeks that some officers ... set up an agreement with nurses at a local hospital for sexual favors.... Questions [include] whether money passed hands for the alleged sexual favors...."

—Los Angeles Times,
October 29, 1976

"It was on ... a Sunday that ... Taylor went to a party ... a private fund-raiser ... held in a gay bar.... Two friends arrived, and he and one friend moved to the bar to talk ... but a Los Angeles Police Department vice officer [a "balding blond man of about 40"] later testified that Taylor and his friend kissed and fondled each other.... The blond officer and 3 other plainclothesmen ... were augmented by 5 more plainclothes and 10 uniformed officers, and the arrests began.

"Taylor later testified that as the arrested men were handcuffed and led to a police van parked at the rear, he heard one officer call, 'We've got room for two more.' Another man, and then Taylor, were taken along, making a total of 21.

"His first reaction, he recalls, was to say, 'You're kidding.'"

—Los Angeles Times,
March 25, 1974

CHIEF SUPPORTS THEM

GAY S.F. OFFICERS URGED
TO 'COME OUT OF CLOSET'

"There are 20 homosexuals on the San Francisco Police Force, police chief Charles Gain says, urging them to 'come out of the closet' and show that gays can be good cops. He promised them his 'full support.'"

—*Los Angeles Times,*
October 19, 1976

URGES TOLERANCE FOR 'INCURABLE' GAYS. . . .

"Vatican City (AP). . . . Without discounting what the church considers the gravity of all homosexual acts, [the Vatican] . . . drew a distinction between homosexuals 'whose tendency comes from a false education, from a lack of normal sexual development, from habit, from bad example, or other similar causes' and a second group 'who are definitely such because of some kind of innate instinct or a pathological constitution judged to be "incurable". . . .'

"It added that Scripture does 'not permit us to conclude that all those who suffer from this anomaly are personally responsible for it, but it does attest to the fact that homosexual acts are intrinsically disordered and can in no case be approved of.'"

—*Los Angeles Times,*
January 15, 1976

"Perhaps the greatest perversion of all is to use the Bible as a social weapon that harms, hurts, and dehumanizes."

—Gerald A. LaRue,
U.S.C. School of Religion,
Los Angeles Times,
June 10, 1975

10:34 P.M. *Greenstone Park.*

NO MOON.

Jim passes the stone alcove, descends through ashen shadows toward the wall against the trees. He sits on the back of a concrete bench, his outline visible in the mute lamplight. A lean shadow floats by. Attractive, masculine. Jim spreads his legs wide. Two other men are lurking. The lean man—dark, angular, with a gypsy face, the most attractive of the three men Jim has lured—sits next to him on the back of the bench; he too spreads his legs, one knee touching Jim's. Another man squats before Jim. The sexual current rising, the third man bends before the lean one. Rhythmically the two kneeling suck the two sitting, Jim and the man next to him staring at each other.

Jim moves away, glancing back at the lean man, inviting him to follow. Jim waits against the wall near the water fountain. The lean goodlooking man approaches him. Gliding together, they kiss, erect exposed cocks pressed against each other. The other goes down on Jim. Inside the warm throat, Jim's cock grows full. Now the other stands for Jim to reciprocate. Jim bends and takes the other's cock in his mouth; he feels the round tight shaft slide past his lips, along his tongue, into his mouth. They alternate sucking each other, briefly each time, and kiss, as if to connect both cocks with both mouths.

Car lights flush the area, pulling shadows from the slain darkness.

The two separate in opposite directions. The car lights shift. Not the cops—only another hunter driving in.

Jim stands on the ledge of the concrete grotto. Motionless, like ebony statues, three men wait below against the wall. Nothing happens, no one moves for a seeming eternity. Four figures stand in the dark pool, Jim on the ledge as if commanding the traumatized hill. More moments pass. Nothing. Minutes. Nothing. Jim feels a stab of desperation. A man moves toward him from the path, climbs the ledge as if to approach him—and moves on. Still, nothing! Despair stabs more deeply. Another outlaw moves toward the alcove. The three others remain frozen. Jim stretches his body, touching his bare chest through the open vest. As the man climbs the ledge, his lips brush Jim's pants at the groin. Despair lifts. The lips press tightly against Jim's crotch.

Jim jumps off the ledge, onto the curving path, a tunnel through the trees. Stifled sighs. Matted leaves. Shadows of men wait. In recurring islands of lamplight, figures materialize for seconds. Men stand against trees, alone, in twos, threes.

To be seen clearly Jim pauses in a wing of yellow light. A man stands before him, his fingers spidering along the bare flesh of Jim's chest. Jim flexes exhibitionistically. Eyes adoring, the man stands back, jerking himself off silently staring at Jim's muscle-tensed body.

Jim moves farther along the path. A man in a leather jacket, shiny even in the dark, abruptly, suddenly, as if in a speeded-up film, kneels before Jim, opening Jim's pants, sucking his cock, hands pulling Jim's hips forward, to push the cock farther in, farther; he gags. Now one finger tries to penetrate Jim's ass. Jim jerks away immediately, pulls his cock out of the other's mouth, pushing him away, rejecting even the hint of penetration.

He moves deeper into the thick-treed area. Past others.

And a muscular youngman. Both pause, wait. But each expects the other to advance first. Neither will. They walk away, not glancing back.

Jim returns to the concrete alcove. A youngman is already there, pressed against the shadows. Jim stands on the ledge, the other takes his cock in his mouth. Another man suddenly there squats sucking the youngman blowing Jim. Jim breaks away, the youngman follows him down the slope to the deserted concrete wall. The youngman offers his ass to Jim's erect cock. But Jim doesn't want to fuck, not now, doesn't want to chance ending the hunt in this area, even for a short while. He merely rubs his cock against the other's smooth buttocks while the other jerks off.

Jim drives to another side of the circular park, gets out, stands by the road. A car stops. The driver gets out. He tries to kiss Jim, to rub his body against his—but he is not attractive enough for that. Jim guides his head down, down. The man accepts his cock. Lights flash around the curving road. The cops? Another hunter?

The outlaw excitement demanding rashness, Jim holds the man's head at his groin. The man continues sucking hungrily as the carlights near. The car stops in the middle of the road, the driver watches.

Jim turns away, as if to enter his car. The others drive off. Again he stands by the road.

Another car. The driver is young, goodlooking. Yes. Jim crosses the road, ascends a short incline toward the playground there, deserted now. The youngman follows him.

A slide. A merry-go-round on the sand. A tangled jungle gym. Skeletons of children's games, somber in the night. Both men sit on the merry-go-round. They kiss. The merry-go-round moves slightly. Their hands explore, holding cocks, balls. The youngman leans over Jim's cock, sucking it. Jim's finger moves past the lightly furred balls, touching, then entering the knotted asshole. The other's tongue swirls about Jim's cock.

The merry-go-round begins to turn slowly.

11:48 P.M. *Montana Street. Hanson Avenue.*

Hunters are scattering from the park in their cars. The soundless signal to shift the arena has been given. Now the placid residential district below the hilltop park will become, totally unaware of its transformation, the center of this floating underground.

Until a year ago, there was an old unoccupied house on one of the corners, its yard cluttered with branchy trees and bushes. Late at night hunters congregated there in fleeting orgies. There were recurrent rousts by the cops; outlaws were lined outside, handcuffed.

Now cars are swirling around the block, stopping, moving on, U-turning. The more daring men get out, stand, walk along the sidewalks.

Jim waits outside his car in the parking lot next to a sleepy apartment house. Several cars drive around, drivers look at him for a signal. A car stops. A man calls out: "You hustling?"

"Yeah." He wasn't, and this isn't hustling territory—but the man's words aroused the mysterious excitement to sell his body.

The man surprises him: "Sorry—but I'm not into paying."

The man drives away angrily.

Another replaces him. Jim walks to the driver's window. The motor of the car continues to purr. Shirtless, too, his pants at his ankles, cock hard, the driver, goodlooking, reaches out to touch Jim's groin. Now he pulls out Jim's cock. Jim touches the other's bare chest, stretching cock. He would like this man to come home with him, but he will not commit himself to suggesting it. Through the window the man's mouth pulls Jim's cock expertly into the deepest part of the throat—the rash scene instantly over.

By mutual signal, they withdraw.

Now a very handsome dark youngman drives by in a mangled sportscar. "You got a place?" he asks Jim.

Jim is very attracted to him; he's glad he didn't go home with the other man. "Yeah—just a few minutes from here," he says. But he won't ask him over, can't commit himself even now.

"Follow you there?"
"Sure."
And so the night will end early, Jim thinks.
And long before the purgatorial dawn he avoids.

12:10 A.M.   *The Apartment.*
Two beautiful male bodies lie side by side naked. They don't touch. Neither moves. Each looks straight ahead, away from the other. Used to being pursued, each waits for the other to advance first. Both are severely turned on, cocks rigid. Now they glance at each other, each wanting the other even more now. But they look away. Their cocks strain in isolation. Nothing.
Nothing.
Jim jumps off the bed, the other reaches for his clothes simultaneously. Looking away from each other, both dress hurriedly, each cut deeply by regret they did not connect.

VOICE OVER: *Interview 2*

I'M INTERVIEWED BY the editor of a radical gay newspaper.

I explain that I never set out to do "research" on my books. *City of Night* began as a letter I wrote in El Paso to a friend of mine, telling him my experiences during Mardi Gras. I wrote *Numbers* in a frenzy of three months after I returned to Los Angeles and spent every day in Griffith Park counting sexual encounters. I wrote *This Day's Death* (the only book of mine I dislike, and increasingly) after I was busted.

The interviewer remarks on the "pathos, despair, compulsion" in my books.

I say: "I feel there's an element of all those in gay life. Despair is very real—and it's not an indictment of the gay world to say so. Consider the imposed schizophrenia, wearing a mask, putting it on, taking it off. . . ." And the imposed religious guilt! It was the basis for confession. You had to tell your "trespasses" to a faceless, whispering voice that kept insisting, "How many times did you commit that sin? How many times?" Locked in guilt even when you had no cause to feel guilty. After confession and fasting, came the Sunday-morning purification. Communion! You knelt to receive the wafer that was the precious body of Christ. It was all over so quickly, especially since there had been so much agony in confession and fasting! And you knew that soon, too soon, you'd be huddled kneeling guiltily in the darkness again before that mysterious little screened window of the confessional and addressing the faceless presence: "Bless me, Father, for I have sinned." Then you'll grow up feeling outraged and betrayed because there's no substitute for salvation.

The interviewer asks me about a section in my book *The Fourth Angel* in which a teenage girl says that "to survive you've got to learn not to feel, even if you have to teach yourself." "To what extent," he asks me, "do you feel you have had to do this in your own life to survive?"

Yes, on the streets I disguise my feelings, I play distant, tough, a role which attracts and alienates at the same time—as defensive, I suppose, as it is arrogant. I keep my two "selves" apart—the writer and the sexhunter; confusing when the boundaries meld. Like recently in Griffith Park when a man in the arena told me someone had written a book about me—called *Numbers*. A few days later he brought me a copy of my book, not knowing I had written it. He inscribed it: "To Johnny Rio— . . ." My character. Unfortunately, when he discovered subsequently who I was, he felt betrayed. . . . Oh, yes, and bodybuilding, coating myself with muscles, is a similar defense.

Now the interviewer evokes the hideous monster: "Do you think this is something you can continue to develop as you grow older, into middle age and old age?"

I answer staunchly: "I'll get better." I say: "I think narcissism can be very healthy. Love of oneself, of one's body, is beautiful." Yet what a commentary—and hangover from stifling religions—that we consider "humility" a virtue, and "vanity" a sin. With so much constantly putting us down—life by its very niggardly nature feeding us crumbs—why should we additionally put *ourselves* down, accept crumbs as our due? Why should we be commended for our humility when we uphold we're dreadful and not worthy of praise, and be condemned for our vanity when we uphold that we *are* worthy of attention? And why two standards? Why should the intellectual manifestations— books, paintings, the other "art" forms—be acceptably exhibited, put out for display, but not the body? I spend hours, days, months, years on a book. I want it to be accepted, loved, admired, praised, sought. Why is my body different? I spend hours on it too. I don't find it strange to want to display it—and without "modesty"—and to have it accepted, loved, admired.

The interviewer: "Perhaps we can talk more about the hint of violence and toughness in your work and whether or not it's true of your own life."

I say: "I do cultivate a certain tough appearance because it attracts people sexually, and I do equate sex with power. But I know the difference between that and the most negative aspect within the gay world—S & M." I have evoked another gay demon: sadomasochism and its fierce psychic grip on the gay world. Yes, we're in a highly mined territory.

The interviewer's voice is agitated; he points out that he himself is not "into S & M." And: "There *can* be a negativism." But he verbalizes the most outrageous rationalization: "On the other hand I think pain can be an added dimension in a relationship."

I say: "One can justify eating dirt by claiming it intensifies one's closeness to the earth. . . . There would be commendable honesty in the S & M world if someone would admit: 'I want to be hurt and humiliated because I hate myself.' The hypocrisy comes when one calls it love. I find the inflicting of pain or the inviting of pain repugnant. I love the rush of being submitted to sexually—but that's different from inflicting pain."

The interviewer counters: "But don't you think it's possible in an ongoing relationship that pain—humiliation—can be an added dimension? I have no reason to disbelieve the people who have experienced it as such."

I say: "I do disbelieve it. Entirely. Pain and humiliation have nothing to do with love."

He asks me to speak about the "dynamic of hustling" in my own life.

Thankfully, I'm not evasive, as I was in an earlier interview. This time I'm true to the streets: "I have a fierce need to hustle." Nostalgia tugs at me. I remember past times: We wore blue jeans, tight T-shirts. We were all so butch, man, and we were proud. But streethustling is fading in elegance and style. Then, we never approached anyone, just waited to be courted, yes. Now, tacky hustlers peer into all cars, call out at the men driving around. Not all, of course, not all. "There's no rush like hustling," I say. "Yet I'm aware that it's involved with repression."

"You feel there's a conflict between your feelings about gay liberation and your attraction to the hustling world?" He asks me whether I think that hustling and S & M can be reconciled to some extent with gay liberation.

Hustling, perhaps; S & M, definitely not—though: "I would be dishonest if I said that there's love between the person who pays and the person paid."

"Are you speaking only of yourself?" he asks me pointedly.

I answer: "About myself, but also about other hustlers. It's a brutal thing to hear hustlers talking about their clients in derisive terms, with so much contempt at times." Yet there's a tendency on the part of the persons who pay to romanticize the hustler; they don't *want* to know what's involved, how the hustler views them; they're pitiful in their insistence that love can be bought. Look. Hustling *is* a loveless act. But there's no reason why sex shouldn't exist without love. The important matter is to purge sex of *hatred*, self-hatred or otherwise.

I go on to tell the interviewer that once I was jarred into viewing the possibility of reciprocal contempt: After paying me to express his own one-way desire for me, a man became moodily silent. Only to make him feel better, I said, "Have you ever hustled?"—extending to him—generously, I thought—my treasured experience. He snapped indignantly: "Never! I was raised in a very moral family!"

The interviewer asks me the question which recurs: "What sort of sexual experience have you had outside of hustling?"

I answer, like at other times, that I have three main trips—hustling, "numbers," and mutual contacts with certain people; that I have explored the outline of relationships only very vaguely.

The interviewer asks me what I feel will happen in my life: "Do you feel a driving need for something else?"

I answer: "For growth." I tell him that in my non-sexual life I'm quite giving, and very loving with friends, but in a love–sexual sense I find it all difficult. The patterns I make for myself there are circular.

The interviewer asks me about my early life.

I sigh. "I was born in El Paso, Texas. My mother was a beautiful Mexican woman, whom I love more than anything else in the world and whose death is a constant sorrowful presence in my life now." *My mother. . . . She had the most beautiful green—really green—eyes, and a smile that haunted you instantly. I loved her—love her, because death has changed nothing, and she loved me, and I— . . .* But that's for another time. Not now. "My father was Scotch—a very angry, brilliant man." *Driven, crushed by wrecked dreams. Sad. . . .* I went to a local college on a scholarship, I hurried through. I was in the army, a period that evaporates thankfully like a dream; I went in a private, came out a private. Then I went to New York and discovered Times Square, and then to other cities to discover Pershing Square, Main Street, Hollywood Boulevard, Selma, Market Street, Newberry Square, the French Quarter. . . . Much later I turned, very briefly, to drugs and was almost destroyed by LSD.

I move on to another subject: exhibitionism as art form—like dancing or writing, I uphold. Glorious to go to the beach, find a relatively secluded spot, and lie there naked, waiting for the perfect voyeur. I hate clumsy, tacky exhibitionism, though; it should be beautiful, motions rehearsed, the body carefully prepared to court the voyeur. I remember a man in an apartment building I lived in; he would stand—concealed, he thought, by trees—outside my window while I worked out with weights. He would appear regularly, like a faithful lover. I wore different trunks for him; I adjusted my workout apparatus to face the window. When we ran into each other outside, we each pretended the other didn't know. It was an elegant love affair. Then I moved away.

The interviewer asks me what direction I see my life taking.

I answer: "I would very much like to be completely free. Intellectually, I'm close to that in regard to sex. But I still play roles."

We discuss promiscuity.

I put it in the context of revolution: "When a courageous black woman in the South refused to move to the back of the bus, that was a revolutionary act—breaking the law in public. When gay people fuck and suck in the streets, that too is a revolutionary act. That's where *we* confront ignorant sex laws." Unfortunately I add: "I think it's a matter of style and taste. Most people wouldn't do it in the middle of a busy street in the daytime even if it became legal. Societal attitudes are strong enough to act as a deterrent; you don't need laws—that's the whole point. There's no law against painting yourself blue or yellow—but few people do it."

I hate that postscript in that interview. I wish I had stopped with revolution.

The interviewer says: "There's a theory that much gay creativity has come from the pressures of the oppression of society from the outside and that if those pressures weren't there the creativity would dry up. I disagree very strongly."

"I disagree strongly too," I say. "That theory might end up justifying the pressures and persecution in order to allow art to flourish. It's true that the pressures have created a discernible gay sensibility; but with the lifting of those ugly pressures another, equally fine art would come, based more on joy than pressure."

I go on to say that I see the sexhunt as an art form too. The beautiful abstract choreography, balletic, symphonic.... Enter the saboteur with his recurrent motif: "Though sometimes," I hear myself add, "after a night of hustling and dark cruising alleys, I think of suicide." I vanquish the saboteur: "But when I'm caught up in the beautiful hunt, I know it's the most exciting experience in the world—and at those times I wouldn't trade it for any other."

12:35 A.M. *Montana Street. Hanson Avenue.*

A SENSE OF loss, unshaped defeat because of the earlier lack
of connection in his apartment pulled Jim back to the
streets—and the youngman he was with is also here again.
The cars in this area have increased. Jim is about to get out
when he sees the cops flashing their lights at cruising cars.
The hunters scatter. Two not quick enough are being
hassled by the cops.

Jim drives into the park. No cars in the lot—the cops
must have been through. But hunters who climbed the hill
may be along the paths. Yes. There. Across the road and by
the stone grotto stands a man, shirt open.

Jim gets out. Now both men stand looking at each other
from across the road. Like cats, Jim thinks suddenly.
Neither will cross to the other's quickly delineated turf.
Now defiantly, Jim removes his vest, stands shirtless,
challenging the other. The other removes his shirt, challenging Jim back. Still, neither crosses to the other's side.
The memory of the dark youngman he just went home with
is still too fresh on Jim's mind. Again feeling cheated by the
deadlock, he drives away. The shirtless man stares after
him.

12:47 A.M. *Sutton Street.*

Although it's past midnight, for Jim it's still Friday; the

night will not end until he goes home to sleep. Before dawn.

Along lower Hollywood Boulevard, transvestites defy the threatening streets. Jim drives to a subway tunnel connecting one side of the street to the other; these underground tunnels recur throughout the city, for pedestrians to avoid heavy traffic.

A man stands like a dedicated sentry by the tunnel's mouth. His eyes search Jim's passing car. Seeing Jim park, the man hurries down the steps of the subway tunnel.

Jim walks to that corner, stands by the railing at the top of the tunnel. Glancing down, he sees the man in the fan of smothered light at the bottom of the steps. The man touches his own groin and runs his tongue over his lips. Jim descends into the murky tunnel; the faint odor of cum permeates the air. The man slides down against the wall. On it is engraved the crude drawing of a giant cumming cock.

Jim offers his cock, the other sucks it. Now chemical, electric signals go out into the street. Silently, another outlaw, alerted, enters the tunnel. In the stifled light, the man blowing Jim doesn't pause. The youngman entering already has his cock out. The squatting man reaches for it too, alternately sucking Jim's, alternately the other's, now taking both cocks in his straining mouth. The two standing lean toward each other over the man blowing them. Yes, the other is very attractive, and Jim allows their lips to come together. They ignore a fourth hunter, who merely stands closely watching in hypnotized fascination as Jim's cock and the other's push into the mouth of the kneeling man. Jim is aware of cum spurting. His? The other's? Both? He pulls his cock out. The other came, not he.

Footsteps. He uses that as an excuse to move on.

Outside, he walks past the dark corridor between two buildings on a side street. No one is there now. Then he hears it, a tapping, insistent, on glass. He looks around. Nothing. The tapping—a definite signal—increases. He glances across the street. In a second-story apartment, blinds and drapes open, an old, old man, ugly, shriveled body naked and skeletal, is signaling on his window.

Jim turns away.

He drives to Western. He looks toward the entrance to another tunnel, this one connecting the street to the bus stop on the freeway. No one there now either.

He parks on Western.

Here, one liberating night, just slightly after 11:00, he leaned against a fully lighted shop window—bicycles for sale all shiny chrome and slick spokes inside—while a man, who had just separated from a girl at the corner, blew him for oblivious seconds. The heavy Western Avenue traffic passed by noisily, blind.

1:15 A.M. *The Street and Alley Outside the Hawk Bar.*

He stands on the street across from a leather-oriented bar that attracts butch men. Soon it will be closing time, and the patrons will move into the lot, the street, the alley. Already, some are staking out their places.

Shirtless too, a man lingering in the alley sees Jim immediately; he moves even slower in the beginning choreography of the hunt. Slowly too—slower—Jim floats under a dark stairway leading to the upper story of an apartment house. The shirtless man glides after him. Under the stairs, the man is about to touch Jim's chest when a third man, unattractive, uncomfortable, hungry, interrupts the connection, perhaps deliberately to separate the two attractive, attracted men. Doggedly, he won't move. Impatient, Jim leaves, expecting the first man to follow him. But misinterpreting Jim's exit, the man drives away. The unattractive man remains abandoned under the stairs.

In the alley, in a recessed entrance to a building, the door boarded, two men are moaning softly. Jim is about to move away when the one being fucked reaches out toward his cock. Jim enters the enclosure. Now the man being fucked blows Jim.

Along the alley, a white, luminous crystal web of carlights entraps them threateningly.

The three bodies press against the boarded door, the connections unsevered. Not the cops.

Jim crosses the street. More outlaws are leaving the closing bar. An attractive man begins to cruise him. Now another, equally attractive, glances at both, situating himself in the middle. Jim walks away hurriedly; the possibility that they might prefer each other, not him, terrifies him. Even with all the night's conquests, one rejection might crush him. . . . He walks past an abandoned house—for sale as long as he can remember. In the shadows an unattractive man is jerking off; everyone walks by, ignoring him.

Jim moves to the other side of the house. Dried weeds crack brittlely under his feet. A blond man with a dark stubble of beard follows him into the velvet darkness. Jim waits. The man holds out a container of amyl nitrite to Jim; he inhales deeply. Instantly, the rushing blood crushes time and reality into sex, this moment, this sexual moment. Sex-senses pulse violently. Back to Jim, the man lowers his own pants, the naked ass squirms against Jim's quickly hard cock, the man guides it with his hand to the vaseline-prepared opening. Instead, in one movement, Jim pushes his middle finger into the oily opening, past the brushing hairs, into the knotted button giving way easily into soft, incredibly smooth flesh inside. Jim pushes another finger into the waiting ass. The bending man reaches back, holding the magic amyl for Jim to sniff again. He does—the sexual pulsing rush encloses him. The man's fingers cup Jim's balls.

Jim pushes a third finger into the crack.

Now in a frenzied whisper both softened and intensified by the pounding fume-stirred blood, the man begs: "Your whole fist! Shove your whole fucking fist up my ass!"

Jim pulls out his fingers, the asshole closes suddenly, the youngman moans.

The implied violence disturbing him at the same time that it arouses him, Jim moves away—replaced by another man pushing into the blond bending man.

At a faucet on the lawn, Jim wipes his hands with dirt and water—fiercely, fiercely.

As he moves along the overhanging branches sheltering the sidewalk, he passes a man sitting in his car, hand hanging out the window. He nods to Jim. But Jim walks on.

Back to the alley. The square passage before the

boarded door is vacant. Jim waits there. Strange to stand there, alone. Strange to— . . . He stops those thoughts, which recur. An outlaw has joined him, and he's desirable. Pressed against each other and against the crossed, nailed boards, they kiss. A light plunges along the alley. The two lean their bodies more tightly against the wall. The light passes. It *was* a cop car!—but the cops didn't see them, are stopped across the street. Their whirling lights whip up the darkness crazily. Men scatter. The lights of the stopped cop car capture faces and bodies like a camera's flashbulb.

Jim and the other cross the alley, to the area under the stairs, a wooden cove. The swirling coplight across the street illumines their faces periodically, lighting their exposed flesh sexually as the two kiss, connect, explore.

Without coming, Jim and the other part. Beyond the stairs, the area is clear. The cops are gone. The quiet street is deserted.

VOICE OVER: *Selective Sins and Exhortations*

"THOU SHALT NOT KILL," says the Bible.

In Kentucky, I and squads of other youngmen in infantry training were taken in ugly green trucks to dusty fields and taught by experts to attach a pointed bayonet to our rifles. Then we stood before a row of hanging dirt-bloated dummies, substitute enemy, and we learned to lunge at those "bodies" while we shouted, "Kill! Kill!" "Louder!" screamed our expert army teacher. "Louder! Kill! *Kill!*" Our bayonets stabbed over and over and then we twisted the butt of our rifles and pretended to smash a face and crush a skull. All in preparation for a time when the dummies would be human beings.

The same Book also says that to "lie with mankind, as with womankind" is an "abomination"—and because of that, generations have despised, incarcerated, and killed homosexuals. But what of people who eat fat? The same Book warns that even the soul of one who does so "shall be cut off from his people." It also admonishes against another minority, those who eat rabbit. But that admonishment has not been converted into law.

Pull out the phrase warning against "leaving the natural use of the woman." Hate homosexuals! Yet the same Book tells us that we "owe no man anything but to love one another: for he that loveth another hath fulfilled the law."

"Rebuke not an elder," says the Bible.

I watch television newsclips of an old-age home. The living dead with stringy, spidery, silky—beautiful—hair and carved cheeks; with quivering hands as if all life is finally rushing in indignation to those fingertips; the desperate alive eyes in the tossed-out bodies scream. . . . "Rebuke not an elder." And worthy citizens draw up a successful petition to commit an old, old woman—shriveled body still fierce with pride and anger—in order to get her uncomfortable presence out of their tidy neighborhood; her property, pieces of her life, tossed out for careless sale. "Rebuke not an elder," says the Book.

Are women who bear boys filthy for seven days?—longer, if they bear girls? Is a man dirty until evening after fucking his wife? Are we contaminated by touching a menstruating woman?

In the morning I look out, and I see the atmosphere like a wired cage, a poisonous presence.

Punish adultery by death! Stone disobedient children!

Are there laws against women wearing gold or pearls "or costly array"? The same Book forbids it. And it states categorically that "the love of money is the root of all evil."

But how can *that* be? Our lawyers and judges and police chiefs aren't so bad off. And look at some of our cardinals and preachers.

Certainly God didn't mean *that*—so forget all that crap about "the love of money." Move on to more important matters. Sodom and Gomorrah! Yes!

"And there came two angels to Sodom."

And the Sodomites insisted that Lot bring them out that they might "know them." Lot offered instead his virgin daughters! "And do ye to them as is good in your eyes," he told the Sodomites. But the same Bible tells us that even to look "on a woman to lust after her" is to commit adultery, and adulterers shall be put to death! Well, to offer one's virgin daughters— . . . Maybe *that* was the real sin. . . .

The solution to those conflicts is clear: Accept the

implications of the first part of the story of Sodom and ignore the latter.

"The woman shall not wear that which pertaineth unto a man, neither shall a man put on a woman's garment." But what about a law against wearing wool and linen together? It's forbidden equally by the same Book that tells us: "Make three fringes upon the quarter of thy vesture, wherewith thou covereth thyself."

If a man dies childless, must his brother marry the widow? Do we—despite our lavish barbarities—forbid the following to come "nigh unto the altar"?—a blind or a lame man? One with a "blemish in his eye"? One with a broken foot or a broken hand? Are there laws to that effect? Shall we make everyone who breaks a hand, register with the police, and shall we incarcerate those who break a foot?

And how can justice be bought by "the root of all evil"?

Of course peacemakers are "the children of God"—but that had better not mean that government and church officials can't justify any war, all wars!

"Louder!" screamed our expert army teacher. "Louder! Kill! *Kill!*"

2:22 A.M. *The Alley and Streets Near the Target Bar.*

JIM KNOWS WHERE the hunt will shift now, and minutes later he's there. A limbo area: The glittering, slender, decorated youngmen from the dance bar and the surly-posing masculine men from the leather and western bar a block away share overlapping areas for a few minutes. Waiting men line a side street and an alley, stand mutely while cruising cars circle the drowsy streets.

Removing his vest, Jim walks slowly along the block. His eyes connect with a desirable tall man he wants. That was his purpose, to display himself here, connect, then to be followed across the street, where he is now, away from the dense area; he walks into the alley, moving toward the back of a vacant house.

Jim and the outlaw who followed him climb the stairless platform. Never completed, the structure has begun to age, a dank odor clings to the naked boards. Stepping carefully to avoid exposed areas on the floor, they move into what would have been an inner room. Skeletal boards randomly dissect the moonless, cloudless sky. An old mattress lies on the patched floor; a mattress brought here by whom? In the gutless house, they remove all their clothes, they lie on the cast-off mattress, head to feet, cock to mouth, mouth to cock.

Jim feels the gathering sperm at his balls; the rushing feeling spreads, his hips thrust into the other's mouth, which receives the jetting liquid. The other's cock, abandoned at that moment by Jim's mouth, shoots into the warm air.

2:51 A.M.   *Outside Andy's.*

Although he just came, the outlaw excitement still rages. Jim drives past Andy's, the all-hours coffeeshop. Leathermen, glitterers, hustlers, queens, all are here, milling outside. Jim gets out at the corner, intending to "hitchhike"—but a man wearing a cowboy hat just circled the block, looking back at him.

Moments later, they sit in the car parked on a dim street. The man licks Jim's torso, the tongue nestling under his armpits, pulling at the hairs there.

3:05 A.M.   *The Garages, Yards, and Alleys Along Bierce Place.*

As he drives to Bierce Place, he glances apprehensively at his watch. Still time before night turns purgatorial purple at dawn.

Several cars cruise the area, many men roam the alleys. An afterhours club, a bathhouse, a gay theater—these lure the hunters here after 2:00 in the morning.

Nearby, neat trim houses slumber cozily, unaware that for a distance of about three blocks and lasting till just before dawn, orgies will recur in their garages, yards; under stairs, unlocked patios, store entryways, open spaces between buildings, and on the street itself.

In the gray night, Jim walks along the alley. The sexual odor of amyl permeates the misty air. Men drift gracefully like dark searching ghosts in a silent ballet; flowing forms unite, float away to another, others. In the garages, darker bunched shadows stir. Under a stairway, at least five men devour each other, slowly, slowly. Against walls and in cars, bodies connect. Suspended in the dark, forms emerge recurrently beyond the misty scrim. Like in a dream. Jim stops his thoughts by surrendering to hands and mouths in protected shadows, his cock only barely hardening.

In the lighted window of an upstairs room over a garage, a naked man signals Jim as he cruises the alley. Jim looks away, walks toward the corner. The naked man has come down the stairs, is now standing in the street. He reaches out for Jim—but Jim pulls away. Although the man is attractive, his exhibitionism is too blatant.

Jim crosses the street, to another alley. Under a sheltered stairway shadows shift. Stirrings in a garage; shadows materialize. Men lean against telephone poles. Jim moves into a vacant garage. Garden implements are dark and strange, like dormant weapons. Immediately someone is with him. Others squat before others. Someone holds a vial of amyl under Jim's nose. He sniffs, the scene explodes in sex.

Now he stands by the partition between two buildings—until he notices that only a few feet away two men are fucking. He moves away.

The lights of cars cruising the alleys entrap the walking figures, suspend them for moments in crystal light filtered through mist.

Now Jim is with a handsome man in an outdoor patio left unlocked. A garden table there, iron-grillwork chairs. Dark windows stare blankly. The two bodies advance, slowly as if not to violate the mesmerized rhythm of the mysterious hunt outside. Both cocks, aroused but spent, touch limply.

In the alley again, Jim looks at his watch.

Not yet near dawn.

VOICE OVER: *Four Factions of the Rear Guard*

1

I ATTEND A DINNER of gay gentlemen and icy ladies.

Our host is a little man who adores collecting people. He looks like a gay monk. On a black and white tiled floor multiplied by mirrors, he's explaining breathlessly in the corridor who the combatants will be tonight:

"Oh, the usual Los Angeles royalty—though *of course* they're *all* from Pasadena—and our darling Dusty, an ex-Busby Berkeley chorus boy—he'll be 5000 years old in February, and the poor thing *still* thinks he's the cutest thing in dyed feathers! You'll *adore* Natasha, she's a Russian duchess, simply *devastated* by the revolution, and now she's a lab technician but she reads cards. And the wife of Herman von Dern? She *never* says an intelligent word. Oh, there *is* a strange little man all in white and one emerald, I *think* he's famous but God only knows what *for!*—he's here with his muscleman protégé, a Mr Somebody (you two might like each other). . . . Oh, yes, and Otto, a clairvoyant from Orange County. Simply *marvelous* with earthquakes. Do you know Billy Adams?—the son of Alexa Alexandra?—the silent-movie star? Most people don't *know* it, but she was a deafmute, and you can *imagine* what the talkies did to *her.* And some others— . . ." He pauses for breath; we're at the ornate door to his apartment. He turns suddenly to me and says: "Oh, and I want to tell you I *adore* your book!"

"Which one?" I ask, somewhat irritated; I've written five, and people still refer to my "book."

"*City of Night,* of course," he says—inevitably. "Oh, it was forward of me to call you out of nowhere—but how else? how else? But let's do go in. Everyone is simply *dying* to meet you!"

Entering, I see the incredible ensemble; here and there are a few very beautiful determinedly sexless women, one in a tuxedo. I'm wearing a tight, very open shirt, and I love how I am being looked at; I am obviously the evening's fresh blood—myself, and the other muscular man, who sits rigidly throughout the evening with the man who "sponsors" him in body contests.

The chairs are all high-backed, of course. Velvet cuddles the room. The light is, oh, golden. A yellow chandelier twinkles flirtatiously.

The ladies and gentlemen are wearing emeralds, diamonds, rubies, pearls—one gentleman exhibits at least a dozen rings on a chain ("his fingers are too *fat,*" our host whispers).

Dusty the Busby Berkeley chorus boy wears a tacky necklace of pukah shells. "They're quite expensive," he informs Count Etienne, a skinny man with plucked eyebrows—no relation to the duchess here.

"Hmmm," says his lordship.

"I paid fifty dollars for the necklace," the ex-chorus boy insists.

Flashing rubies and emeralds, the count says, "Oh, *nice!* But you know, dear, you have to have a certain *bubbly* personality to get away with *those* things—*you* have it, *I* don't."

Dusty waits for his turn. It comes. His lordship is narrating the shock he felt when an ordinary policeman came to his door by mistake. In Pasadena!

Dusty strikes: "And the Pasadena ladies looking out

their windows said, Oh, my God, she's entertaining the military now!" He loops the pukah-shell necklace around his wrist.

Drinks about the room are like colored water in goblets: green, red, amber. Photographs of the great stars line bookshelves; the gorgeous artificial faces next to dead flowers.

When the count comments favorably on my body, I ask what he does.

"Mostly I'm a count," he answers.

And the Busby Berkeley chorus boy strikes again: "Cunt?"

His lordship smiles tolerantly. The rabble— . . . "Count, dear, with an 'O.' "

"Oh," says the ex-chorus boy, and goes on to tell about the death of Hollywood and glamor.

"So many funerals," sighs Billy Adams, the son of the mute star. "So many stars dying. Gone, gone. I went to Mandy Mandeville's funeral. She looked terrible—so shriveled, so tiny. They used to be bigger. Oh, but at Forest Lawn this adorable youngman insisted I buy a plot there—before need. And I did."

"Did you buy the youngman or the plot?" asks the host.

"It overlooks Glendale," the famous son of Alexa Alexandra says.

"How chic," says his lordship.

The icy ladies sip their drinks frostily. They look like Russian spies in an American movie.

"My *God!*—I thought you were dead," Dusty the ex-chorus boy says to a new guest, a man who once played the evil scientist in dozens of movies.

Natasha the Russian duchess wants to read the cards for me—but there's only an incomplete deck, *two* incomplete decks. So she mixes them—different-sized cards. In her chubby hands, they flutter to the floor. "Fuck it," she says.

The clairvoyant tells me he doesn't need the cards to tell me I have powers I haven't even discovered yet and I'll win the contest I'm entering.

But the old gentleman "famous for God knows what"—

and he *is* all in white, with just one huge emerald—says, no, no, it's *his* muscular friend—who hasn't said a word—who is entering the contest.

Oh.

Somebody tells me he loved my book.

"Which one?" I ask.

"*City of Night,* of course."

"Do you still hustle?" the ex-chorus boy asks me naughtily.

"Yes," I say defiantly.

"You know," he goes on. "I occasionally dial the telephone on the corner of Selma, and I speak to the hustlers—so exciting!"

My God, I've talked to him!

I want to affront them all, they're so uptight, reactionary. "I also go to alleys."

His lordship says he couldn't get involved with alleys because, being inbred royalty, he has to guard against disease. "It would *kill* me," he says. From his coat-of-armed blazer jacket he pulls out an ivory fan, which he spreads expertly—*swushhh!*—as if to chase away deadly germs, especially those that may be coming from the ex-chorus boy.

I tell the count he could go to clean alleys.

"What kills *me,*" says Dusty the Busby Berkeley chorus boy, "is that all the niggers are driving Cadillacs."

The gentleman in white asks him didn't he wear feathers in his last film?

"What happens in the alleys?" the clairvoyant asks.

"Some clairvoyant," sighs the host.

"Fucking and sucking." I don't like how I'm sounding, but I want to protest this stagnation.

"Oh, it was all more fun and sexy before the so-called sex revolution," says Billy Adams, the famous son, "before all this sexual revolution mess. *We* kept in our closets."

"My family lost their *estate* in a revolution," his lordship sneers icily.

"Mine too," echoes the duchess; "that's why I'm a lab technician."

The table is set: Silver plates shine under hypnotized candles.

The sexless beauties look like killers.

Now here's a guru in flowing robes—just out of jail for attempting to shoot his lover. *"Om, om."*

The beauty in the tuxedo gets told not to smile—she hasn't—or she'll ruin her lovely baby face. The gentleman in white suggests that his "friend" and I armwrestle.

The guru asks me what I suggest for his sagging middle.

Someone tells the cool beauty that if she sneers she'll get wrinkles too.

Om.

Dusty laments the openness of everything sexual now. "I like it more naughty," he giggles.

The gentleman in white agrees snippily: "The closet is perfectly comfortable, thank you!"

For dinner we have meatloaf.

2

In his palatial home, the famous director courts an army of drifting youngmen. All are sure they'll become big stars. Not one has, not one will.

I hate the man, his contempt. So much wasted power! He uses it to extend a tapestry of dreams cruelly to the hungry youngmen, only to withdraw it quickly and send them to others in a sliding order back to the streets but, now, with memories of evaporated glory.

"My films extol the old truths," he says in an interview. "That is what is needed, a return to morality."

3

I meet a famous star. He gets drunk. Under the dinner table his hand gropes me. His fingers dig into my fly. I'm trying to be cool, not to embarrass anyone. Others at the table are unaware what's happening under it.

Except for the star's bodyguard-lover.

Alerted by other similar times, he stands abruptly behind the star and looks down. The star withdraws his stumbling fingers.

"I knew it," says the bodyguard-lover.

"Piss," says the star.

The bodyguard leaves.

The star gets drunker. His overtures to me increase. "Please come home with me." He's pitiful, this famous, rich, powerful man. Pitiful. Always falling in love with those who can't love him, who will only use him; surrounded by an entourage of invited sycophants who drain his need for love; always, always inviting to be used. No, I can't go with him, I say.

He leaves the party. But he calls back on the telephone. Please come to his house, just to talk. Just so he will be with someone. *Please.*

Driving to his mausoleum of a house, I see in the flash of my headlights his bodyguard-lover, spying.

Fuck it. I promised I'd come, to talk. And there he is, the lonely star, at his door.

The house is cluttered like an overbought antique store. Chandeliers like crystal spiderwebs. Devouring velvet chairs. Figurines and statues battling limply for attention. Plastic corpses of flowers.

"I want to show you my bedroom," he tells me.

I decide I have to leave.

"Please."

His bed is on a platform. It's a cross between a throne and a circus tent; drapes held at the top with a golden crown. Rows and rows of clothes hang in enormous open closets like squads of frozen guards.

He tries to kiss me, but I'm not attracted to him. "Hey, man," I say.

"Please."

He knew all along I'd reject him this way, I think suddenly. He knew it all along.

As I'm leaving, he offers to take me to Palm Springs if I stay.

4

"It's a white party," the man informs me. "Everyone has to dress completely in white." The party will be in his lovely rustic home.

What the hell. I get into it. I wear a white-bloused, see-through open Cavalier shirt, white boots, and pants with two rows of buttons in front.

A greenhouse with exotic flowers. Listen to the delicate water spray, like kisses. Oh, a brook! And alcoves. Look! A large swaying hammock. And minstrels in white, playing flutes.

Men and boys in white jockstraps wander along the multi-leveled gardens. A man turns up in tennis drag. Men sit along the tiered ledges watching the parade.

A few women idle about, ignored. There's a sultan in see-through pants. There's a man in white ballet tights, genitals exposed. A dazed-looking youngman with a very bad complexion and wearing nothing but crossed belts on his skinny body wanders aimlessly.

I think suddenly of a dull, white purgatory.

Over a hundred guests in white.

A producer arrives with harnessed "slaves." There's appreciative applause from the tiers.

"It's just lovely. Lovely. So innocent," says a man standing benignly on a balcony like a voyeuristic high priest.

3:40 A.M. *Albertson Avenue.*

A FEW MEN WALK along rows of elegant antique stores. More drive around the blocks, cruising in their cars. Jim is about to park and get out—to be seen fully, as always— when an ominous squad car invades the area. Now the tide of hunters will recede here to surface elsewhere.

As Jim drives off, he sees a man he was with last week; the man stops abruptly, ignoring the rampaging cops and signaling that he wants to make it again with Jim. But it was too complete, that one encounter.

FLASHBACK: *A House. Last Week.*

On the street the man had appealed instantly to Jim's hungry narcissism. Leaning out the window to comment on Jim's body, the man, slim, with angular features—he was dressed in casual modishness—looked much younger, Jim knew intuitively, than he actually was. Agreeing to get together, Jim followed the sports Mercedes into the hills, to a house loftily distant from the others, its Spanish balconies poised over a lush hill.

Inside, the man moved up carpeted steps. The house had the easy elegance of wealth and style, the only discord the colors slashing each other in paintings on the walls. The man led Jim into a huge bedroom in the upper level of the house. There was a sitting room, a bar, a dressing room. Jim saw a photograph on a table, the photograph of a little boy; the man as a child? his son? Gliding past the table, the man turned the photograph down. He lighted tall candles about the room. It swam in gold mist. Instantly the room was bordered by retreating candlelight; it became a framed picture.

"All this is unreal, this house, this furniture, it means nothing. None of it is real." The man spoke softly, his words flowing into the amber light. "*You* are what is real. You and your muscular body." His voice became even softer, as if not to stir the gold twilight. "Tonight I found you finally, I knew you when I saw you. I knew that here with me you would walk into that dressing room and find clothes worthy of your precious manhood." And then he pronounced one word slightly louder than the rest, a word formed precisely, carefully, a mantra:

"Stud."

Jim was pulled into the dream, it melded with one of his. He often becomes a fantasy figure in sexual encounters. That fulfills a part of him, yes, because he knows that no object is more adored, idolized than that in a dreamer's fantasy of sex.

Ageless in this light, the man opened a bottle of wine at the small bar. The cork crumbled. Dropped crumbs floated in the purple liquid. Frowning, as if that tiny incident had violated too much, the man discarded the bottle. He reached for another, opened this one easily, and served two glasses. The glasses were so frail they were invisible without the purple liquid. He handed one to Jim, sipped from the other.

Purposely Jim had not spoken since they met, knowing that jarring demons lurk within the fringes of a fantasy. He stood showing his body in studied casualness.

The man reclined against the backboard of the bed. "I would lie here," the soft voice floated, "looking at these magazines— ..." He reached for magazines, four, five, strewn strategically on the floor. He leafed through one, the special one. Jim saw the photograph of a determinedly masculine muscular man in a narcissistic pose before an adoring figure not quite as masculine, looking up from a kneeling position.

"This one," the man's voice glided into the candle mist of the room, "the muscular one is you."

No, the model did not look like Jim, but he and the man in the photograph were of the same type, probably the same size. The model wore tight, faded jeans—a tear at one thigh, another at the knee, boots buckled at the ankle, a thick carved belt, a vest under a denim jacket. The figure idolizing him wore ordinary clothes.

The man turned the pages of the magazine. In each succeeding photograph the model wore less clothes; the other remained fully clothed, his adoration increasing in poses of worship.

Jim glanced at himself in a mirror on the wall. He flexed, slightly.

"I would be looking at these, and you would appear from that room— . . ." The man indicated the open dressing room. ". . . —and I would recognize you from my dreams, this time with my eyes open." Again he formed the magic word:

"Stud."

Mirrors embraced Jim in the dressing room. His image was shot back and forth, like projected slides, onto the gleaming glass screens. Without surprise, he saw on the dresser what he had known would be there. Neatly set out— waiting for how many nights?—faded jeans torn at the thigh and knee, strapped boots, carved belt, vest, denim jacket, a jockstrap.

Jim removed his own clothes. He put on the jockstrap, looked at himself, put on the ripped pants, and he looked at himself, then put on the boots—only those were slightly large—and he stared at himself, then put on the vest, and stared, and then the denim jacket and stared at himself— multiplied poses from every angle, a room of glossy pictures. Responding to the images, his cock strained against the fabric of the tight jeans, the engorged head under the jock-covered cock almost emerging from the tear at one thigh.

On the bed, the man continued for moments looking at the figures in the magazine. Suddenly he glanced up at Jim, and inhaled.

"Stud."

Jim stood relaxed before him, the first pose. The man leaned back. Jim flexed, the second pose. The man's eyes blinked, entrapping each image, like the closing shutter of a camera. The soft voice resumed. "A man, a beautiful man, rough, a man, and he knows it, and I'll worship his muscular body, his manhood, a man's body, idolize it, and he knows it, beautiful stud, and he knows it."

Jim's moves were slow, choreographed carefully in the mirror. Now he advanced toward the man.

Too quickly!

The man's voice cautioned:

"But he won't let me touch him, not yet, just let me look at him, worship him at a distance."

Jim moved back.

"Stud."

In the mirror across the room Jim saw himself, the fantasy framed. He basked in sexual power, his power to personify the cherished fantasy in this fusing of two dreams.

The pages of the magazine turned. The model removes his clothes. Jim held the denim jacket over his bare shoulder, the vest off for now, to be replaced. He dropped the denim jacket, put on the vest; stood loosely, stretched, flexed, relaxed.

"Ignoring me and staring at himself while I stare at him, and he knows I idolize him, he knows it."

Jim unbuckled the belt.

"Tempting me, tantalizing me— ... Slowly, slowly." From the bed, the man edged toward Jim. Jim moved back a step.

"Making me long for him, knowing how he looks."

Jim raised one booted foot onto the bed. The man's hand glided toward it. Jim did not withdraw. The man's hand clasped the boot, an anchor in the swimming fantasy.

"Stud."

Jim withdrew his foot. Now he opened the top button of the pants. The man's head inched toward the concealed groin. Again Jim moved back.

"Making me wait, seeing himself so beautiful, so masculine."

Jim opened another button. The top of the jockstrap was stark and white against his brown flesh. He allowed the pants to open in a V. Two triangles of tanned flesh flanked the full pouch. The man turned to another page in the magazine. Jim reached out and drew the man's head forward, not roughly, no, importantly not roughly, but slowly. The head surrendered easily to the jock-covered groin.

"Lick it." Even those words, Jim spoke with careful softness.

The man's tongue gradually moistened the elastic material. The cock expanded under it and pushed at the edges.

Moving back from the man's rapt eyes, Jim raised his foot, propping it on the bed. The man removed one boot, then the other, the socks, the pants.

Jim stood naked except for the vest, the jockstrap.

"Stud."

"Lick it."

The man's tongue outlined the straining column under the material. Jim glanced at the mirror and saw the man, reproduced with him in the amber glass, burrow his head into the covered groin. Hard, flushed red, the head of Jim's cock slipped out of the pouch. Before the man's tongue could touch it, Jim pushed his cock slowly back into the pouch.

"Not letting me touch it until he's ready, just looking in the mirror, knowing how much I want him."

Jim saw his own reflection pull the man's head slowly forward, directing the mouth to suck the erect cock stretching the elastic cloth. The material was so moist that the flesh was visible through it. The man sucked the cloth-covered cock, stroking it in his throat and with his lips, back and forth, back and forth, rhythmically.

"Pull the strap off with your mouth," Jim told the man. Not a blunt exhortation, the words were spoken in the subdued tone that matched the slow rhythms, consistent with the choreography of his sensual dream.

The man's teeth and lips drew the strap down. It clung loosely to Jim's thighs, then slid over his feet. The man bent. Jim raised his foot, the strap on the tip of it. The man removed the strap with his mouth.

Leaning back on the bed, the man held the strap against his lips, kissing the portion that had enclosed Jim's cock. Then he held the strap in his hand.

Slowly, Jim guided the man's head to his groin, held it there for moments, inches away.

"Now he'll let me, what I've longed for, and he'll be looking into the mirror, looking beautiful and manly, and he knows it."

"Suck me," Jim said. Even the command was calm.

The man's sucking was cadenced, a long stroke, a shorter one, a long one, a short one, matching the rhythmic thrusts of Jim's arched body.

The man turned to the last page of the magazine.

"Stud."

Jim removed the leather vest and stood over the man.

The man looked up at him. One hand touched the magazine, the other worked its fingers over Jim's cock, back and forth, back and forth, back and forth.

In the framed mirror, Jim saw his own cum spill in slow arcking spurts as the man directed the white liquid onto his clothed body, on the jockstrap, on his face, on his lips, over the open magazine, and on the photograph in it of a muscular man standing naked over a clothed man surrounded in bed by magazines of photographs of muscular nude bodies.

3:46 A.M. *Terrace Circle.*

No, Jim does not want to go with him again. He prefers to leave the memory perfect.

The outlaws scattered from Albertson Avenue have fled to Terrace Circle, a residential district of neatly decorated, attractive houses. Perhaps half the residents—more than that—in these six or seven blocks are gay.

Along leafy ledges, men walk the dark streets. Even the sound of loud footsteps is out of place, disconnected. A lighted window; a man on the lawn stands staring into it at a naked man inside.

A man before the open door of his house calls out to Jim: "Wanna come in? Me and my roommate are getting people together for an orgy. Can't start till we have ten. You'll be the seventh."

"Why ten?" Jim asks.

"Less than that's too little, more's a mess," the man answers.

Jim shakes his head, not turned on by the prospect of a strict orgy. A car parks next to him. Jim stands in the middle of the block. The driver shifts to the passenger side of his car. His head strains out the window toward Jim. Jim moves closer.

Suddenly there's the motion that announces cops in the area. The lingering becomes hurried, like a slightly speeded-up movie seen earlier in slow-motion. Forms slide into garages, others move into cars, cars desert the area, doors of houses open here and there, sheltering the threatened outlaws.

And here they are, lights flashing, two squad cars. Four cops rush out, gathering men at random; they'll question them here or take them to the station for "investigation."

Quickly, the man in the car by Jim opens the door for him, Jim gets in; the man drives a few blocks away. He parks. "We're safe now," he says.

Anger wrenches Jim at the thought of the attacking cops. This time his cock hardens immediately when the man bends over it.

Minutes later, back on Terrace Circle, the cops are gone, and new men and cars are cruising the area.

Driving away, Jim avoids glancing at his watch.

4:12 A.M. *Greenstone Park.*

Speeding! He drives into the park, to end the night's hunt.

He walks along the dark path. Past hunters, shadows among the trees.

He returns to his car and drives down the hill.

Before dawn.

VOICE OVER: *Cops and Muggers*

WITHOUT EXCEPTION, every cop who entraps or persecutes homosexuals, every judge who vindictively sentences them, every prosecuting attorney who pushes vengefully for gay convictions, every rabid police chief who rants against homosexuality—without exception each is to some extent at war with his own sexual fears, and those fears are very probably grounded in latent, self-hating homosexuality. The intensity of his unexplored self-doubts determines his danger to true law and order.

The main reason for becoming a vice cop on the gay detail is one of suppressed sexuality. Often led by a bleating police chief, the vice cop becomes a tight member of a rival gang against homosexuals.

Entrapment—illegal—is rampant and provides cops a sexual exorcism. They dress suggestively in outrageous clothes. Choosing their quarry very selectively, they offer money for sex. They entice cruising gays with overt sexual signals. In public places they fondle themselves. They can thus "pretend" for a short period to be what they fear they are. Instead of making it, they bust the submerged part of themselves.

A midnight call from a friend: "I've been busted!—the

guy propositioned me! Please get me out!" And you feel the surrogate horror—tonight it's not you.

The recurrent assertion (included routinely in virtually every homosexual-arrest report) that cops are responding to "citizens' complaints" is belied by the recent findings of two Los Angeles students, now attorneys, that, out of the total of 646 primarily gay-oriented lewd-conduct arrests occurring in a period in summer, only two were based on "civilian" complaints—and both of those complaints were made by the same security officer in one department store. Policemen effectuated the rest of the busts, over 600 of which were by plainclothesmen or vice cops. *Gay promiscuity is visible only to homosexuals and to the cops.*

Technically, one could bust a cop on a citizen's arrest for enticing and soliciting—creating the so-called "criminal lewd act" the cop ostensibly seeks to curb. That cops flagrantly entrap is underscored by two lawyers who in 1976 gave lie-detector tests to twelve men claiming entrapment under the sex-solicitation statute. Only two of those so arrested failed the test. When so much promiscuous gay sex does undeniably occur, why is entrapment used? Because the real objects of the cops' hatred are *all* homosexuals—not "criminal" acts. Anyone in a gay area is vulnerable.

Every male homosexual lives under the constant threat of arbitrary arrest and a wrecked life. Available space in a cop vehicle—a factor as circumstantial as that may determine whether or not a man's future is mangled. Gay publications advertise insurance against arrest; homosexuals make sure they have change with them at all times for emergency jail calls. The anxiety this creates—not knowing whether one will return home with a partner, harming no one, or end up in jail—is a prime factor of the gay experience and results in rebellious promiscuity.

Two attorneys knowledgeable in the field estimate that in Los Angeles County alone approximately two-hundred men are arrested each month on lewd-conduct charges; this results in the dreaded, life-usurping, permanent registration with the police—as a "sex offender." One hundred more men are arrested monthly on gay-prostitution charges. (In a bow to capitalistic enterprise, male prostitution is not considered a registerable sex offense, but free, mutual solicitation is.)

A man is in a bar, another sits next to him, smiles. "Hi." "Hi." Knees touch. "Wanna get together?" "Okay." Outside, the first man is confronted by another man; both the man who invited him and the one approaching are cops. "You're under arrest!"—and the nightmare begins. Handcuffs. You see the despising face that smiled and encouraged earlier. Jail doors lock. Found guilty of lewd conduct, you'll have to register as a sex offender—all because you accepted an invitation to sex!

At best, to arrest anyone for suggesting or agreeing to a sexual contact, or for having one, is insane; at worst, it's criminal. Homosexuality is not a victimless crime—the homosexual is the victim, the cop the criminal.

A man sits in a gay bar with his sister, whom he's finally told about his sex life. He's happy, she's accepted it lovingly; she had wanted to see his world, and now they're celebrating their new closeness. A vice cop mistakes her from behind for a drag queen and pulls her roughly back by the hair. The brother protests. Cops batter him to the floor. The seriously beaten man is jailed. "Resisting lawful arrest," the cops claim.

A youngman is in a small town outside L.A. Lonely. He's never made it with a man before, but wants to. A man offers him a ride. He gets into the car. The man is fondling himself, the youngman answers. You're busted. The judge threatens to hold you incommunicado for three months—for "psychiatric examination," insisting that all homosexuals are insane.

Lights flash in a bar. Outrageously dressed men identify themselves as cops. Handcuffs snap on whoever is near. A cop dangles one more set of handcuffs. "You!" he chooses at random. And you become a "sex offender" for life.

Each time a chief of police rants in public against homosexuals, he unleashes a wave of lunatic attackers into known gay areas. Murderers, muggers, robbers raid homosexual areas with weapons. Cops, who systematically harass cruising gays, pointedly ignore calls for help in menaced areas. (Early in 1976, the Internal Affairs Division of the Los Angeles Police Department was quietly investigating a matter that could turn against them: At least one off-duty cop was reputedly beating up homosexuals in Hollywood.) Why, then, do homosexuals continue summoning the police to report crime with homosexual overtones? Because there is in all of us, gay and straight, that indoctrination which makes us continue to demand that cops be the good guys, no matter how often they prove otherwise.

A man is cruising. Two men drive by and call him a "fucking queer." Through their window, you swing at one angrily. They turn out to be vice cops, and you're charged with assaulting an officer.

A report written by a vice cop in an arrest charging two men with a felonious oral-copulation contact punishable by up to ten years in prison was challenged by the defense on the basis that from the position he located himself (on a winding, heavily treed path at least twenty feet away from a branch-sheltered alcove where he placed the two defendants), he could not have possibly witnessed the details he so heatedly described in his report. Excerpts:

". . . Officer observed X standing on the trail. X had no shirt on and his pants were around his ankles and his right hand was on the shoulder of def Y. Def Y was on both knees directly in front of def X. Def X's penis was inserted in the mouth of def Y. Y was moving his head back and forth in a back and forth motion with his eyes closed. . . ."

In a tiny theater attracting gays, a cop screams: "Roundup time!" Six cops go on a rampage knocking men to the floor.

A man in a public restroom sees another playing suggestively with himself. He answers the signal. Another man rushes in, knocks the first to the ground. You're busted and sentenced to fifteen years in prison because you have a previous record and the judge says you're a "menace."

A youngman in prison on a "sex charge" sits before shifting slides of nude men on a screen. Each time he becomes aroused, he feels the nausea-wrenching pain of "therapy."

Imagine the horror of living with that constant fear, those threats. Imagine being forbidden by law to seek out a sexual partner. Imagine that—and you begin to understand the promiscuous rage of the sexual outlaw.

Each time a homosexual is arrested, law and order suffers.

In a city in which, in 1975, homicides rose over 600 for the first time—an increase of 17.5% over 1974—the Los Angeles Police Department was still able in 1976 to spare 103 men and over $100,000 to raid a gay bathhouse! Only 22.1% of all burglaries reported in 1974 were solved; yet, according to a 1974 *Los Angeles Times* account, the City Attorney's office was handling up to 500 gay-bar arrests yearly, many of those involving men merely holding hands or dancing together!

And: In the same area of Los Angeles where thirty-one lewd conduct arrests were made in one year—in one theater—a psychopath has raped and murdered at least nine terrified helpless old lone women.

And: In Hollywood and downtown Los Angeles, where vice arrests are routine, a maniac has slashed the throats of at least nine men.

It becomes clear that apart from providing cops a negative psychological outlet for their sexual frustrations, easy gay arrests, harassment, entrapment, and convictions—legally sanctioned sadism—disguise police inability to control violence. Boosted by the smashed lives of homosexuals, statistics blur murders, rapes, muggings, robbery. (A well-known attorney claims to have found indications that, in one heavily gay area, the police may have removed stalls between urinals in a public restroom in order to provide easier contact between males, and thereby increase arrests.)

Conceivably to sustain this blurring of serious crime, a barrage of cop public relations promotion is aimed at stirring up sexual demons in the general public, to convince them to accept the staggering waste of manpower and money. (Cops even use costly helicopters against cruising homosexuals!)

In a long, expensive trial, and on conflicting testimony that in any other case would have brought a dismissal of charges, a deputy mayor—who testified, with the corroboration of the city's respected mayor, that he was investigating complaints of gay harassment by vice cops—was convicted by a Los Angeles jury of "lewd conduct" in a tiny porno theater. In one of the highest violent-crime areas in the city, six vice cops "just happened" to be in that minuscule theater that night. Thus a man who was ably serving the community was forced to resign. Officially he became a "sex offender"—destroyed by the careless testimony of a man who will spend a portion of his life "pretending" in toilets to solicit sexual encounters.

Without realizing it, the people who support this cop-vendetta do so at the expense of their own security. They are duped—deliberately, calculatedly, callously—to condone real violence, crime which will turn viciously on them.

The more homosexuals are harassed, the more violent crime will rise—and in proportion, because of depleted law-enforcement resources.

Beyond all that, does police harassment stop sexual outlawry?

No. It increases it—creates it—by resultant defiance.

The police count on that.

4:16 A.M. *Montana Street. Hanson Avenue.*

A van stops. Two men. "Wanna three-way?"

Jim is glad for the straightforward approach. He doesn't want games. He is anxious to go home, but he wants— needs—one more contact for this night.

The man who asked him about the three-way is very attractive—and Jim is instinctively sure they're not cops. He will reciprocate with him, but he can't see the other clearly. So, to protect himself, he says, "I could get into it, but I don't do anything, myself."

The second man leans forward—he's equally attractive as the first. "You've got a gorgeous bod. Can we follow you?"

Yes.

4:24 A.M. *The Apartment.*

Before dawn.

Immediately, they're in the bedroom. All naked. Lovers from San Francisco, the two have lean bodies, sensual faces. From the pocket of his shirt, the taller of the two, both dark, brings out two amyl ampules—poppers—and a metallic inhaler.

Jim lies back on the bed—two mouths lick his body; it

awakens completely. He flexes on the bed, sending blood rushing to his muscles. Hard naked bodies shift about him. The tall man's cock is inches from Jim's mouth, and Jim is tempted to take it between his lips; but at least for now he wants to indulge the one-way expression of desire for him by the two.

He stands over them, legs spread. The shorter of the two men pops the amyl ampule, holds it up to Jim, the chemical odor holds him tightly, seals these moments of wild sex. He can hear the blood pumping in his head. The sex scene seems bordered, like a photograph, for close observation. The others sniff the ampule stuffed into the inhaler.

Standing, Jim directs the two heads to the areas of his body he wants explored by the eager tongues—flexed biceps, flexed pectorals, tensed stomach, tensed thighs, calves, cock, balls, ass. Now he lies back on the bed, and the glued mouths move with him. Each of the two is alternately jerking his own cock, the other's, Jim's. Now both mouths meet at Jim's genitals; the lips of one pulling lightly at the pubic hairs, the other's eating the head of his cock. The amyl encloses the scene even more tightly.

Like the others', Jim's cock is hard, hard. He stretches on the bed. The two others flank him, head to feet. They suck his cock and balls, their lips and tongues touching over Jim's groin. Now Jim's mouth receives the tall man's cock, then shifts to the other's, back to the tall man's, now the other's. He leans back, body stretching, ending for now the reciprocal acts. Now the taller poises his ass over Jim's straining cock, and the shorter man directs Jim's prick into his lover's ass. Jim enters it. The man raises and lowers his ass on the sliding cock. The third man holding the cock in place, Jim and the other shift their bodies on the bed. The tall man now lies on his back, legs held wide open by his lover into a wide-flaring V.

The shorter man licks Jim's ass. Jim pumps easily, pulling out his cock all the way, pushing it in again, out, in.

Before he can plunge in again, the shorter of the two lovers holds Jim's cock, redirects it to his own ass. The tall man sits up watching. The shorter man's ass is tighter than the other's; it won't open at first—and then it does, slowly, barely allowing Jim's cock entry, opens slowly, slowly. Now the taller of the two pops the other ampule, holding it, crushed, to each alternately.

Lifted by the amyl's waves of sensuality, Jim continues to delve deeper into the other's tight ass, feeling the flesh of the asshole gathering closely about the head of his cock, now about the sensitive ring of flesh below, now about the vein-pulsing shaft. Cum gathers with the sudden joyous rush of amyl as Jim fucks the smooth hole. As the tall man licks the point of contact—Jim's cock and balls and his lover's ass—Jim leans over, straining awkwardly, to suck the tall man's long cock, creating a line of raw sensation between his own cock and his mouth. Now Jim's hand directs the long cock toward the mouth of the man he's fucking.

The tall man kneels before the shorter man bent over. The shorter one receives the cock as Jim thrusts over and over into his ass in exactly the right rhythm, the ass opening to his cock, closing, opening, the softness inside kissing it. Jim looks down—sees his own cock, beautiful and hard and round and long, sees the hair-brushed flesh opening and closing to it, feels the shorter man's full cock pulsing in his hand. Sees and feels flesh and sex.

Male, male, male.

Jim pulls the man's legs wider, to enter the deepest part of him. Jim's lips meet the tall man's, tongues connecting moistly.

Bodies shift. Both lovers kneel head down, buttocks raised on the bed. Jim fucks one, fucks the other, returns to the tighter one, to the other again, the tighter one.

The taller man is jerking off his own cock, and his face is under Jim's groin. As Jim pulls in and out of the other's ass, the tall man licks the lunging cock and the other's parting asshole.

Jim's body contracts! Pulls forward like a gun! Death is challenged. Cocks explode! Jim's cock shoots into the ass. The tall man shoots into his lover's mouth, the other shoots a gliding arc of sperm into the air.

"Oh, God!"

Naked bodies lie back, motionless. They lie there for moments. The odor of sex and amyl hovers over the room.

Now the two lovers dress.

"Goodbye."

"Bye."

"Bye."

In the shower, Jim's soaped hands adore his muscular body. This night's hunt. And what was found? He concentrates on the sound of the jetting water. How many hands? How many mouths? How many cocks? How many assholes? How many lovers, strangers, men? He feels the specialness of his outlawry, and an exquisite joy.

He turns off the water. And what was found? What was searched for? Depression knots tightly at the center of his being.

He stands naked before the mirror. The joy returns.

Without looking out the window at the dawn, he pulls the drapes against it.

He lies naked on the white sheets. His hand cups his cock.

Saturday

10:08 A.M. *The Apartment. The Gym.*

HE WOKE CHARGED with energy from last night's hunt.

He has breakfast—several eggs mixed with milk, honey, and protein powder; all-grain bread with butter; and—his one indulgence to "trash food"—coffee. He takes a fistful of vitamins.

Ordinarily he doesn't work out on Saturdays, but kinetic power demands it today.

He'll pump his arms.

He inclines a long board on the back of a weighted chair. He grabs a loaded dumbbell. Propping his upper arm and elbow on the decline, he curls the dumbbell with careful slowness, feeling the resistance. One arm, then the other. One set each. Another. Two sets. Four, five. Seven sets. Exhaling in audible bursts, filling his lungs with oxygen, he forces more, low sets. One more repetition. And one more. Just . . . one . . . more.

He inspects himself in the mirror. He's ready.

Outside, the sun is white over shaggy palmtrees.

11:05 A.M. *Greenstone Park.*

He chooses Greenstone Park for the first few minutes of sunning. Relatively subdued in the afternoon—at times completely placid—it is still always potentially a sexual arena.

On the open spoon of grass next to the parking area, a few subdued exiles have gathered to sun in trunks. Jim doesn't join them.

He walks under the concrete grotto and onto the path. So different in the daylight. Sun penetrates the trees in warm patches. Choosing one just large enough to contain his body, he lies on the beach mat, thermos filled with protein beside him, and strips to tiny trunks, almost a posing strap. Minutes pass under the tanning sun. Half an hour. He's glad for the isolation, himself and the sexual sun. Footsteps. Jim opens his eyes narrowly. A hunter is staring at him. Jim stretches his body.

"You've got a beautiful body," the man says.

Jim feels the outlaw excitement stir.

"I've seen you hustling on Selma, I've got some money, I don't live far," the man invites.

Just that was enough for now. "Sorry, man, I'm in a hurry today. Another time, okay?" Jim tells the man.

The admiration, the offer of sexmoney—newly charged, Jim drinks from the thermos jar. For moments more he lies luxuriating in the hot sun and the awareness of his own body.

12:23 P.M.   *Griffith Park.*

Griffith Park is the capital of the sexual underground. Sprawling, all alcoves, grottos, paths, glens, branch-formed "caves," craggy inclines. Miles of sexhunting along declining paths, hills to the sides of the road. When on very hot days the area is closed to cars because of fire hazard, hundreds of outlaws hunt along the lower part of the park or move on foot in a jagged exodus up the hill.

Jim knows the seasonal and hourly vicissitudes of the year-round park, areas shifting with the sun.

Driving up the winding road, he scouts the area. He is wearing his exercise cutoffs, the bikini under it, no shirt, climbing boots. Dozens and dozens of cars, parked tightly by the sides of roads, or driving up and down, radios blaring. Hundreds of outlaws. Many young, attractive. Many beautiful, displaying semi-stripped bodies.

Jim parks in one of his favorite places. He walks to the edge of a foresty area. A "path" declines slightly toward thickening trees. He pauses. No one else is here now, but he descends the short path, into this depth of the park.

As he moves into the green, he hears the sound of his feet pressing the ground. He pauses. He clears his hearing of other sounds. Then he starts walking ahead, this time to gather the sounds his body creates as it passes through the green. His shoulder brushes the branch of a tree, just as his foot presses blades of long uncut grass. Moist. Blades glisten. A brittle twig at the end of the branch cracks. He sees the blades of grass bend under his feet, press into the ground, slide against each other as he passes, and then they begin to rise. Dry brown and yellow leaves on the underside of low brush break. They lie on the ground, dry, along with others, moist, the dry ones turned up, edges stabbing-sharp. A long branch pushed back with his hand resists, pushes, then gives, snapping back, shaking the leaves of another tree. A few leaves fall dead, joining the others on the ground. The branch hits a twig. The shadow of the branch, trapped in a spear of cutting light, streaks the moist green earth, then stops, tangled into other shadows. Jim stops. He stares at the unmoving shadows of tall trees. Where the sun invades, they form diagonals. The tall trees stir only at the high top, goaded by a breeze. There is the vague sound of dry rustling. He inhales. He listens. The sweet musty odor of moist wood and greenery—he smells its definite presence. It mixes with the sounds of grass, leaves, moisture, twigs, branches, shadows, stillness. He looks into the greenness ahead until he sees carved green forms within the frieze of green. He stares down at the ground. He moves his foot on the moist and dry leaves. They stir. Then he moves on.

Back up the path. Ready to commit himself to the hunt, he crosses the main concrete road, to a hill. There are two main accesses to its summit, a gradually ascending dirt road, which requires ten minutes' climbing, and a rougher one over rocks and under snagging branches, which takes two minutes. Jim chooses the faster. Perspiration beads his oiled muscles.

12:34 P.M. *Griffith Park. The Hill.*

On the hill are several choice spots for sunbathing, the best ones for good sexual contact being feet away from branchy hollows of trees.

The first spot. An unattractive loose-fleshed old man lies there naked, his hand on his spent groin. Abandoned and desperate and alone—one of many lingering, ubiquitous, wasted, judging ghosts in the gay world. Jim avoids him.

Another spot. Another naked man—attractive; he looks up at Jim and invites. An older man, fully, hotly dressed, as if to conceal his body among so much nakedness, stares at them over the bushes. Jim darts into a yawning cove of branches. The naked youngman wraps a towel about his waist and follows. In the leafy cave, he pulls Jim's trunks down, then the bikini; Jim removes the other's towel. Cock rubs cock. The other blows Jim, then straightens up. Jim is about to go down on him when he sees the fully dressed man entering the cove. Jim and the other stop their movement, adjust towel and trunks. Long, long moments, and the man won't leave. Annoyed, Jim breaks away.

At the pinnacle of this hill, two men lie in trunks, side by side, holding hands.

Jim walks to the opposite side of the hill. In another place, barely enclosed by low bushes, a boyish youngman spreads his legs, his own fingers exploring his ass invitingly.

Jim moves on until he finds an unoccupied spot. He drinks from the thermos of protein, spreads his beach mat, removes his trunks and bikini, and lies under the sun, the bikini bunched loosely at his groin. The man who earlier intruded on him and the other has followed him here. Jim ignores him. The man moves desolately away.

Eyes closed, Jim hears rustling branches, quickening sighs. Footsteps emerge from the nearby brushy area.

The sun kisses Jim's body; he dozes for moments. The sound of footsteps rouses him. He doesn't open his eyes. The footsteps approach, closer. Closer. His eyes remain deliberately shut. The footsteps have reached his side. Now a hand pushes away the bunched bikini from his groin, a mouth envelops his cock. Still, Jim doesn't open his eyes. The sun, his sweat, the mouth sucking. . . . Now he eases the mouth away. Footsteps depart. Jim's eyes remain closed.

Moments later he stands, stretches naked—aware electrically of a presence in the immediate area.

In the bushes to his left, a light-haired man is standing under the sun-mottled leaves; he looks very handsome, young—and vaguely familiar.

The youngman motions to Jim. Jim puts on the cutoffs and moves down the path. Now he sees the man clearly. Attractive, yes, but not as desirable as Jim thought at first; he will make it with him, yes, but he's not sure he'll reciprocate, as he thought earlier. The body is perhaps too thin, the face, though young, is already too sexhungry in its gauntness. But the eyes—so blue. Blue. Again, Jim has a sense of passing recognition.

In the hollow alcove, the man kneels before Jim, taking his cock urgently, sucking it almost desperately, face shifting, rimming him, tongue returning hungrily to the balls, cock; gasping, almost in panic. Now the face looks up at Jim; the man implores: "Spit on me! Piss in my mouth!"

Jim looks down at him, at the impossibly blue eyes. Jim shakes his head. No. The man's eyes!

"Please! Treat me as rough as you want! I'll drink your piss, I'll— . . .!"

Jim retreats from the blue, blue eyes. Adjusting his trunks, he moves out of the hollow. He turns back impulsively. "Is your name— . . .?"

But the man moves swiftly along the path, in search of someone else.

FLASHBACK: *Griffith Park. Ten Years Ago.*

A very beautiful youngman, slender, sandy-haired, full lips. It was his first time in the park, he told Jim, who was not nearly as muscular as now, had more of a gymnast's body then. And it was Jim's first season in the park. Before, his primary scene had been as hustler.

They almost didn't make it. Although the youngman

was beautiful, Jim thought him too young, perhaps seven-teen, maybe even— . . . And Jim is very seldom attracted to the very young. But the youngman, alternately shy and youthfully aggressive, insisted. Please. They walked down a long path. They lay on the leaves, both reticent—Jim because of his inability to advance first, and, too, because of the other's newness and youth; the other because of inexperience. But they managed. They moved slowly, cautiously, simultaneously—and they kissed; he was one of the very first men Jim had ever kissed. They kissed very, very long. Mostly that. Lying on the green, brown, yellow leaves, they didn't even undress fully. They merely touched each other, gently, as if for the first time, a slow innocence. That was all. And they came pressing against each other. Just that. Jim never forgot the youngman. Nor his blue, blue, impossibly blue, eyes. Nor his name. Danny.

VOICE OVER: *Consenting Adults, Explorer Scout*
Girls, and Glittering Bisexuals

1

"JUDGMENT AFFIRMED."

With only two words, the Supreme Court said that homosexuals are not necessarily entitled to the right of privacy ensured by the Constitution. It did so tacitly by allowing to stand, without hearing, a decision of the United States District Court for the Eastern District of Virginia upholding a Virginia statute making homosexual acts between consenting adults, even in private, a crime punishable with up to three years' imprisonment and not less than one. The state has the overriding freedom to promote "morality and decency," their honors declared, adding, "We cannot say that the statute offends the Bill of Rights."

The case was brought up by "John Doe" plaintiffs to test a statute declaring anal and oral sex a felony, whether in public or private. Because the statute did not differentiate between heterosexual and homosexual acts, the two-man majority on the Virginia court of three judges—one dissenting—clearly had to skirt the issue of concurrently barring such acts for heterosexuals. This it did gingerly by arguing that in the case of *Griswold v. Connecticut* (1965), which the plaintiffs had used as their primary basis for argument and in which the Supreme Court struck down a statute forbidding the use of contraceptives, their decision had asserted the right of privacy *only in marriage*.

So much for that.

Now they could deal with homosexuals: ". . . since [homosexuality] is obviously no portion of marriage, home or family life," the majority opinion thus ignored gay fathers, gay mothers, gay children, "the . . . question is whether there is any ground for barring Virginia from branding it as criminal. If a State determines that punishment therefor, even when committed in the home, is appropriate in the promotion of morality and decency, it is not for the courts to say that the State is not free to do so. . . . Fundamentally the State action is simply directed to the suppression of crime. . . ."

"Moreover . . . the State is not required to show that moral delinquency actually results from homosexuality," the judges somersaulted. "It is enough . . . to establish that the conduct is likely to end in a contribution to moral delinquency. . . . It would indeed be impracticable to prove the actuality of such a consequence," they acknowledged, but, fuck it, "the law is not so exacting," their honors snapped testily.

Nudging aside the doctrine of separation of church and state, the Virginia majority traced anti-homosexuality to the Bible, quoting the familiar admonishments from Leviticus and including the exhortation that homosexuals "shall surely be put to death." Certainly their enlightened honors were not signaling the state for more drastic punishment?

In a humane and intelligent dissent, District Judge Merhige chastised the two majority judges: ". . . in the absence of any legitimate interest of rational basis to support the statute's application we must, without regard to our own proclivities, . . . hold the statute . . . to be violative of . . . the Due Process Clause of the Fourteenth Amendment to the Constitution of the United States. . . .

Private consensual sex acts between adults are matters . . . in which the State has no legitimate interest."

Pointing out the majority's nifty separation of heterosexual acts from homosexual acts, Judge Merhige continued: "To say . . . that the right of privacy . . . is limited in matters of marital, home, or family life is unwarranted under the law . . . is inconsistent with current Supreme Court opinions and is unsupportable. . . . That the right of privacy is not limited to the facts of *Griswold* is demonstrated by later Supreme Court decisions. . . . [In *Eisenstadt v. Baird* (1972)] the Court declined to restrict the right of privacy in sexual matters to married couples . . . [and] to a great extent vitiated any implication that the State can . . . forbid extramarital sexuality. . . . The right to select consenting adult sexual partners must be considered within this category . . . whether heterosexual or homosexual. [The State of Virginia] . . . made no tender of any evidence that even impliedly demonstrated that homosexuality causes society any significant harm. . . . To suggest, as defendants do, that the prohibition of homosexual conduct will in some manner encourage new heterosexual marriages and prevent the dissolution of existing ones is unworthy of judicial response. . . . I can find no authority for intrusion by the State into the private dwelling of a citizen. . . . the issue centers not around morality or decency, but on the Constitutional right of privacy."

In words as succinctly eloquent as any pronounced in support of true judicial understanding, the dissenting judge admonished: "What we know as men is not [to be] forgotten as judges."

Nevertheless:

"Judgment affirmed," said the Supreme Court about the Virginia majority opinion—and dismissed, without hearing, the appeal. (Supreme Court Justices Brennan, Marshall, and Stevens would have heard the matter.)

Affirmed: The ancestral judgments of frightened men. Affirmed: The spilling of blood demanded by the Bible. Affirmed: The burnings and incarceration of the dark and "enlightened" ages. Affirmed: Prosecutions, blackmailings, muggings, attacks, literal and symbolic assassinations and murders. Affirmed: The psychological and physical torture of gay children—and adults. With two dull words the Supreme Court affirmed that grotesque spectrum of sexual ignorance.

Even in states where private consensual sex acts between adults would continue to be protected, the impact of the upheld Virginia decision was major. In effect condoning anti-homosexuality, it goaded cops and other gay-haters everywhere on their psyche-terrified rampages, it armed quivering bigots to draw up referendum petitions to revoke legitimization of freedom of sexual choice.

And it would certainly bestir the revolutionary fervor of sexual outlawry on the streets.

Shortly after the Supreme Court affirmation, "straight" marauders in Los Angeles lay in wait in the parking lot of, appropriately, a church. As cars in the well-known gay area cruised the street, from the shadows gangs attacked with rocks and bottles.

Not a single cop showed up.

2

Cops did show up, however, when a group of teenage female Explorer Scouts began appearing at Los Angeles precincts to help out with law-enforcement matters. After all, when dozens of men are out busting homosexuals, massage parlors, and book stores, an awful lot of work goes unattended—and these young girls would certainly aid. Ranging from fourteen to eighteen years of age, the girls were part of a group known as LEEGS—Law Enforcement Explorer Girl Scouts—numbering about 250, and affiliated *not* with the Girl Scouts but with the Boy Scouts. As it developed, for a few there was an extra "E" in the acronym: The girls and the overworked officers were exploring far more than "crime."

Or so would a small Los Angeles-area newspaper, the *Valley News*—scooping everyone else—proclaim in its banner headline:

LAPD SEX SCANDAL

MORALS PROBE REVOLVES AROUND POLICE, GIRL SCOUTS

Certainly not!

Hadn't there only a short time back been a memorandum—circulated among Los Angeles police and "constituents"—from a deputy chief, no less, warning against the employment of homosexuals as policemen and setting out with alarm the reasons why this must never, never be?

". . . The man or woman in blue is responsible for finding lost children . . . ," wrote the deputy chief, "instructing and counseling the young. . . . Police officers, like school teachers, engage in intimate and delicate relationships with children. Consider some regular Police programs. . . . Police Explorers, Student Workers, and Summer Camps . . . place an officer in the position to teach and influence young children . . . to mold the youthful ideals and morals of the youth of our country. All these areas pair children and the police in a very close relationship. A homosexual placed anywhere within this area would be a violation of parental and social trust. Additionally, police officers are often required to fill the role of counselor to juveniles regarding sexual matters."

Indeed!

For some time, teenagers of both sexes were being used in affiliation with the Los Angeles Police Department. Among their duties was keeping watch from atop buildings on busy Hollywood streets. Equipped with smart walkie-talkies, they could communicate to patrol cars any "unusual" activity, whatever that included. They also went on cop beats and block patrols, these busy teenagers, and they learned crowd control. They were taken camping on some weekends. There, reportedly, was where "exploration" of another kind may have occurred—perhaps while one or another of the cops was filling "the role of counselor . . . regarding sexual matters."

Rumors had floated around police stations that some cops were involved with underage girls. Then one of the LEEGS girls, herself reportedly not involved, told a police lieutenant that the weekends had turned into "sex orgies." Approximately 30 Hollywood Division uniformed officers and 6 teenage girls, some as young as fourteen, the informant to the *Valley News* alleged, were involved. An investigation by the internal division of the police department had been going on, quietly, for a month, a police captain acknowledged, and the results might involve criminal action. He denied that there were any "sex orgies," that fourteen-year-old girls were involved, and that the incidents had occurred during camping trips.

Badgered at a news conference, an assistant police chief insisted doggedly that none of this constituted "a sex scandal": "There was no rape, no seduction, there was a lot of agreement. We don't have any outraged parents, which is kind of disappointing, I guess. We don't have any outraged young people. We've got outraged police officers. But I don't think you can call it a sex scandal." He emphasized that only private situations were involved, all with off-duty officers, none in the LEEGS Program themselves. And so, one could at least allow a sigh of relief that no explorer perched on a rooftop had allowed *her* eyes to stray from the busy streets.

Goddamnit, there was no sex scandal!

16 FACE CHARGES IN
LAPD SEX SCANDAL

In its new headlined story, the scooping *Valley News* indicated that the alleged 30 police had, not unexpectedly, shrunk to an alleged 16; the number of teenage girls, including 4 juveniles, was holding strong at 6. Nine of the 16 cops might face felony charges of unlawful sex with a person under eighteen, 4 to 5 might be charged with misdemeanors of contributing to the delinquency of a minor. All 16—unnamed—faced disciplinary action, and some, now, insubordination and failure to cooperate with the internal-affairs investigation. Raising the age one year on each side, the deputy chief now alleged the exploring girls were fifteen to nineteen years old.

Soon the 16 police dwindled to 3 facing felony counts, while 6 others might still be charged with misdemeanors. And: The girls, the acting chief now declared, were between sixteen and eighteen. (When? Two years ago? Now? That was left unclear.) One could expect that before the matter was over, the "girls" would be middle-aged matrons.

The girls resigned, the cops remained on duty.

At a press conference, the chief of police—whose refrain for opposing hiring gay cops had been What-about-when-they-deal-with-boys?—offered to discuss sex—"tomorrow."

There was much joking about the cops and the hypocrisy exposed. "Since when does there have to be violence in order for sexual misconduct to occur? Many a child molester is a kindly old soul," read a letter in the *Los Angeles Times*. Another: "Comforting to learn that the officers have been permitted to remain on duty—hopefully protecting us from gay bars, nude beaches, and massage parlors." And: "For those of us liberals who wanted heterosexuals to have an opportunity to prove themselves worthy of public trust, this has been a sad year: . . . heterosexual sex scandals in the U.S. Congress . . . heterosexual sex scandals in the Los Angeles Police Department."

Amid the understandable glee in the gay community, there was much bitterness: Had 30 gay scoutmasters been allegedly involved with 6 teenage boys, would any police spokesman have insisted there was "no sex scandal"? Would the investigation have been conducted quietly? Would the accused still be employed instead of having been taken, handcuffed, to jail cells and released, if at all, on staggering bails? Would it have mattered that the boys had given their consent—might even have sought out the scoutmasters? That there had been no violence? That there were no outraged parents?

No. The police would have generated the outrage, names and photographs would have been released, television cameras would have explored campgrounds for discarded bubblegum wrappers, cops would lecture against the gay menace. There would not have been a promised discussion of the sex scandal . . . "tomorrow"—it would have been discussed yesterday, today, and tomorrow and tomorrow.

The reality was that straight cops were involved in the scandal. The matter had been exposed only because of the chance-taking of an obscure newspaper and a daring reporter. From news story to news story it was becoming clear that the legal charges against the men involved were fading fast. (Misdemeanor—not felony—charges were finally filed against 5 cops, now identified and ranging in age from twenty-four to thirty-four, for unlawful sexual intercourse and contributing to the delinquency of a minor. A one-year statute of limitations had precluded possible prosecution of any of the others; several were relieved of their duties, some suspended pending hearings, and one was totally cleared.) But the frantic hypocrisy of memorandums and rationalized bigotry, of frenzied speeches warning of the danger of gay police officers in dealing with children—that had been revealed. The hypocrisy was glaring, and that was important.

And yet—difficult as it would be, and very, for gays relentlessly hounded by the police—it was important that homosexuals "support" the cops trapped in the "explorer-girl sex scandal"; yes, to point out that to prosecute those sex-defiant cops was *almost* as unfair as prosecuting homosexuals ("almost," because the cops would be dealt with a leniency not extended to homosexuals; "almost," because the factors of hypocrisy and life-destroying persecution of gays could not be easily forgiven). After all, the sex had all been consensual between the cops and the girls, whether 14, 15, 16, 17, 18—or 45 years old; perhaps some of the girls were police groupies? It was the same hungry hypocritical evil of fake "morality" that devours homosexuals daily that was, for a change, nibbling at the cops.

The acting chief of police had emphasized over and over: All the activities had been *willing*, there had been *no force*, there had been only *consent*.

He was echoing, word for word, the basis for gay rights.

Was it too much to hope that the prosecuted officers would see the connection between their situation and that of homosexuals? Would they see—and therefore be stirred themselves by outlaw indignation—the trap of *all* sexual hypocrisy?

3

A growing sexual hypocrisy is the chic-y pose of "glittering bisexuality." It's everywhere, like sequined pollen. A magazine does a spread on a separated count and countess announcing their affairs with both men and women, a rock singer proclaims his bisexuality, unisex costumes flourish like space mushrooms, a resolutely gay writer insists he's "bithexual," and the "glitter bars" are crowded with "straight" couples and singles. Not rare in such bars to hear the question put by one man to his male dancing partner:

"Are you gay or straight?"

Well, isn't bisexuality the ideal condition—employing "the best of both worlds"? It is only one of at least three "ideal" possible worlds; and to uphold it as *the* ideal is to deny the specialness of both male and female, and to diminish both the heterosexual experience and the homosexual experience—and the true bisexual experience.

Because of its easy, safe, chic acceptability (especially among the upperclasses, i.e., hairdressers and fashion designers), the *claim* of "bisexuality" to mask homosexuality offers a ready escape from the need to assert one's sexual choice truly, fully—and radically. Just as no more reactionary figure exists than the member of a minority who self-protectively "passes" for one of the majority, so the homosexual posing as "bisexual" dissipates the revolutionary commitment required to smash repressive laws and attitudes. None of this is to deny the existence, nor the right of choice, of genuine bisexuals.

And a daring word in support of the heterosexual man. At a time of often justified battering from straight women and gay men and women, and attacked as if he were not essential to the survival of the species, the heterosexual man must be granted his definitive place too. But his sexual specialness is being seriously assaulted. Her thinking fashioned increasingly by the new, slick women's magazines, a type of straight woman may even expect her heterosexual lover to look and "be" like the predominantly gay models (defined by bogus biographies, fantasies presented as real) pictured within those pages. She is in effect being "taught" to yearn for a gay man in a straight man. Here, too—as in the context of gays taught by straights—expectations and realities clash, disastrously, for all.

To accept both the "male" and "female" aspects of one's being while finally asserting a sexual preference for one sex is liberating—and different from being homosexual and posing hypocritically as—or passing as—"bisexual" simply because it is not dangerous to do so.

Where all sexual boundaries blur, it is at the expense of all sexual experiences.

There are homosexuals, men and women.

There are heterosexuals, women and men.

There are, increasingly, transsexuals, men and women.

And there are genuine bisexuals, women and men.

All distinct experiences. Each different. Each unique. Each special. Each potentially "ideal."

1:12 P.M. *Griffith Park. The Hill.*

JIM LIES ON the beachmat. It wasn't Danny, he tells himself, it wasn't him. But he knows the earlier one has disappeared today. Suddenly he feels an objectless panic. He touches his muscles.

He's grateful for the presence of someone else now: A tall husky goodlooking man waiting in the same grotto. Jim sees him snort from an inhaler. The magic sex vapor. He holds it out toward Jim, inviting. Jim moves back into the hollow. The man holds the inhaler to Jim's nose. Jim is instantly enveloped in a wave of sensuality. Already, the man is going down on him. The chemical rush spreads—Jim imagines he is the other, and himself—that he is blowing himself, reaching the places on himself that he can't reach, seeing himself as if he were two: He feels his own hard cock in the other's throat as if it is his own throat which has opened to swallow his own cock.

Again the amyl. Again the time-stopping, sexually isolating moments. The other has lowered his own pants, a round cock juts out. Jim snorts more deeply of the amyl and bending down sucks the other, imagining it's his own cock in his own throat.

Now both men stand tightly pressed. Jim feels the other's cum smearing both their stomachs.

Minutes later Jim moves along the path. The boyish youngman who lay barely concealed, legs spread inviting, is still in the same spot; but now another man crouches over him.

The unmistakable roar of the hated helicopter!

The cops!

Men move for cover. Jim continues along the sheltered path.

The helicopter circles ominously, whipping up the dirt along the paths.

1:38 P.M. *Griffith Park. The Road. A Path.*

On the main road the hunters have increased.

Jim drives past the exhibitionistic lookout: A "U" in the road, where, parked strategically, men in cars flash naked bodies at each other across a gorge. Most of the areas along the road are taken; several cars in each—and Jim never joins others already there—an attitude as arrogant as it is defensive. Finally, on the upper part of the road, he stops in an area shaded by trees; three cars just drove away. Behind, rocks rise into a brushy hill.

He stands exhibiting himself. A very handsome man drives by. He looks back. Jim answers the signal. The man U-turns, parks behind Jim's car, and gets out. He's even better than Jim thought; he's very muscular, obviously a bodybuilder too.

Jim walks slowly toward the path behind—slowly, to make sure that the other follows before he commits himself to the rocky climb. The other does. They climb steep rocks, move along a short dirt path, climb more rocks—higher into the hill. Still higher. They have silently conveyed to each other that they want more than the furtive moments a readily accessible place might provide. They climb still more. Now they reach a tightly sheltered pocket of trees. They have to stoop to enter it.

1:47 P.M. *Griffith Park. The Isolated Cove.*

Standing before each other—mirror images—they flex in the fantasy poses of body magazines. Briefly, they touch each other. Now they remove their clothes. Naked in the remote cove, they kiss, hands outline carved muscles.

Now the other's downward-sliding tongue draws a moist line along Jim's flat stomach to his groin. Jim cups the other's hard pectorals. The other's mouth glides slowly lower. Jim looks down, seeing his own firm thighs, the other's; his flat stomach, the other's; his stone-hard cock, the other's. Their muscles. Jim squeezes the other's nipples very softly; the other sighs.

Both stand, separating so they can study each other's flexing bodies, looking at the muscles they will soon touch, lick, fuse with—aware, each, of the rush of blood into aroused organs, as into weight-pumped muscles. The man's tongue dabs at Jim's nipples, now it slides from one to the other, around, in tiny, soft brush strokes, moving under the arms, into the armpits, mouth nestling there, tongue rousing the moist hair, lapping gently at the gathering sweat, tongue returning to the pectorals, down the torso, nestling in his navel, moving downward moistly to the pubic hairs flecked with spilled sun.

Alive, alert, Jim can almost feel the tiny buds on the other's tongue as it moves down in circles on his tingling flesh; tongue inching steadily downward, until—at the moment that Jim, leaning back sighing, anticipates the mouth will enclose his cock—it moves up again, instead, startling anew the flesh at his nipples. The man bites. Jim pulls back. The other licks the barely stung nipples with a light-brushing tongue—which now glides up to meet Jim's, mouth open. They kiss, tongues extending, withdrawing, tongue sucking tongue. They part again, to see each other fully; again to study the muscles they will again explore.

Their hard chests gleam in the spotty sun.

Jim glances at the hairs shining on their legs. He reaches over to touch the other's protruding cock as the other bends, mouth swiftly enclosing Jim's bare cock. Jim feels the skin of his cock pull back, the head exposed raw to sensation, feels the other's saliva lubricating the cock, feels the tongue finding the ring-like indention between the head and the shaft; the tongue swirls there.

Jim reaches for the other's cock. Visual images, physical sensations meld. Where is he feeling the other, where is the other feeling him? He wants the other's cock in his mouth, but the other will not release his yet. The head of Jim's cock pauses at the back of the other's mouth, as if that is as far as it can penetrate. But expertly the other's throat opens, and the cock, poised only for moments, slides in, head, vein-pulsing shaft—as if to burst within. Holding it there, the other constricts the muscles of his throat, squeezing Jim's blood-gorged cock tighter, lips touching his balls. Jim's eyes devour the spectacle—his pubic hairs against the other's mouth, his balls firmly against the other's chin; his cock hotly inside the other's throat.

Now the other releases Jim's cock. He straightens up; his cock is so rigid rising from the furry pubic area that it almost parallels his stomach. Again, apart, they flex.

Jim bends over the other's waiting cock, but his mouth retreats deliberately without touching it yet; instead his tongue moves in a "T" from the other's pectorals to, then along, the trickle of hair down his stomach, to the cock again. Pubic hairs touch his lips. The full cock slides into his mouth, his hands rise grasping the other's tensing pectorals. The sexual flesh engorges his mouth.

They lie on the leaf-mattressed ground, head to feet. The other's mouth nestles below Jim's balls, velvet tongue edging toward his ass; it glides tantalizingly over Jim's buttocks, avoiding the opening. Jim releases the cock in his mouth, takes it again, releases it again, takes it. The other swallows Jim's cock—and suddenly releasing it, the mouth slides back to the buttocks, presses against the parting, the lips kissing it. The other's mouth opens, the tongue protrudes, his hands pull Jim's buttocks softly apart to expose the inner opening; the tongue touches it softly, draws back and forth.

Jim's lips hold the head of the other's cock, his tongue circling the sensitive ring of raw flesh. He stares at the flesh less than inches from him. His tongue slides over the other's tight balls; he encloses one in his lips, then the other. Sensations blend with sensations; as if what the other is doing to him, he is doing back; as if what he is doing to the other, the other is doing to him. Time stops.

Their eyes are open wide, studying naked muscles

outrageously flexed; limbs, organs. Jim touches the other's flaring thighs, his fingers awakening the soft field of hairs; his hands about the other's buttocks, stretching them, touching the knotted hole with his finger—as the other explores his with his tongue. Masculine, beautiful, muscles, male. Quickly the bodies shift, head to head. Lips grasp flitting tongues. Naked, cocks, male, outlaws. They inhale deeply the sweet odor of their mixed, clean sweat. They taste it on their tongues.

Again they part to look at carved pectorals, thick arms, wide shoulders, tight waists, round legs. Naked muscular bodies. They press together again, cock on cock, hands sliding up and down, around, front, back; mouth on mouth, mouths on nipples, mouths on cocks, on balls, thighs on thighs, mouth on mouth. And now mouths on cocks, cocks in mouths; they blow each other rhythmically, the inward thrust of one's mouth matching the outward pull of the other's, alternating. Is it his own cum Jim feels gathering from all over his body, or is it the other's? Both? He feels it, rushing as if from his feet, along tensed calves and hard thighs, buttocks; feels it rushing, sliding, up the spine to his cock and into the other's mouth, along spine, buttocks, thighs, calves, feet—and back to the other's cock and into Jim's mouth and back to the other's in an electric fused circle.

Jim breaks the circle, pulling his head back to capture visually the moment of challenged death—and the other's orgasmic liquid arcs in a pearly spurt into the air. Jim's body contracts, feeling his own cum flowing into the other's throat—once, again, again—and Jim takes the other's cream-smeared cock in his mouth—both men still coming, as if the universe itself were gathering into their bodies, their mouths, their cocks.

MONTAGE: *The City*

FIVE HUNDRED AND ninety-seven miles of freeways in Los Angeles! Longer than from here to Phoenix by almost two hundred miles!

The Santa Ana Freeway, Santa Monica Freeway, Ventura, Hollywood, Harbor, Golden State, San Diego Freeways!

Wheeeeeeeeee!

Onramps and offramps and sweeping connecting archways clinging to gravity. Magnificent concrete arcs. Freeways leading everywhere! At night cars stopped to avert recurrent disasters—crushed trucks, stalled cars, an ostrich (once) blocking the lanes—form a ruby necklace of braking red lights.

This great city's pulsing arteries, five hundred and ninety-seven miles leading to nice-death at death-loving Forest Lawn, to childsex at Disneyland, contrived disasters at Universal Studios, simulated corpses at wax museums, throw-back premieres, impossibly gorgeous rose gardens, the grand Watts Towers asserting peasant love. Progressive colleges and universities, repressive colleges and universities.

Those hundreds of tangled miles of freeways try valiantly to embrace the contradictions of this technicolor city. Freedom and repression in a palmtreed battlefield—with time out at the beaches. Loving and hating, the gentle and the violent, glorious beauty and hard-core ugliness. Beaches and forests and deserts. The elegance and the raunch. Manson and the new Governor Brown. Om and Amen. Body and Soul. Extravagant nude bodies and Hare Krishna zombies.

Rebellious dopers and the red-necked grandsons of Okies, crushed—as the dust bowl couldn't—by lower-middleclass splendor.

Brrrrmmmmmmmmmmmmm!

Every Wednesday night, the red-neck children, with pimples like hard-earned badges, drive customized cars (just off the blocks—stick shifts held like roaring hard-ons) up and down a blocks-long area of Van Nuys Boulevard; they parade their chrome creations like small dinosaurs, low-riding. Vans like squat futuristic castles. A pubic ritual of growling engines. On the sidewalk, little groupies applaud the pimpled charioteers.

Brrrrmmmmmmmmmmmmm!

And downtown Los Angeles is the casbah of the walking dead among courageous tambourined missions *insisting: Survive!*

Yes, hundreds of miles connecting splendid names—Westlake, Silverlake, Hollywood, Echo Park, Bel Air, Laurel Canyon—and ugly names—Azusa ("A" to "Z" in the U.S.A.!), Tujunga, Downey, Tarzana, for godssake!

Carpets of magnificent flowers. Those proud birds of paradise with golden beaks. Those blue and purple lupin. Those joshua trees with bunches of blossoms like candelabra! Flowers that will eventually cover the razed lot where L.A. cops burned the S.L.A. on TV.

And palmtrees. Bless the lofty proud palmtrees!

Bless the unflinching movie-struck hordes in coffee-houses discussing where they felt that breakthrough emotion that freed them, man, *you* know, to, *you* know, man, *act!* ("And Justin said, man, 'Let it come out, let it come out—all of it, every bit of it—that's what acting, and living, are all about!'")

Sweep off the freeway!

Sunset Strip, best gallery of pop art in the world. Electric posters, giant electric mouths opening and closing, electric tongues protruding, winking electric eyes, electric crushed rainbows. Sexy cardboard electric men and women. Jeweled neon. Phosphorescence as art form.

Revolutionary murals in East L.A. And a dazzling frieze on La Brea: Greek statues, painted like movie stars, lounge among L.A. palmtrees; The Thinker, unusually muscular, is tanned bronze.

And four thousand and forty-three and seven-tenths acres of land donated to Los Angeles by, bless him, Colonel Griffith J. Griffith.

Griffith Park in the midst of the great city, acres of forested hills, miles of driving roads and hiking paths. Golf courses, tennis courts, sex haunts, meandering horse trails, merry-go-round, springs, picnic areas, exhibitionistic heaven, train rides, Travel Town, Mineral Wells, flowers, voyeurs' delight, wild trees, squirrels, sexual paradise, wild deer, bird-watching; and a saintly hermit lived in the park undetected for months.

There's a makebelieve sky at Griffith Park Observatory. Every hour they create a star-spilled sky on a magic cyclorama.

The sky that used to be.

On the beach, a man plants an exotic red cloth poster decorated with magazine pictures of Coca-Cola bottles, Marlboro men, Volkswagen vans, refrigerators, furniture. In a booming voice he gathers tanned bodies about him on the sand. Beard and hair scratching at the sea wind, he prophesies:

"I predict the sun will set tonight, and I predict the night will come, I predict the night will fade at dawn, and the sun will rise again, I predict people will die and new ones will be born."

Acceptance as prophecy. Survival as habit.

2:12 P.M. *Griffith Park. The Road. Another Hill.*

BACK ON THE main road—and a new wave of men has poured into the tide already in the park—the two muscular men smile at each other. Both hesitate to enter their cars, resisting the ancestral pull to become strangers again after the intimacy; each waits as if for the other to extend the connection into another time, another place, another level. But neither can, that ancestral fear of rejection pulls. Still smiling, still hesitating, still looking back, they inch toward their cars, slowly, wait at open doors—and then they drive away.

As superb as the sexual sharing was only moments earlier, Jim is aware immediately of an instant panicked emptiness. Only one moment of time was conquered, the experience ending when it began. Another eternity challenges him. So he drives to another side of the park, to another hill in the arena.

Suddenly the fragment of a broken memory cuts. . . . Danny.

The sun's heat laps at the park and him as he climbs the rocky barren hill. Only at the top are there trees. The brush is sear, brittle, weedy along the jagged "paths." Almost at the top, Jim looks up and sees a copper-tanned, tall man standing naked on a rock. Because he's attracted to him—

and because others are here, wandering the area, in trunks, or clothed, or lying nude in depressed clearings of rocks— Jim turns away sharply, obviating even the barest possibility of rejection; but he makes himself available like this: He slides under a gathering of trees nearby. A man is blowing another. Jim moves out quickly.

He stands among open rocks against sharp blue sky. A towel now wrapped around his middle, the tall man follows him there. They stand on the brown rocks. "Fuck me," the man says to Jim. Despite the earlier long orgasm, Jim feels his cock react. To prepare for the act, the tall man sucks Jim for moments. Now he sprawls on a towel-draped rock, his legs spread invitingly, one finger moistening his ass with suntan oil. "Cummon, baby, fuck me!"

Goaded exhibitionistically by at least two other men who stand watching eagerly—and now another is straining to look over the brush—Jim manages to slide his cock, not entirely hard, into the tall man. Legs straining, the tall man came the instant Jim's cock entered him. Jim withdraws his soft cock, wiping it on the man's towel.

He climbs down the hill hurriedly, drives up to the restroom outside the Observatory—and washes his cock with soap, preparing it for more encounters.

2:47 P.M.   *Griffith Park. The Arena.*
There are men all over the sexual turf—some men shirtless or tanktopped, in bluejeans; others in trunks, shorts, cutoffs, bikinis; and some—even in the hot, hot sun— stand rigidly in black leather by motorcycles like surly chrome animals.

Along the road, Jim sees a hugely muscular man he's seen often in the park. Elegantly theatrical in leather shorts, strapped sandals, he walks a beautiful, sleekly muscular dog, like an extension of himself. The man glances quickly away from Jim's car, recognizing it and him, just as Jim glanced away from him, each trying to beat the other at looking away. One's obvious narcissism challenges the other's. Although each wants to, they will never come together.

Leaning against the side of his car a few moments later, eyes closed, Jim is startled by a man's voice—he must have walked up from the bushes behind.

"Remember me?—you jerked off in my mouth up the road a few weeks ago," the man says.

Jim doesn't remember him.

"Want to do it again?" the man asks.

Jim doesn't. "Sorry, I just came."

The man moves away.

Replaced by an attractive one, blond.

Moments later Jim and the blond youngman face each other in the sheltered brush below. Each is signaling the other by brushing his exposed groin. But there's an impasse—neither moves. "Suck me," Jim says finally. "That's what I want *you* to do to *me*," the other says. Instant enemies, they move back to their cars.

Now Jim will commit himself to what he calls "the arena." Parking among many cars near a turn in the road, he breathes deeply. This "arena" demands the fullest commitment because the very abundance of choices in the shifting choreography creates the most precarious balance between success and rejection. Although he knows it will be crowded with dozens of hunters, Jim can enter it— ostensibly but not actually violating one of his "rules"— because it is so wide and sprawling that it is not as if he were "joining" one group.

He moves into a hollow clearing. Crumpled papers, a semen-caked handkerchief (relics left by other outlaws) lie on the leaves. Jim waits, alone.

A goodlooking man enters—is about to approach Jim, when another, equally goodlooking, moves in. Panic grabs Jim. Before he can leave—goaded by even the possibility that the two will prefer each other—he sees them, yes, moving closer together. He feels a cold knife rip the length of his body. He walks out, almost running.

In his car, he re-oils his muscles, pumps his arms by clenching his fists behind his back, drinks protein from his thermos, touches his body. Rejection. But maybe if he'd stayed, they would have *both* turned to him. Maybe, having signaled him already, the one wanted to signal the other, to make it a three-way. Maybe— . . . Rejection scorches coldly.

3:05 P.M.   *Griffith Park. Along the Road.*
   Anxiously—to wipe away the earlier incident—he drives to the area of the water tank. He walks under the bright sun down the path. Three bodies are clustered by the tank; he turns away.
   On the path he stands alone. Floating men approach, look at him, pass. The delicate balance wavers further. It doesn't matter that so many have admired him, adored him—yesterday, last night, today, minutes earlier, no. Not even the glorious orgasm earlier matters, this moment. Each moment bears its total reality in his hunting existence—*now*. The past evaporates.
   He returns to his car, drives to another spot. He stands there, showing off. A car drives in. The man, young, gets out, begins to approach him—then gets back in his car and drives away. Desolate and alone, Jim feels a hollow scream inside. What happened? He reminds himself of the beautiful muscular man in the isolated cove earlier. Ended. Rejection is present now. He tells himself: I'm looking too tough, I'm showing off too obviously, I'm looking unapproachable, I'm— . . . Rejection.
   A convertible sports car parks.
   "Hi." A handsome youngman.
   "Hi." Jim's hand drops brushing his own groin. He walks down the path, toward the bushes, committing himself, as he rarely does, rashly. Breath held, he waits.
   The other does not follow. He drives off.
   Despair deepens blackly.
   Moments later the same handsome youngman in the sports car returns. Jim is about to get into his car, to drive away, to reject *him*, when the youngman calls out to him: "Look—you're not a cop, are you?"
   And so that was it. "No."
   "You've got the best body I've seen in a long time," the youngman tells Jim.
   Suddenly everything is all right again. In the bushes with this youngman, Jim feels the outlaw joy return in a swelling tide.

4:04 P.M.   *The Movie Arcade.*

As he drove out of the park, the vague rejection faded even more. He keeps telling himself that, yes, of course, the two men in the arena wanted him in *a three-way,* and that's why— . . . Still, there are blisters to soothe.

He goes to a magazine store off Hollywood Boulevard. In the back is a darkened movie arcade.

Now wearing Levi's and boots, but still shirtless, Jim moves idly past magazines exhibiting naked bright-colored sexflesh, giant organs and orifices, like mangled fish in distorting closeup. Instantly, he feels a man's eyes on him. Jim pauses at a rack as if to leaf through a magazine. Squatting, the man reaches for one on a lower rack. For moments his mouth pauses before Jim's groin.

Jim walks to the back of the twilit arcade. Cubicles like confessionals house porno movies; for one or two quarters each few minutes, a grainy reel flashes writhing images on a tiny individual screen inches from the viewer. Some cubicles are vacant. Others contain two or three people bunched together—no film running. Along the walls three or four men just stand. Others wander among the booths and aisles.

Jim enters a vacant booth. Waits. The man who followed him blows him. Another man watches. Jim pulls his own cock away from the squatting man, holding it out for the other to suck too. But the other wants only to watch.

Moans rise over the rough metallic whirring of old, old projectors.

A goodlooking man squeezes into the same booth. The squatting man alternates between sucking Jim and the other. Over the head bobbing on their cocks, the two standing stare at each other untouching.

MIXED MEDIA 2

"Four San Francisco teenagers recently got the surprise of their young lives. Tooling around in their souped-up car looking for a little fun, they spotted two homosexuals leaving . . . a well-known gay bar. The youths roared to a stop, jumped out of their car and began to push the homosexuals around. Suddenly a brawny band . . . lit into them. . . . The teenagers fled into the night, only to return ten minutes later, begging for their car. 'Look, man, we don't want no trouble.'

"The group they most assuredly did not want trouble with was the Lavender Panthers, a stiff-wristed team of gay vigilantes who have taken to the streets . . . to protect their confreres against just such attacks. . . . The basic band numbers 21 homosexuals. . . . Besides their goal of halting the attacks, the Lavender Panthers want to gainsay the popular notion that all homosexuals are 'sissies, cowards, and pansies' who will do nothing when attacked."

—*Time*,
October 8, 1973

"In re issue of hiring homosexuals as police officers. . . . Homosexuals have a corrosive influence . . . they attempt to

entice normal individuals to engage in perverted prac-
tices. . . . they prefer individual pursuit of professions and
hobbies, whereas the heterosexual is team-oriented in both
work and play. . . .

"In a recent court case . . . the court states, 'Members of
the police force must be above suspicion of violating the
laws that they must uphold.' "

—Excerpt of memorandum
from a deputy chief of police
of the L.A. Police Department
to a police captain,
December 12, 1974

L.A. POLICEMAN
CITED IN ASSAULT
COMPLAINT BY D.A.

"A Los Angeles policeman was named Thursday in an
assault-with-a-deadly weapon complaint . . . in the shooting
of a private investigator."

—*Los Angeles Times,*
May 14, 1976

OFFICER CHARGED
ANEW IN BEATING
OF CYCLIST, 28

"Charges that a Los Angeles policeman beat a suspect
so badly he lost his left eye were refiled Tuesday after the
case against him had been dismissed when a fellow officer
regarded as a key prosecution witness failed to appear in
court."

—*Los Angeles Times,*
March 31, 1976

MURDERS RAISE QUESTION
ABOUT OFFICERS' CONDUCT
ILLEGAL ARMS,
INTRIGUE MARK
SLAYING CASE

"A double murder trial in San Bernardino [California] County has raised serious questions about the conduct of federal, state, and local law enforcement officers."
—Los Angeles Times,
May 31, 1976

LONG BEACH TO
CHARGE SOME
POLICE IN SPREE

"Misdemeanor charges will be filed against some of the Long Beach police officers involved in a drunken spree during which civilians were attacked. . . ."
—Los Angeles Times,
April 23, 1976

LONG BEACH ORDERS INQUIRY
ON SUSPENDED THEFT PROBE
COUNCIL TELLS 2 OFFICIALS
TO LOOK INTO CHARGES THAT
POLICE HALTED THE EFFORT
WHEN IT LED TO CITY HALL

—Los Angeles Times,
June 30, 1976

SAN DIEGO POLICE
OFFICER CONVICTED

"A veteran police officer was convicted Friday of receiving stolen property and of conspiracy."
—Los Angeles Times,
March 27, 1976

LAPD CRITICIZED FOR GIVING
TOO MANY OFFICERS
HIGH EVALUATIONS

"The Los Angeles Police Department has been criticized by the City Personnel Department for grading too many of its top officers 'excellent' and 'outstanding' and far too few as 'satisfactory.' "

—Los Angeles Times,
June 14, 1976

POLICE DISHONESTY CALLED 'EXTENSIVE'

—Los Angeles Times,
December 29, 1972

L.A. CRIME THREE TIMES HIGHER THAN REPORTED,
U.S. SURVEY SAYS

"Washington.—Crime ran nearly three times higher in Los Angeles in 1972 than the number of violations reported to the police, according to a survey conducted for a justice department unit."

—Los Angeles Times,
April 15, 1975

COPS HAVE A BALL AT THE BALL

"At least nine persons . . . were arrested at a big Los Angeles drag ball . . . —the largest number of arrests and the most police activity at such an event in Los Angeles since the early fifties . . . all for lewd conduct.

"[One of the arrested], wearing an elaborate drag costume, came to the ball by taxi, and on his arrival a plainclothes vice officer opened the door, . . . paid the sizable cab fare, and then another plainclothesman opened the . . . door for him. [The arrested man] was under the impression the two men who had been so helpful were employees of the ball and, when he found himself a quarter short on admission, . . . asked one of them if he might borrow a quarter until he could get one from a friend inside. . . . One of the men gave him the quarter, asking, 'What's in it for me later?' [The arrested man replied,] 'We can work something out.' [He] was promptly handcuffed and arrested for prostitution."

—The Advocate,
December 20, 1972

[*Same year and month:*]

COUNTY HOMICIDES SOAR AT
ALL-TIME ANNUAL HIGH
NEARLY 1000 RECORDED DURING 1972

". . . the Los Angeles Police Department logged the 500th killing in the city, the first time that figure has been reached in one year."

—Los Angeles Times,
December 13, 1972

SERIOUS FLAWS
IN INVESTIGATIONS
OF CRIME FOUND

"Serious shortcomings in the criminal investigation process of police and sheriff's departments throughout the country were found in a two-year Rand Corporation study released . . . by the Justice Department. . . .

"Among its major findings were:

"—Substantially more than half of all serious crimes receive no more than superficial attention from investigators. . . ."

—Los Angeles Times,
February 14, 1976

"A San Bernardino [California] Appellate Court upheld the convictions of two young men [aged 23 and 21] for kissing in public. The court called [their] behavior 'lewd and dissolute.' The pair were arrested at a freeway rest stop. . . . Defense attorneys argued unsuccessfully that the law was 'unconstitutionally vague' and that similar conduct by a man and a woman would not have resulted in arrest and conviction. The defendants were . . . ordered to register as sex offenders. . . . Officers [had] observed them kissing for an hour and forty minutes."

—*Los Angeles Times,*
September 12, 1976

" 'At some points during the night, it's absolutely ludicrous,' said a vice squad officer [speaking about male and female San Francisco street hustlers]. 'The only people on the streets are them and us.' "

—*Los Angeles Times,*
January 5, 1977

LAW PROVIDES
LESS PENALTY
FOR MORE HARM

"It wasn't easy, but California legislators have managed to create a law which, depending on the inclination of prosecutors, would mean that the more you injure a person, the less you will be punished."

—*Los Angeles Times,*
February 14, 1976

". . . Under SB 42 [a bill altering California's indeterminate sentencing procedures] fixed sentences will be applied to all crimes, except those that carry the death penalty or a life term.

". . .The first class [of sentences] covers terms of 16 months to two or three years, for crimes such as attempted robbery, assault on a peace officer, forgery, grand theft and many more.

"The second class involves terms of two, three or four years and includes felonies such as robbery, perjury, arson, voluntary manslaughter, sodomy. . . ."

—*Los Angeles Times,*
November 18, 1976

" 'It is unfair to label homosexuality in and of itself a mental illness,' says Dr. Judd Marmor, . . . candidate for the American Psychiatric Association Presidency. . . . 'Psychiatrists are not immune to the prejudices of their culture.' "
—*Time,*
April 1, 1974

"With no one important [romantically] at the moment, Marisa [Berenson] has . . . turned to the untouchables. 'I, for one, have become a big fan of homosexuals. . . . So also [is] her friend Loulou de la Falaise, designer St. Laurent's creative assistant and a member of Normandy's *petite noblesse.* 'I've become a fag moll really,' she laughs. 'There's nothing more fun than fags.' "
—*Newsweek,*
August 27, 1973

"You have failed to establish that a bona fide marital relationship can exist between two faggots."
—Written reason given by the U.S. Immigration and Naturalization Service to an Australian male homosexual for denying him a visa as the legal spouse of a U.S. citizen, 1976

DOCTORS VOTE TO CUT STIGMA OF DEVIATION

"Washington (AP).—The American Psychiatric Association said Monday that a mail referendum by its membership had upheld the decision to remove homosexuality from [its] list of mental disorders.

"At its regular meeting [on] December 15 [1973], the association's board ruled that homosexuality could no longer be listed as a mental disorder and urged that homosexuals be given the same civil rights protection guaranteed other citizens."
—*Los Angeles Times,*
April 9, 1974

5:02 P.M. *Hollywood Boulevard. Selma.*

BEHIND THE THIN shroud of smog, the California sun scorches coldly white. Hollywood Boulevard is crowded with tribes of outlaws—hustlers, sexhunters, queens.

Jim hugs each desiring glance on his shirtless body. Leaving the movie arcade earlier, he suddenly needed to sell his body.

"What's happenin?"

The blond hustler stands outside the Gold Cup Coffee Shop.

"Not much—with you?"

"Making it, making it."

The announcement of continuing survival.

Smiling, they separate. Ignoring a man who looks too much like a cop, Jim moves on to Selma.

He stands studying that terribly unextraordinary-looking street.

So much of his life, here. So many memories. They surface like ghosts. Ghosts. . . .

The man who dialed numbers on his telephone while lying on the floor, Jim standing over him; the man dialing, hanging up, dialing again—then speaking hoarsely into the receiver: "Right this minute, I'm lying on the floor, and this muscular hustler is going to jerk off on me, and he'll force me to eat his hot cum—and—and— . . . Oh, oh!" The phone dropped on the cradle. Later Jim asked him, "You always call your friends when you're making it?" "Friends!" the man said. "Oh, no, I just dial at random until I reach anyone!"

And the gentle man who wanted to send Jim to school.

And the tough young kid with bulging arms; he drove a defiant, jacked-up car. He looked like a hustler himself, but he bought hustlers. He cuddled in his car with Jim, and came.

And the impeccable little man who merely wanted to massage Jim's body, and offered him more if he "fell asleep."

And the man who— . . .

So many others, remembered, forgotten, remembered. Nights. Mornings. Afternoons.

And one particularly desolate night.

FLASHBACK: *Christmas Eve. Two Years Ago. Selma.*

A cold Texas-dusty night. To crush memories, Jim was hustling. The wind flung palmtree leaves on the streets. The day had been fiercely orange.

A man in a car kept circling the block, not stopping. Finally he parked a few feet away from Jim, got out, and approached him as if to study him better. They spoke for a few seconds, making arrangements. They drove to the man's home. What happened, Jim doesn't know—but it festers like a permanent cut.

Suddenly, after leaving the room for a short while—and before he had even touched Jim—the man returned and said he had just a found a note from the man he worked for to pick him up in a few minutes. As strange as that, as abrupt. Jim felt an iron-fisted depression. The man gave him half the agreed amount of money—"for wasting your time"—and drove him back to the palm-littered streets. Moments later, when Jim had almost managed to force himself to believe the man's strange story, he saw the same man circling the block.

5:08 P.M.   *Selma.*

Jim speaks briefly to hustlers he recognizes; they warn him about cops or "weirdos" on the street today. Two other shirtless hustlers sit on the steps of the Baptist church. As he passes the phone booth on the corner, he hears it ring. Curious, he answers it.

The voice asks: "How big is your cock?"

Jim laughs, hangs up.

A prissy, slightly effeminate old man with a pampered hairdo and impossibly even white teeth has parked a few feet ahead and is standing on the sidewalk staring at Jim. Jim touches his own chest. The man moves over to him: "What a beautiful body you have!" Jim feels a delicious warmth. "And thank God you're a *man* and not one of those skinny boys," the little man goes on. Because that stirred the specter of aging—though a compliment—Jim's warmth decreases slightly, returns fully when the man continues: "Too few masculine men are left. Oh, what a body! I adore muscles!"

They agree on twenty dollars, and that Jim will "do nothing." The man's name is Roo. He was once a chorus boy—"singing, dancing, camping"—oh, long, long ago "when Hollywood was *really* Hollywood!" Now he gives singing lessons.

5:25 P.M.   *Roo's Home.*

A neat, inexpensive house—a piano draped with an old-fashioned fringed shawl, flower-embroidered. A photograph on it, a small bronze statue.

In the equally ordered bedroom, Roo asks Jim to put on a posing strap. "Like in the *really* sexy magazines, before they had to show *everything!*"

Jim does.

"Beautiful!" the man applauds.

For Jim, nothing further would be needed. Roo paid him even before they got here, is now admiring his body. Jim could leave now, fully satisfied by this scene. But he knows Roo wants more.

There's a loud knock on the front door.

"How rude!" Roo closes the bedroom door behind him.

Jim hears excited talk:

A rough voice: "Listen to me, Roo, I need twenty bucks right away. *Now,* dammit, I need it bad, and I'm in a hurry, Roo!"

Roo's voice is deliberately controlled—but tinged with agitation, and fear: "No, no! I don't have any money. And I have someone with me," he warns.

"Dammit, Roo!" The voice gets rougher.

"I said no!"

"You wanna blow me? I got a few minutes; you wanna blow me for the twenty bucks?"

"I told you, I'm with someone— . . ."

"Roo— . . . Motherfucker— . . ."

"All right. I'll give you a check. They'll cash it at that corner store."

"And give me some cigarettes, I'm outta cigarettes."

"All right, all right—just go away. *Please!*" A few seconds later: "Here."

The door slams.

Flushed, Roo returns to Jim in the bedroom.

"You're gorgeous," Roo resumes, his breathing slightly uneven. He kneels before Jim. "Shut your eyes, don't look at me." Jim closes his eyes. He feels Roo's suddenly toothless mouth on his cock.

Jim didn't come. Roo came secretly, trying to disguise even his quickened breathing.

Jim goes to the shower, the water harsh and cold on his body. Through, he stands wrapped in a towel; stands by the living room door looking at Roo's skinny form at the piano.

Now Jim sees the photograph—a faded picture of an old white-haired woman—and the bronzed object—bronzed baby shoes tarnished with age.

The tiny, shriveled, used form of Roo sits at the piano and sings—beautifully—an old romantic song.

VOICE OVER: *Hustlers, Clients, and Eminent Psychiatrists*

"MALEHUSTLERS.... DRIFTERS, tough, street-smart. And smarter, but pretending, sometimes, to be dumb. Students and middle-class youngmen, though on the rough streets not as many as, briefly too, become callboys (the callboy faction being safer, more 'conservative'—only muted revolution there). A precarious existence—you're new one day, old another. The clients remain, the sellers are pushed aside; a fresh wave of hustling outlaws flows regularly into the city.

"The customers.... The myth says they're all middle-aged or older, probably married, shy. But that's not true. Those exist, yes, abundantly; there are, too—though far, far fewer—the attractive and the young who merely prefer to pay, especially among those who want to cling to the myth that masculine hustlers are 'straight.'"

I'm speaking about male streethustling to a group of eminent California psychiatrists and psychologists who meet irregularly. I sit at one end of the table and face about twenty men and women. Occasionally they will whisper briefly among each other.

With as much defiance as honesty I say:

The world of streethustling holds great power over me,

and the others in it, a world we love; I've experienced it—survived it—for years—much longer, I'm proud to say, than most. It's a world clouded in generalities. Hustling is one of those activities that has to be experienced first-hand to be fully understood; sociology doesn't work.

The first man who picked me up while I was hustling—the very day I arrived in New York—approached me with these words: "I'll give you ten and I don't give a damn for you." That was a good street price at that time. His words—and, as it turned out, he *did* give a damn; a very moving, tough man—opened up a world of sexual power through being paid, and they took me to streets in New York, Los Angeles, San Francisco, New Orleans, Chicago, St. Louis, Dallas—even, to smash my sheltered childhood, in El Paso, my hometown, where I was picked up by a junior-high teacher of mine, who didn't recognize me.

Even when I had good jobs, I was on the streets recurrently, pulled back as if by a powerful lover. Even when *City of Night* was riding the best-seller lists. I've seen copies of my books in the houses of people who have picked me up anonymously. At times just the offer of sexmoney is enough. Those times I don't need, actually, to go with anyone.

There is a terrific, terrible excitement in getting paid by another man for sex. A great psychological release, a feeling that this is where real sexual power lies—not only to be desired by one's own sex but to be paid for being desired, and if one chooses that strict role, not to reciprocate in those encounters, a feeling of emotional detachment as freedom—these are some of the lures; lures implicitly acknowledged as desirable by the very special place the malehustler occupies in the gay world, entirely different from that of the female prostitute in the straight. Even when he is disdained by those who would never pay for sex, he is still an object of admiration to most, at times an object of jealousy. To "look like a hustler" in gay jargon is to look very, very good.

One of the myths of the hustler is that he is actually looking for love. Perhaps, under the surface, deeply. On the surface there is too often contempt for the client, yes, at best pity—sometimes, seldom and at times only fleetingly, affection; yes, I have felt that. The client, too, at times resents the hustler because he desires him. I think of the hustling streets as a battlefield; two armies, the hustler and the client, warring, yet needing each other.

Outside of a busy coffeeshop where hustlers gather in clusters throughout the night, an older man in a bright-new car parked and waited during a recent buyers' night. Youngmen solicited him anxiously in turns, stepping into the car, being rejected grandly by him, stepping out, replaced by another eager or desperate youngman. Smiling meanly, the older man—one of that breed of corrupted, corrupt, corrupting old men—turned down one after the other, finally driving off contemptuously alone, leaving behind raised middle fingers and a squad of deliberately rejected hustlers—some skinny, desolate little teenagers among the more experienced, cocky, older others; skinny boys, yes, sadly, progressively younger, lining the hustling streets; prostitutes before their boyhood has been played out, some still exhibiting the vestiges of innocence, some already corrupted, corrupt, corrupting—an increasing breed of the young, with no options but the streets—which is when it is all mean and ugly, when it is not a matter of choice; wanted for no other reason than their youth, their boyhood. . . . And yet, later that very night, I met a man as old as the contemptuous other one—but, this one, sweet, sweet, eager to be "liked," just liked, desperate for whatever warmth he might squeeze out, if only in his imagination, in a paid encounter, eager to "pay more"—to elicit it—simply for being allowed to suck a cock. . . . Hustling is all too often involved in mutual exploitation and slaughter, of the young and the old, the beautiful and the unattractive.

The standard street price is twenty dollars—but this fluctuates; you ask for as much as you can get (and designate what for). You go for less depending on your needs—bartering is not rare. Another lucky day you'll go for more—$25, $30, more. Like the stock market, streethustling has daily highs and lows.

The relationship among masculine hustlers is a very

delicate one. It relies on repression. A fantasy in the gay world is of two street hustlers making it with each other. There's the notion that today's hustlers are tomorrow's payers. Both concepts are largely inaccurate. Many masculine streethustlers still think of themselves defensively as "straight," a role those attracted to them expect, even at times demand, they play. Often girls hang around necking with hustlers on the street until a client for their boyfriends appears. Though some hustlers may move back and forth into a cruising area for an unpaid contact of mutual attraction, in hustling turf among other masculine hustlers they must remain, rigidly, "buddies" (like Paul Newman and Robert Redford).

Now about hustlers becoming payers later on: Perhaps that's true of callboys with notoriously less hangups. I'm talking about the masculine, straight-playing streethustler; he knows, from his vast experience and those shared by others like him, of the hustler's contempt, pity—at times even hatred—for the client. It would require a psychic upheaval for him to be able to shift roles masochistically. And the malehustler is a proud creature, though less so now.

A few years back, he was almost without exception masculine; it was almost always assumed he would "do nothing back." Within the past few years—drugs, gay liberation—two other breeds have thrived—the masculine bisexual and the androgynous, usually willowy but not effeminate, young hustler. Of course, the queens have existed since the time of the dinosaurs.

Street techniques vary, but there are general aspects. The hustler usually stands on one of several known corners, or walks idly along the streets, or mills with other hustlers outside known food stands, coffeeshops. Steady hustlers have their favorite corners. A client will stop his car and signal a hustler. Depending on his style or lack of it, the hustler will then stand by the car until the man speaks first or will just hop in.

Fantasy is important on the streets. If a client asks whether you're married, you say yes if you're smart, because he wants that. If he asks if you've been in the marines, or the army, or the navy (curiously never the air force), yes. If he asks if you've ever worked in a carnival, or posed for pictures, or been in a rodeo, yes, yes, yes.

Danger of course is always present, a constant factor. Plainclothes cops offer money, make the entrapping proposition, then bust. There are the marauding gangs of hoods who raid hustling streets. And the psychotic figures attracted and repelled by hustlers. . . . The psychic danger of constant loneliness.

For many drifting youngmen, hustling is their only means of experiencing worlds otherwise totally locked to them. For moments their desired young bodies are the keys to those worlds. Their fleeting youth is their one bid for attention. Beyond that, their lives will fade. But during those moments, hustling, they matter, importantly. The drabness lifts.

Postscript

Recently *Time* magazine created a new style of male-hustling. A story on "pornography" referred to the thriving heterosexual massage parlors lining the south side of a certain Los Angeles boulevard, and to the male prostitutes hustling on the north side. The latter was not true. There had existed, yes, a "limbo" section on that thoroughfare, where one stood or hitchhiked along certain blocks or lingered outside an all-night coffeehouse. Although occasionally you might find a client there, it was not a hustling area, more mutual cruising than anything else. Days after the *Time* mistake, the area conducive to hitchhiking was suddenly converted into a hustling turf rivaling that on Selma—at a time when the arrests were decimating hustlers on that street.

Now, on weekends, malehustlers—thumbs held out in varying personal styles—stand at virtually every parking meter along the newly thriving thoroughfare, sometimes so busy now you have to walk for blocks to find a place for yourself. Cars drive around the blocks slowly, choosing.

This new style has the advantage that you're there legally—hitchhiking, not "loitering" (though cops have already begun their jealous harassment). The disadvantage is that you often get a ride from someone who doesn't know, or more often pretends not to know, that the hitchhikers are hustlers—a situation that has given rise to a breed of men who get off simply on giving hustlers a ride. You will see the same hustler a few minutes later hitchhiking back to the first turf—two small islands at the end of a stretch of a mile-and-a-half of street.

In summer especially, the heavy influx of drifters creates a sad spectacle. Goodlooking anxious youngmen—a whole spectrum, from the slender and blond to the tough and dark—wait eagerly, even signaling cars on slow nights, buyers' nights—eager youngmen being driven up and down the same street and hoping for a firm connection for the night.

And another change, this one internal—call it the subtle stirring of the radicalization of the malehustling contingent. Existing on the fringes of the gay world, male hustlers have always been dual outsiders, outlaws from the main society, and outcasts within the main gay world of hostile non-payers and non-sellers. Desired abundantly, and envied, they are nonetheless the least cared about. Routine mass roundups of hustlers occur with no outcry, virtually no manifestation of concern within the vast gay world—while a comparable gay roundup anywhere else will see mushrooming conferences called by ever-ready gay "spokesmen" before television cameras. An attorney points out that, compared to non-commercial gays, a disproportionate number of arrested hustlers will actually be jailed—because few can afford to pay for representation—hustlers are easy spenders, living from day to day—and because hustler arrests bring no free publicity for the lawyer who might defend them.

Still, during a gay parade on Hollywood Boulevard, groups of malehustlers of a breed notorious for their posture that they are not gay—"just hustling for bread"—cheered marching contingents of open homosexuals. When three hustlers were arrested for popping firecrackers near invading cops, a pressurized anger stirred palpably among the others. That very night on Selma, a group of girls sped by in a car and yelled, "Queers! Queers!" at the masculine, toughlooking hustlers milling about on the streets. Only a few years earlier that breed would have answered with a ball-wounded, "Come back and I'll show you who's queer!" Not that night. There was an almost total indifference. One of the most masculine of the streethustlers southerndrawled at the shouting women: "Yeah, we queer, so what?" It was as radical a statement as had ever been voiced on that street.

Concurrently, the camaraderie—an increasing camaraderie—among hustlers is easing in its strict role-playing, slowly but perceptibly. Unacceptable before—disastrous to one's masculine hustling image—comments are now lightly exchanged routinely admiring of each other's attractiveness or specialty—muscles, handsome faces, unique clothes style, even reputed cock size. There is still the uneasiness, the sexual uneasiness, among masculine hustlers, but more and more cross turfs back and forth, from hustling to mutual cruising of other males; indeed, a type of non-hustling, non-paying goodlooking youngmen now roam the hustling streets attracting equally goodlooking malehustlers, not with money but with their own good looks.

What remains unchanged are the lurking dangers of cop entrapment—and the brevity of the life on the hustling streets. A hustler's life *is* brief. Some hustlers begin in their young teens. New hustlers still arrive almost daily and find favorite spots nightly, on Selma or on the new turf *Time* created. The first weeks you won't wait around long, stepping in and out of cars friskily, waving back at your friends still waiting. Abruptly, the time of waiting stretches, the number of rides diminishes. You meet each other on the street and one of you asks, "What's happenin?" and the other answers noncommittally, shrugging, and asks back and the answer comes, "Not doin too good tonight, slow night." Even as you speak, fresh competition hops into cars, waving back at you. There is the awareness—perceived as yet by only the two of you—that on the street you're becoming a has-been before you ever were, really a "has."

On Selma late one night a young hustler, there week after week, passes, nods in the easy camaraderie that happens among street hustlers recognizing each other. "How's it goin?" "All right—with you?" He shrugs, "Could be better," and adds quickly, boosting himself, "Just made five bucks, the guy just played with my cock for a couple of minutes in his car, said he didn't have no place, I didn't even have to take my dick out—yeah, I made five bucks in a couple of minutes," spotting the same man still driving around the block choosing, "five bucks for a couple of minutes, can't beat that."

He was right—you couldn't beat five bucks for two minutes, that's $150 an hour! Right up there. More than psychiatrists make, at least now.

Unfortunately his clients, and the world that crowns youth only briefly, will make it impossible for him—unlike psychiatrists—to hook his clients for years.

Another night. Another corner. And a young hustler comes by; perhaps eighteen, wearing that beauty that exists only because it *is* eighteen. But wait: the special street-youthfulness is tattered. He's perhaps nineteen; perhaps even twenty. He recognizes me from other streets. "Hey, man, can I ask you a question?" I pull back in panic. I know what he's going to ask, he's already verbalizing it: "How old are you?"

I lie outrageously—but even the fake age makes him react—in implied admiration, yes, of my street survival, but his reaction wounds anyway, deeply: "Wow!—and you *still* got a good hustle." He's congratulating my survival, perhaps even envying it a tiny bit: For him at that age, what? "Am I dressed okay?" he asks me abruptly, nervously opening his shirt an extra button. "I mean, I'm not making it like I used to. I've been hanging around three hours today—and nothing!"

I'm still wounded by his question, his reaction—the specter of age is floating under the street light. But I feel wounded for him, too. I have my body cunningly constructed for street survival, and I have options—but he, at nineteen or twenty, the freshness of his youth is already tarnished. He's a thin, no-longer-boy.

Exploited? Oh, yes, unquestionably. Just as later tonight

he may exploit; he may rob and beat up the next man who picks him up, or—but this is less likely—be robbed and beaten up himself. Most probably, both will make a bargain and go through with it.

And the influx will continue, the new faces and young bodies fresh among the straining older ones; an influx created at least in part—and hypocritically—by grotesquely bloated cop reports issued periodically and aimed, despite disclaimers, at making all homosexuals look like rich predators luring innocent youths. Because: A twelve-year-old boy can earn up to $1000 a day as a prostitute, a recent, incredibly absurd cop report—front-paged rashly without questioning by Los Angeles newspapers—claimed (imagine!— a new upper-class!—aging rock stars and twelve-year-old male prostitutes in Gucci gear!); a report issued in the wake of a sex scandal involving underage scout girls and cops and in the face of threats to cut the vice division's budget. A thousand dollars a day, hustling! That means there are many rich perverts just waiting to molest your little boy unless you give us a lot of money to bust them wherever they hang out, the insidious message is conveyed.

Left out is the fact that most of the men who pick up the very young on the streets (and unlike many who prefer the older ones) do not belong to the so-called "gay community" of upfront homosexuals, those who frequent gay bars, parks; no, they are loners, closeted victims of repression, quite often married, having children of their own, leading otherwise "straight" lives.

A thousand bucks a day hustling, man!

So dozens of boys line the streets, going for ten bucks on a slow night, even less when you're desperate for a place to sleep; finding kindness sometimes, yes, often, but just as often finding contemptuous men; and realizing that, finally, it's a buyer's market on the streets because the number of men who pick up hustlers remains relatively stable—they own cars, homes, have jobs, businesses, do not form a floating group—whereas the hustlers arrive in waves; new ones for the same buyers, the "older" hustlers thrust aside in as little as a few weeks.

Old youngmen and boys haunt the streets.

Then the cops raid the hustling turfs.

Netted, trapped, the youngest and most frightened of the hustlers will tell their captors whatever they want to hear. One thousand dollars a day? Yes, sure—a lot of rich fags out there. (But you have no money to get a lawyer.) A customer every fifteen minutes? Oh, yeah. (But the familiar corner became your enemy.) Thousands of customers? Yes—and all rich, famous, powerful, on TV. (But you can't call one to bail you out.) And so the terrified boys are offered up in sacrifice to exaggerated reports and shrieking headlines: HOMOSEXUALS PREYING ON INNOCENT BOYS!

Getting attention. These often lost, pitiful youngmen. Getting attention only when they're busted—and in order to whip up the frothing homophobia whenever the cops need it. Only then. Not before—or even after—when the options might be opened by genuine official concern for the young—the money-sucking agencies, bureaus, divisions, departments vomiting rancid sociologese and pieties; spewing nonsense; extending no real options to these boys (if they *want* options—because choice must be respected—and the psychic lure of the streets is strong, the life even glamorous in its trashy way, and you're a special, desired survivor—if you last) against whatever existence may bring about—unhappiness and exploitation, whether in the farm fields, dingy restaurant kitchens, or on the mean hustling streets.

The explosive, self-serving cop report issued, the citizens quivering anew over the "gay threat"—the boys will probably be back on the enticing streets, because, ultimately, nobody cared otherwise in the hypocritical agencies, bureaus, divisions, departments. Still young, many too young; boys and youngmen more knowledgeable now—because youth is no guarantee of innocence (as bands of preteenagers increasingly preying violently on the lame old attest), just as age is no affirmation of corruption.

Mutual exploitation—the old corrupt, the young corrupt. That is the nature of the ugly, devouring, beautiful, lonely, exciting, devastating, dead-end, glorious hustling streets.

No, you don't get rich on the streets—though you have good periods and at first it seems you might. True, a few hustlers will find one person who genuinely cares for them, even helps them into another life. But that's rare on the streets. Other hustlers will drop out, when the intervals of waiting stretch into nights—get jobs, marry, have children, perhaps even be relatively happy, more than likely eke out lives of screaming frustration. Others may move into the vaster gay world of non-commercial encounters, even form relationships. Some are only summer hustlers, returning "home" when the season is over. But the resourceless ones—yes, most of them—what happens when they're through on the exciting, tough streets, those once-goodlooking, once-youngmen cocky in their desirability, remembering the cars that braked eagerly, the often-beautiful homes their looks opened so easily? They disappear.

And on skid row—if you care to look—you may now and then see among the others a singularly doomed old man. Something makes you look again. Lurking in the weather-scorched brown face is the lingering breath of a special magic, the thin, sad ghost of the conquering youngman he was.

6:56 P.M. *Griffith Park. The Twilit Road.*

JIM RETURNS URGENTLY to Griffith Park. He drives up the road, but the upper paths have begun to thin. For twilit moments the blatant exhibitionists will flourish. Shadows have spread a mantle over the green. The exodus of cars moves downward to join the pageant of sex at the bottom of the park.

Driving back, Jim pauses at a sandy crest overlooking the city. He stands there. Below, smog smothers the streets. Palmtrees stretch their full length to the sky.

7:14 P.M. *Griffith Park. The Lower Areas.*

Daily, the areas of the sexhunt are reduced mainly to two—the upper ones virtually eliminated as night begins to float in, shadows tangling first at the top of the road.

At the bottom, dozens of cars gather along the periphery of the park, still light with hot sun. Hunters move on foot into the forested brush nearby, knowing each hollow, each path. Throughout the area, lone figures stand—just stand—waiting, dots in the green sea. Several men move slowly along the paths paralleling the main road, only their lower bodies visible, upper bodies hidden by branches.

Soon twilight will hover over the park. For moments

everything will be luminous. Shafts of brilliant dying light will pierce the freezing green. Then a frail curtain of mist will descend.

Jim gets out of his car, climbs the short path, and enters the sex-charged silence along the trees. As always, he moves to where there are no others at first—along the rim of a path leading to a cave of leaves. He enters it. Two men are fucking.

Jim moves through thickening mist, past darkening shadows of hunters. Sexsighs waft the woody area. No one stops now to another's approach, no one even pauses in the acts. This is their underground among crushed leaves. Hunters' expert eyes will soon penetrate the rapidly falling dark, finding each other. Without a word, bodies move in a silent symphony.

Jim is contained now in a cluster of hands, mouths, cocks.

Entering his car to drive out of the park, he sees two men in cutoffs leading two young handcuffed outlaws to an unmarked cop car.

At that moment Jim knows his hunt will continue deep into the night.

VOICE OVER: *Getting Involved*

I SEE TWO MEN savagely beating and kicking a third. It's happening on a well-lighted thoroughfare at 10:30 P.M. in Los Angeles. Neat homes and apartments flank the violent scene incongruously. I back my car up as quickly as I can maneuver in the thick traffic, blowing my horn loudly, flashing my brights on and off.

Startled, the two muggers scatter. In my car I follow them until they disappear along a series of cramped garages. It is not a gay area. I return to the attacked man—slight, middle-forties, conscious but shocked by the lightning violence. He doesn't require immediate medical aid. With him in the car I drive around in search of the muggers. A man is rushing into a car. I memorize the license number.

On Hollywood Boulevard, we see a squad car. I yell at the cops about the mugging. One yells back they can't stop because they're on an "emergency call." I persist, they motion me to a side street.

We tell them the muggers are still in the area, and that we have a possible license number. Sorry, they can't do anything now because they're on their way "to break up a fight." But: Go to the Hollywood station over a mile away, make a formal report, and *then* the license number and car description—which we just gave them—will be radioed back to them, and *then* they can act. Unreally, their car drives away.

At the station, one cop behind a desk is slowly taking a report from two giggling pretty girls. Other cops hover about the desk. The dazed bleeding man with me slumps on a wooden bench.

I try to get the attention of several of the milling cops. Time is important, two muggers beat this man— . . . Someone'll get to me as soon as possible.

We wait. Ten minutes. Twenty minutes. Two cops whistle as two women in tight, short skirts—probably decoys posing as prostitutes—stroll in. A black transvestite gets booked. A crying, screaming, hysterical youngwoman is led through the lobby by two cops. She keeps begging: "Mommy!" Curious cops peek into the room where the others have taken her, turn away, shaking their heads and smiling. *"Mommy!"*

Thirty minutes. Almost forty minutes have passed.

An older, heavy policeman saunters in behind the desk. He ignores the bleeding man. I tell the cop what happened.

"Would you get on a witness chair and swear the man you saw at the car was the same man you saw beating that guy?" he demands.

Of course not! But they might check the area out right away. The license number— . . .

The heavy cop summons the dazed man over. "Hey, why'd you pick a fight with those guys?" he asks.

The wounded man winces in renewed shock. He'd been walking home from a nearby store, heard running footsteps, felt a crash of blows. His wallet, watch, keys, a package from the store—all stolen.

The cop disappears with the paper I've written the suspected license number on. He returns, says nothing.

Finally he proceeds officially to take down the report, slowly, staring away occasionally, now past us, now at a drunk babbling in the lobby.

"Call you if we have anything," he says.

It's now about two hours since the mugging. As we leave the station, a world as hostile as the violent streets, the wounded man says, "I had two nightmares tonight—

when I was beaten and when we tried to get the cops to do something about it." With a bloodied hand he touches his face to confirm the reality.

The next day I write an account of that ugly night. The *Los Angeles Times* prints it. I open the article with a quotation published the day before the mugging. In a news story, the Los Angeles police chief had said:

"There is no way our Police Department can do the job by itself. Crime prevention is a cooperative effort and without citizen involvement we can only be half successful."

In response to my article, two cops call to tell me that an official investigation will be made. Another calls to apologize on behalf of his fellow officers involved; I thank him sincerely. The mayor of the city asks for an official report on the incident.

An officer is sent to interview me. I make it clear that I don't want to file a complaint, just air the matter. The investigator chooses to focus on the two cops on the boulevard.

No official word for weeks.

At about the same time that I could not get a cop to pursue two muggers, Los Angeles vice cops were pursuing "sexy hostesses"; the cops had placed an ad in several underground newspapers soliciting "hostesses." They then rented and furnished an office to interview about one hundred fifty applicants, who were told their expenses would be paid on "gambling junkets." The rest? "Yes, it's entirely up to you, honey," an officer was quoted. The selected women were invited to a party; it would be to their benefit to be liked by the "gamblers" there, the deliberate message was conveyed. Now the cops rented a plush hotel suite, with bar, buffet, poker setups. They posed as gamblers and elevator operators and waited to spring on the "sexy hostesses" they had lured. Fifty-four women were arrested for soliciting. Subsequently, pointing out that it would be unlikely that a jury would be convinced there was no entrapment, the city attorney dropped all charges against the women. "An awful lot of effort for this," he said about the wasteful operation.

Finally the official silence surrounding the mugging I

had witnessed is broken by a fierce letter to the *Times* from the police chief:

"... The *Times* published an article [in which the writer stated that] eight days prior to publication [he] had come to the aid of a fellow citizen who had been attacked and robbed. As chief of police, let me publicly commend [him] for those efforts.

"His article, however, so bitterly denounced police-officer conduct as to cause me to order an immediate investigation. The findings ... resulted in the disciplining of two officers.

"[The writer] and the victim encountered [the] two police officers en route to a fight-in-progress call. The officers continued on their way after advising [him] and the victim to report the occurrence to Hollywood area police headquarters. The judgment displayed by those officers was not in keeping with department standards. This explains why they were disciplined.

"Curiously enough, [the writer] accepted their advice without serious protest. ... If [he] merits the department's gratitude for his initial actions, I find him no less deserving of reproach for his extravagant charges of police indifference and apathy.

"He and the victim waited thirty or more minutes before a desk officer was available to take the crime report. ... To attribute that delay to officer rudeness, boredom, or disinterest is wholly unwarranted.

"I imagine [he] ... became [a] happier man on seeing his labors in print. Unfortunately, a multitude who read his story probably believed it.

"[He] is a clever writer [of] artfully constructed phrases ... employed in support of conclusions he obviously was determined to reach in impugning the competency of the many officers present.

"... His arrival at the headquarters coincided precisely with a change of watch. The lobby was crowded with ... officers going off duty or about to assume patrol duties. This unhappy condition accounts for the 'many milling officers.' ...

"Now the desk officer he eventually talked with was

also serving as equipment control officer. This duty required him to account for all equipment assigned to the 49 officers going off duty, and issue like equipment to the 30 officers comprising the next watch. The equipment control officer can complete this task, if he's lucky, in from thirty to forty minutes—about the same length of time that [he] was kept waiting.

"It is true that the desk officer 'disappeared' once he had started to take the crime report ... to check out a license number given him by the writer as a lead to a possible suspect.... As it turned out, neither the car nor the driver in any way was connected to the crime.

"On countless occasions, I have urged all citizens who witness a crime to notify the police immediately. Had [he] done so instead of attempting to intercept one of the suspects, as was the case, a prompt arrest may have ensued.

"When interviewed by a department investigator, [he] realized and agreed that the desk officer had not tried to avoid taking the crime report. He also stated he had no desire to file an official complaint against that officer ... a recipient of the Medal of Valor....

"... The ... article left tens of thousands of your readers with ... distorted impressions created ... about the competence of our officers and their concern for the public good. All were completely vindicated by the investigation except the two officers earlier mentioned."

The following week the *Times* publishes my reply:

"... The tone of [the police chief's] letter is clearly critical of my article. He goes so far as to conjecture that I became 'a happier man' for the experience.... I continue to be disturbed by the matter of apathy and the violence which increasingly invades every area of our lives.

"[He] actually chastises me for accepting 'without serious protest' the advice of two officers. I did indeed protest. What would the result of further 'serious protest' have been? [He] would do both private citizens and police officers a laudable favor to define that phrase.

"He ... criticizes me for taking time in 'attempting to intercept one of the suspects.' Only seconds elapsed in what was, more precisely, an attempt to identify the suspects....

"... There is nothing in [his] letter that points out where I told less than the truth as the victim, and I experienced it.

"He writes: 'All were completely vindicated by the investigation except the two officers earlier mentioned.' All? I focused attention on only three specific officers, and these were the ones inquired about by the investigating officer.

"[He] attributes the thirty- to forty-minute wait in the taking of the mugging report ... to a change of guard. If only violence would stop for a comparable time!

"[He] is correct in saying that I had 'no desire to file an official complaint' against the desk officer. What he omitted is that I never intended to file any official complaint whatsoever against anyone. I made clear to the investigating officer that my purpose was solely to bring attention to [this] ... not to see anyone reprimanded. ... It gives me no personal gratification to learn that two inexperienced officers ... were chastised in this matter.

"Finally, [he] commends me for coming to the aid of a fellow citizen. I appreciate his kind commendation. However, beyond that, a further disturbing implication arises. What a sad irony that we have reached a time when one is commended for doing what should be totally expected, the coming to the aid of any threatened being, whether he or she be a private citizen mugged or a police officer in trouble."

A few days later I receive the following letter from the Commanding Officer of the Internal Affairs Division of the Los Angeles Police Department:

"An investigation has been conducted into your report of misconduct by members of this Department.

"The investigation established that the concerned employees failed to take appropriate action when you notified them that a crime had just occurred.

"You may be assured that this Department does not tolerate such conduct and that appropriate disciplinary action has been administered.

"Thank you for bringing this matter to our attention.

"Very truly yours."

But nothing changes.

A year later, an attempt to get the police to thwart a potentially murderous attack, this time in a gay area, would be met with contemptuous indifference.

8:44 P.M.   *Greenstone Park. The Area of the Garage on Oak Street. Greenstone Park.*

HE ATE AT home—a large steak, salad, green vegetables, milk. Honey. He showered. Changed to another set of Levi's and boots. Instead of a shirt, he wears the open brown-leather vest. He prepares a fresh thermosful of protein to carry with him.

Where now? To Selma to hustle? To Greenstone for "numbers"? He could go to one of the many gaybars, but generally they're too frozen for him—"waxworks," he calls them. The charade of drinking depresses him, and he doesn't care for liquor. The streets are the areas of defiance.

Saturday night. Clear, hot.

He goes to Greenstone Park.

No cars, no shadows in the concrete house, no one along the paths. Only a silent, waiting eeriness. A limbo-time, when the hunt is shifting over. He stands desolately on the stone ledge. Now headlights wash over him for seconds. But the car drove on, stabbing further into the desolation. Didn't the man see him? He waits. The same car comes around again. Again it drives by. Still, no one.

Jim walks along the deserted path, curiously courting the awareness of encroaching isolation, as if he were studying the features of a sleeping lover. Listening to the silence. Staring into the darkness. Feeling his own presence, electric, in the silently whispering dark.

He returns to the concrete grotto.

Along the path a shadowy figure emerges slowly. Jim moves into an arc of light. The figure advances, looks at him, and avoids the concrete grotto—and Jim—by climbing over the slight incline to one side. Without looking back, he crosses the road to the other side.

Am I looking too tough? Jim wonders. Unapproachable? He remembers the two in Griffith Park this afternoon who turned to each other in the arena while he was there. His present need increases.

Time.

He feels a retreating hint, like a brushing wing, of the hellish judgment the streets and dark parks can hurl in empty hours, the hunt turning vengeful. He reminds himself that times of similar despair have invariably been followed by surfeit, mere islands in an ocean. And, Christ, he tries to laugh at himself, there's no one here to be desired *by!* . . . Just that one man who ignored him. And the driver of the car earlier.

He glances at his watch.

He drives to the area of a costume bar on Oak Street. The bar caters to makebelieve motorcyclists, makebelieve construction workers with steel helmets, makebelieve cowboys, even makebelieve foresters. The bar itself doesn't thrive until after 2:00 in the morning, when it becomes an after-hours club. But nearby, in an abandoned garage, outlaws gather sporadically throughout the night.

Two cars, single hunters in each, are parked before it.

Anxious for his sexuality to be acknowledged, Jim gets out of his car. He waits before the crumbling garage. Its sides and back are cluttered with weeds, papers, cans, broken bottles. Barbed wire perhaps at one time meant to keep out the outlaws has been pushed back sternly, a tangle of iron and weeds. The site of orgies late at night is now a deserted battlefield. Across the street is another world, a clutter of apartments and small houses. The garage is flanked by empty weedy lots.

Neither of the drivers of the two cars gets out. Still, Jim waits. Longer. One car drives away. The other driver remains seated. Jim walks by slowly. The man gives him no signal.

Suddenly Jim returns to his car, drives around the block. When he returns, another car has joined the one still there. Again, Jim stands by the tangled barbed wire.

A third car drives, pauses, drives on.

Jim *feels* the brutal passing of time. Nothing is happening! It does not matter that earlier he was paid for sex, that he was abundantly desired in the park, does not matter that he has survived, triumphantly, season after seasons that have spewed others out of the demanding arena. The beautiful orgasm he shared in the park earlier with the muscular man—that does not matter either. It doesn't matter that he knows he could not have become less desirable in minutes, does not matter that Saturday's early-night hours are slow in certain areas in preparation for the late-night surfeit. It doesn't even matter that he has not encountered many hunters yet. No, none of that matters. What matters is the empty reality of these moments, wiping out past and future, each vacant minute a failed test stirring doubts.

He flees the desolate garage. He drives past two subway tunnels and a back lot where hunters gather. No one there.

Back to Greenstone.

He curses the stoplights along the short distance. The anxiety to be desired—to be rendered alive—swells.

Three cars are parked across the road from the concrete house in the park. At least three outlaws are here, and probably more. Jim parks hurriedly and walks into the stone grotto. No one there. He waits in the dirty light. A shadow materializes by the wall below him. Making himself further visible, Jim mounts the ledge overlooking the path. The shadow advances toward him. Desperate to end the sexless spell, Jim cups his own groin in signal—not yet even seeing what the advancing shadow looks like. The man moves closer, steps over the stone hedge. Jim's body strains. The shadow moves on, away.

Another man passes, walks on too.

Why!

He evokes explanations stored from what some have told him about other times. "You look so hung up on yourself." "I thought you were hustling." (Though this is not hustling turf.) "I didn't think you'd be interested in me." But no "reason" works, none contains the growing panic. Nothing short of the needed contact will lift the steely depression.

He sees a man suddenly in the grotto with him. Jim removes his vest, stretches his bare torso. But this man too walks on. The icy stasis hardens.

A new car parks on the arc across the road. Jim locates himself so that his body is highlighted. The driver of the car gets out. Jim sees him crossing the road, an attractive man with longish dark hair. In the grotto, the man looks closely at Jim. Jim touches his own groin. The man squats in the shadows. Warmth begins to course throughout Jim's body. Life! He unbuttons his pants, pulls out his cock, and brings it to the man's mouth. The man's lips part, and then, violent in its abruptness, the moment bursts—the man turns his head away swiftly rejecting Jim's cock, stands up, spits harshly, and rushes back to his car.

Mysterious and powerful, the rejection brings Jim crashing. Suddenly he despises the beloved world of the hunt.

He walks along the silent path, along ashy trees.

A slender youngman approaches. Demanding contact, Jim opens his own fly, begins to work up his cock—but it won't respond. The youngman reaches out tentatively.

"Touch me!" Jim's urgent whisper ricochets in the darkness.

The youngman slides down, he takes Jim's cock in his mouth. Other shadows gather. One edges the tall youngman away and bends over Jim's cock. Jim pulls it out, moves it to another waiting mouth. The empty spell is broken.

He feels resurrected.

VOICE OVER: *The Gay Parade*

IT WAS INDEPENDENCE DAY. Not only that, it was the 200th Fourth of July. In Los Angeles there would be as many parades, it seemed, as there are palmtrees hovering over this God-loved city. There would be the big parade down ritzy Wilshire Boulevard, but it would have to detour at Beverly Hills, which, snobbish even on the day of Democracy's birthday, had decreed its streets would not be clogged by rabble—and there would be local parades and celebrations, WASP ones in Pasadena, black ones in Watts, Chicano ones in East L.A. And the gay parade.

The gay parade.

How curiously radical that still sounded. Even ten years ago, a cop might bust you for holding same-gender hands in public. It all *still* seemed too far out for many—hadn't the dinosauric *Los Angeles Herald-Examiner* lamented editorially the week before that so horrendous a time had arrived as would permit—on independence day!—a parade of perverts?

Of course the parade would be down Hollywood Boulevard. Where else but on the turf they've tried deviously with ordinances, openly with violence, to wrest from us year after year? Hollywood Boulevard. Site of how many gay battles fought cruising and hustling, being chased away by the envious cops, and returning to cruise and hustle, on the same corner, your favorite? Our street, conquered with how many busts for loitering and soliciting and trespassing? how many charges of lewd conduct? how many citations for, even, jaywalking? Bought with how many cop interrogations and trips to jail to be hassled, questioned, booked, held, charged? Oh, yes, bought, and paid for, yes, in symbolic lavender bloodbaths, this beautiful ugly street, with its butch army-surplus store for workers' boots and muscle shirts; dandy shops for glitter concerts and times when you want to show your supertrim build; the store displaying the ubiquitous statue of David, in two groin sizes; this street with its cartoon-vamp-style shop featuring superb sequined clothes just right for a drag ball; this Boulevard with its outdoor food stands ingeniously right for loitering, cruising, soliciting, hustling, jaywalking-to, and lewd conduct.

Yes, we had fought dedicatedly and sometimes bitterly for this royal street, and now it was more symbolically ours than any other place in the world. And if they dig a cavern to replace it, we will cruise in it.

The day is warm, and there's the atmosphere of a fair. Thousands of gays on the Boulevard wait festively for the parade, or form informal "parades" along the sidewalks—dozens of homosexuals holding hands openly, some dressed in colorful regalia, some subdued; for some the less clothes the better, exhibiting tanned bodies proclaiming our unabashed sexuality. And ever-loving Lesbians, some butcher than even the butch muscled men, some femmer than the manikins in the Frederick's of Hollywood windows; yes, and the older gays—homosexuals, *please!*—are here, though not as many as one might hope for—not here, the older ones who still secretly cherish the ancient guilts, light symbolic nightly candles to Judy.

The cruising today is furious but not serious. Furious because perhaps ninety per cent—a solid majority, for once—of the thousands here are gay, not serious because, after all, we have come to see our very own independence day parade. Still, I hope an occasional couple will slip, or has slipped, behind a wall or between buildings to do it, and I myself feel the revolutionary temptation. But this is not really that kind of day.

The atmosphere veers toward euphoria, a euphoria that comes from pride in being open—even if your courage was bolstered only for this day and by the great numbers of us here. Well, what better day for this display than the Fourth? After all, we too were at the Boston Tea Party— one out of ten of us, or one out of six, depending on what Colonial Kinsey kept count.

I would not march in the parade. I wanted an overview, wanted to move, listen, see, absorb it all—and, besides, I don't really like "joining" anything. Walking down the festive street, I felt a crazy mixture of pride and apprehension. Apprehension because I couldn't help remember past gay parades—the tacky floats populated with withering bikinied boys throwing kisses to the clouds, moldy gay leaders riding in chauffeured limousine convertibles, flanked by a squad of marching acolytes. Oh, I had longed then for the ostensible unity and dignity of the civil-rights parades, everyone simply marching and singing, no floats, no limousines, Martin Luther King walking with the people.

God knows the first perceptible augury of this gay parade was grim. A gay gentleman renowed for his grindingly monstrous "taste" had days earlier arranged to register an elephant—an *elephant*—in a local hotel; one had to assume the elephant was gay. Television cameras had devoured the spectacle to spew it out later on their news screens, the elephant registering at the hotel to hail "Gay Pride Week" (proclaimed generously by the mayor, thank you, for gay accomplishments!). An elephant *and* gay pride. Yes'm, but *how?* Well, you see, you *see*, how can you take those fairies *seriously?*

Then, absorbing the good atmosphere, tingling with fine vibrations—we were even being friendly to those we had no sexual interest in, we waved, smiled, said hello—I thought, So what if there is tackiness in the parade? Look at the Legion parades. Carefully, I explored my feelings, sensing a lurking demon; I found him, pushing me into that pitfall of all minorities, that we must not allow ourselves the freedom to be awful—and the implicit freedom to call whatever *is* awful "awful."

Here it comes!

The gay parade!

Even the most reactionary part of me needn't have feared. There was plenty of dignity, and, embarrassing to admit—man—I felt the itchy sentiment that signals real pride. Here you are, and here they are, and here we are. I remember Ma Joad's proud speech of the Okies' eventual triumph in "defeat." We keep coming, she said, because we're the people. (I didn't even let interfere with my mood the bitter knowledge that many of those very same Okies had unleashed mean red-neck children and even cops to pillage our sexhunting grounds.)

Waving banners evoking some of our best moments, the gay contingents march in happy disarray, no regimentalized ranks for us, thanks. A group proclaims perhaps our finest day—the day of the Stonewall Inn riot. Students, young and happily defiant, chant, sing, hold hands, kiss. Even a contingent of straight supporters appears, predictably tiny but nevermind. Again the awareness occurs of what a radical happening this is within the context of only ten years ago. All those homosexuals, butch and femme, marching openly proclaiming:

> Two, four, six eight,
> Homosexuals are great!
> Three, five, seven, nine,
> Lesbians are really fine!

Not smashing poetry, no, but sweet to the ear this gorgeous summer afternoon.

Of course marchers cruised those on the sidewalks, and vice versa. Occasionally a group in the street would catch sight of someone particularly attractive on the sidelines, the word would pass, eyes would flank as if to a military eyes-right/left order, but happily. And wasn't that what it was all about? Freedom, freedom to be, do?

Oh, there was tackiness all right—and why not? I asked

the pursuing demon. Tackiness may be an element—wayward but there, and harmless—of the gay sensibility. There's that fucking elephant again, followed by a small faction of "the society of enlightened enthusiasts" of said elephant-loving gentleman.

Fuck that—and ignore the fact of the gay leader on the goddamned convertible. Who cares when there's the beautiful, dazzling, simply fabulous, gorgeous, lavish, lovely, glamorous, scintillating, glittering, stunning Queen of the Long Beach Drag Ball and her princesses and she's seen you on the sidewalk and smiles and tells the princesses and blows a kiss at you *at the very same moment* that the bare-chested bodybuilder next to you is inching toward you while you inch, too, to touch thighs?

Faces grim, cops assigned to escort the parade grind their motorcycles in angry commentary. They roar the dark machines threateningly close to the often-bare tapping feet of the spectators on the curbs. The only allies of the cops here today are the bellowing jesuspeople, pitiful scraggy zombies who leapt easily from acid bummers into Bible hallucinations. They shout the curses inked on their placards: "Homosexuals are Damned." "Satan is the Homosexual god."

Everyone ignores them, as they ignore the cops.

And then a moment's epiphany: Defendants enmeshed in the iron spiderweb of courts and idiotic laws—busted during a notorious gay bathhouse raid—march along the street: a woman chained to a man, each flanked and handcuffed to a gay man in cop uniform—a chilling spectacle, a reminder to how many spectators of their own arrests? Then the group pauses, and the two gay men playing cops turn to each other and embrace lovingly, and kiss. The roar of the real-cops' motorcycles boomed like shots, the drivers—faces drained—had understood but resisted the message that would have cost them thousands of dollars on a psychiatrist's couch.

Then a touching group: A scattering of parents of gays.

A part of the parade, gay motorcyclists, real bikers, cut snappy figures on the street with their machines. The butchest, dieselest, lady-dude God ever made—tattoo on bulging biceps—matches them turn for turn.

Half a block more, and the parade will end. I felt a letdown. We had showed a part our numbers—and our colors—and everyone had felt, could not have helped but feel, the crackling energy, the electric charging pride. But now it will end. Along the block where the parade has already passed, others feeling the same urge to extend these bold moments rush impulsively into the street to join the parade.

Uncoiling the tight tension, four cops attack one man. One cop jumps him—mounts him—two other cops wrench his arms, another aims a bully club at his legs, three others rush in to join the rampage. (Later the man will be busted and charged with interference and resisting arrest, but a series of photographs recording the cop actions will clear him and pave the way for his suit charging violation of his rights.)

Other spectators attempt to join the parade.

Instantly the cops are on them. Joyous laughter roars into anger along the sidewalks. Then: Shots! No—just firecrackers. Waiting, ready, dozens of anxious cops storm the Boulevard. Red lights on squad cars spin dementedly. Sirens whine shrilly. The outraged cops are finally making their statement against the bewildering spectacle they witnessed—homosexuals openly parading, men kissing men, women kissing women, and "cops" kissing "cops." And so the cops pushed and shoved, just longing for a bashed head, a felled body—thrusting forward with their bully sticks held before them in transferred manhood, allowing no one to join the parade.

They march, clearing the street. A throng of gays flanks them. "Pigs, pigs! Fucking pigs! Pigs! Shit pigs! Pigs, pigs, pigs, pigs!"

The cops had blocked two streets, sealing off the parade route. It was the only gesture they could come up with to make their presence known, to reassert their hatred. Thirty cops on one side, thirty cops on the other. Sixty black-uniformed cops holding sixty wooden cocks protectively before them.

Now twenty-five squad cars invade the gay turf, this gay battleground.

Defiant gays mill before the lined cops. The remem-

bered frustration of having to remain silent while cops
hassled and insulted and threatened, cops secure because of
their bully sticks, bully guns, bully chains—the bullying
made possible because they know you can't answer back—it
was that frustration that found its voice: "Huccome yawll
standin there with yer cocks stickin up?" "Hey, why don't
you suck a cock and then you won't have to hold that
stick." "Don't you remember me?—you danced with me
last night at— . . ."

Hands tightening on their sticks, the cops tensed
perceptibly forward. What was happening? Weren't *they*
the cops?—and L.A. cops, to boot! Nothing in their cop
training—no, nothing in their *lives*—had prepared them for
this. Gay men and women not afraid of them? Imagine! Gay
men and women, and even an obviously straight woman,
taunting *them*? Not only that, but questioning *their* masculinity. And it hurt. Oh, it hurt. After all, how much more
clearly could they prove their masculinity? Hadn't they
bashed the skulls of queers who resisted arrest, and even of
those who didn't? How many handcuffs had they clicked
smartly in raids on queer bars? And if the guy you said was
groping the other guy wasn't really the right one, so
what?—he probably groped or got groped yesterday. So
nothing during those days of barracks intimacy, good days,
buddy days, nothing in Police Academy had prepared them
for this—not the showers, the recreation periods, the sweaty
teams. Certainly nothing during the inspections by the
chief of police, eyeing them from head to foot slowly—for
flaws in their uniforms, of course—nothing had prepared
them for *this*. Jesusgod, *they* were the cops, and *those* were
the queers. Why then did it feel as if *they*— . . .? *What the
fuck was happening here?*

So they held their bully clubs.

For a glaring moment seeing their drained faces, I felt—
almost, almost, *almost*—a scent, almost a scent, of pity for
them, those inheritors of the straight-world's hatred of
homosexuals, a hatred exacerbating their self-doubts. But it
wasn't even that simple. What myriad resentments, against
the life they were forced to live, within their profession of
paranoia, the locked boundaries of a cop's ugly world—

what myriad resentments were aroused by the people whose worlds they could touch only as bullies? . . . But no. It was quickly drowned, that spark of pity for them, drowned in the memories of bashed heads and violence, in the graphic representation of their utmost lack of courage, the bully "courage" that depends on arbitrary authority, on a badge, only that; the greatest cowardice.

More sirens infected the air. Red lights flashed like popping bulbs.

Shirtless, lolling, a cluster of malehustlers gathered in tense good humor. Also heckling. Then a firecracker burst. Another. The cop sticks rose. Cops rushed the three hustlers. Handcuffs clicked tightly.

"Pigs, pigs, pigs, shit pigs, pigs!"

Barely inches away, I felt the inundating rage sweeping the street, and I had a vision of the inevitable gay apocalypse—of thousands of homosexuals rushing against the helmets and the sticks, the guns—thousands of gay men and women riding a tide of pent-up rage released at last. Abruptly that vision of apocalyptic violence stopped. Yes, that would be righteous—but was that indeed what the gay apocalpyse would be?

Perhaps. Yes, perhaps.

Suddenly I laughed aloud. But might it not be, instead, the ultimate, the liberating, public sex orgy?

"Please, please, gay brothers and sisters, please disperse, this is your gay monitor, walk to other corners. Please, leave the street, leave the street peacefully, this is your gay parade monitor, please let's avoid any violence."

Someone laughed bitterly. It was over.

For now.

11:47 P.M. *Selma.*

RESURRECTED OUT of the dread death, rejection—the vacant period ended—Jim still needs the further assurance which only hustling can give him. And it's Saturday night, the busiest night on Selma.

There, a slow-moving squad car is flashing brash lights on the slowly scattering outlaws. Jim waits in his car. The cops leave. The outlaws return. Jim gets out.

Now he waits by the steps of the Baptist Church, imagining his tanned body stark against the white columns.

Pretty, street-hip, a youngwoman, 20—older, younger—glances at him, moves on, looks back, smiles, returns: "What's goin on?"

Jim is friendly. "Getting along." He recognizes her as one of that breed of straight girls attracted to malehustlers, making it from day to day, knowing—perhaps turned on by it—that their "old men"—the hustlers they often live with—sell their bodies to other men.

"You know something?—you remind me of my old man," she tells him. "Remember him? Called himself Reno, cause he got divorced there. He worked the streets about half a year ago. Hey, man, are you straight, bi, or gay?" she asks him bluntly.

Jim only shrugs.

"Shit," she fills in for him, "I think you're whatever you're fucking at the time, yeah?"

"Right," he laughs.

"I live just off the boulevard; come by, huh?" She writes down her address.

As she walks away, he puts the address in his pocket, but he knows he won't call her.

He walks along the street. At the corner, by an old house now apartments, he sees a familiar, lovely figure, a small, thin, blue-haired old woman, about seventy, her frame still youthfully erect, her gait friskily disguising what is probably a hurt knee. As usual, late at night, she's walking two leashed dogs—mongrels. "Hi, there," she calls to Jim. He greets her warmly. "Cops out tonight," she tells him. "A couple of squad cars just came by. And watch out for a late-model Plymouth, looks like vice to me." Jim thanks her for her usual warnings. "Well, you take care of yourself, hear?" she tells him and tugs at the leashes and moves on.

A car has stopped just ahead. A Plymouth—and the driver had not driven by before, didn't really look carefully at him. Jim turns away from the man now signaling him.

A proud Mercedes, elegant, luxurious, stops, the driver waits for Jim to approach. Jim removes his vest, to challenge the car's arrogance with his own. The driver calls out: "Want to come to my place?"

"It depends what for," Jim says.

"So I can really look at your fine body."

"Still depends on what for," Jim draws him out.

"What do you charge?" the man completes the ritual.

Jim answers, the man agrees. But:

"I'm sorry. I just remembered I promised to drive a friend somewhere," Jim lies. "Sorry." That was all he wanted, needed, the admiration, the offer of sexmoney. That he used the other for that, he regrets, yes; but— . . .

VOICE OVER: *Beyond the Fag Hag*

JUDY GARLAND BAPTIZED us in rainbow-colored tears. Not the fabulous performer, no, not her—but the symbol of the eternal, crushed, defeated—but-come-out-fighting—loser she became for the homosexual. Like her, he masochistically acquiesced; kick us and we'll hurt, but we'll come back singing for more with a sob in our voices, they said through her.

It was all right, after "the man that got away" got away, because "over the rainbow" would be some illusive happiness—like heaven for the meek. With offerings of blood-red roses, homosexuals flocked to her performances, and loved her as a symbol in proportion to how much they hated themselves.

Suicide attempts!
Sleeping pills!
Uppers and downers!
Bouts with ugliness!
Judy, we love you!
They wept for her and she wept for them, and she laughed at them and they laughed at her. When she died,

the fags would fly their flags half-mast, she joked to her daughter.

And retreat they did when she did die.

The old faction wept on Fire Island. Their lowered flags flapped bravely in the wind. Somewhere, over the rainbow.

In New York, the weekend of her funeral, the first gay riot occurred.

"Over the rainbow" was not good enough. Here, now. *That* was the reality. The acquiescing hurt was fucked. During what ordinarily would have been a routine mass harassment of gays in a Greenwich Village bar called the Stonewall, homosexuals resisted the cops for the first time. This time The Man didn't get away.

Garland the symbol of gay oppression was truly dead.

Victims themselves, fag hags are sad figures in the gay world. They range from the grand ones—ex-movie queens, the ghost of beauty barely clinging; to the frigid women, usually sexless by choice—brittle, smart, sophisticated, afraid of straight or sexual men, afraid of other women; to the tacky, shrill women rejected sexually.

By converting men to bitchy children, all fag hags use homosexuals for substitute revenge: the dinosauric ex-movie queen, revenge for the men who used up her beauty and fled when youth fled too; the icy women, revenge for the children they'll never have; the loud ones, revenge for the men who will not touch them.

And the gay men who "court" these queen bees? A very small but very visible, often chic group, happy to celebrate the ex-beauty's lost sexuality and to claim her "divine"; happy for fused father–mother figures eternally virginal; with the undesirable women, sympathetic in mutual con- tempt. And for the fag-hag's castrating hatred, these men will pay them back by "adoring" them but never desiring them.

What of other women—straight, sexual, not fag hags?— what of them in relation to gay men? (A sad fact of the gay world is that, with notable exceptions, there is little significant rapport between gay men and gay women.)

That there is hostility from many straight women

toward male homosexuals is as true as that there are homosexuals who despise all women—and who thus sadly cut themselves off from at least half the range of human experience. In women, there is the resentment stirred by the cultural shock at the realization of a competing gay man, ancestral societal attitudes suddenly violated by a man who desires not her but a man; the woman feels irrelevant, her sexual power denied. (This may account for the rush reportedly experienced by some women in competing sexually with a man for another man.)

The gay man's resentment of women is also multifaceted; it may come partly from resentment, at whatever stage of his homosexual awakening, at being taught—even forced—to respond sexually to someone he does not desire; and women who—without encouragement—attempt to "change," or even "cure" or "save" him, certainly humiliate him.

Emerging out of the women's consciousness movement is a new figure, neither fag hag nor surrogate mother nor hostile competitor. Abandoning arbitrarily assigned, restrictive, sexual role-playing—allowing the woman to be strong *and* to feel, the man to feel *and* to be strong—she frees the male from an equally restrictive, equally arbitrary opposite role. The same sexual evil that oppresses women oppresses homosexual men—and straight men.

And will the new, freed woman produce more or less homosexuals? Neither. Just healthier ones.

(Ironically, transvestites and transsexuals—still attired in fifties grandeur of short skirts, tight halters, sequins—may be the last of the repressed "women." "The type of woman who turns me on is gone now," a heterosexual writer lamented recently at a party. "Now when I want to feel *macho*, I pick up a transvestite." And a downtown Los Angeles bar catering to transvestites and transsexuals refuses to serve real women!)

A very special intimacy, respect, and true love can occur between a gay man and a straight woman secure in her own sexuality; a unique, uncluttered closeness that makes no sexual demands, does not use the other in

vindictive substitution, and acknowledges—not denies—
each other's humanity, individuality, and sexual choice—the
special sexual beauty of a woman, the special sexual beauty
of a man.

12:31 A.M. *Santa Monica Boulevard and Highland Avenue.*

HE PARKED ON a side street. Now he's hitchhiking on a busy corner, limbo territory, both hustling and unpaid cruising. A van stops. The driver is very goodlooking. A hairy mat crowds the edge of his white T-shirt. Jim gets in. The man places his hand lightly on his own groin, a signal Jim answers by placing his on his own.

12:38 A.M. *A Side Street Near West Hollywood.*

There is a mattress in back of the van, parked now in a lot. Both men strip. They take each other's cock in their mouths simultaneously. Jim doesn't want to come, although he feels his cock preparing in the other's throat, the other's growing in his. At that very moment, Jim pulls his mouth away, the other's cum spills on the mattress.

The man drives Jim back to the same corner. "My name's John. What's yours?" he asks Jim, to stamp an identity on the contact.

"John, too," Jim answers. At that moment he wishes he

had come in the other's mouth and had taken the other's cum in his.

12:51 A.M.   *Santa Monica Boulevard and Highland Avenue.*

As he stands hitchhiking vaguely, his thumb just barely held out at his thigh, he considers going back to his car and driving to the most popular of the glitterbars. Floor sprinkled with tiny silvery lights, colored strobes pounding to disco rock, it attracts a wide spectrum of the gay, bisexual, and, increasingly, the straight worlds. Beautiful boys and youngmen primp there; handsome masculine ones often in cutoffs and tanktops cruise. And gorgeous straight women, vaguely costumed, dance alone sometimes, sometimes with men, sometimes with women—men and men, men and women, women and women gyrating in graceful, studiedly orgasmic movements. But Jim decides against going there. Saturdays it's jammed, and there is only the mildest revolution there.

Perhaps he'll drive to the beach. On warm evenings, hunters gather about the area of the shadowy pier.

FLASHBACK: *The Beach at Night. A Week Ago.*

Shadows fused in the double darkness under the crumbling boards of the pier.

Jim walked to the edge of the ocean, sprayed with silver foam. He is always aware of the mysterious darkness beyond the water—black; locking secrets. An outlaw followed him, now another, the three a shrinking triangle moving to the sensual sighing of the ocean.

At the edge of the shore, Jim removed his clothes and lay on the still-warm sand. No fog tonight, the moon naked too.

One of the two other outlaws stripped wordlessly next to him. For long, they lay side by side, touching. A few feet away the third man lay clothed on the sand watching them.

12:55 A.M.   *Santa Monica Boulevard and Highland*
              Avenue.

But the beach is unpredictable, especially on weekends. He might drive for miles and find it deserted.

A car stops to give him a ride, but he waves it away and returns to his own.

VOICE OVER: *The Gay Sensibility*

I'M SUPPOSED TO represent the "underground voice" in a program on Sensuality in the Arts. It's gone badly—two movie stars have read and posed too long, and one man has actually been hooted; I comfort myself by telling myself that he deserved it for being an asshole. The large audience, tacky, middleclass, predominantly straight, here mainly to see the movie stars, is noisy and restive. I'll be followed by a strutting harlequin of a man, who's pissed because the program is going on too long—he's right about that—and people are going to leave without hearing him. Why I agreed to be here, I suddenly don't know. I'm embarrassed, and I consider splitting. But my friends are here, and I've already been introduced.

Fuck.

In the first row a woman is knitting furiously. Madame DeFarge?

I start my talk:

For centuries homosexuals— . . .

(The chattering subsides somewhat. Oh, oh, a queer.)

. . . —have been prosecuted and persecuted. The law tells us we're criminals, and so we've become defiant outlaws. Psychiatrists demand we be sick, and so we've become obsessed with physical beauty. Religion insists we're sinners, and so we've become soulful sensualists. The result is the unique, sensual, feeling, elegant sensibility of the sexual outlaw.

(The woman in the front row plunges a needle into her threads; she eyes me with one crazy and one normal eye.)

What produces this sensibility?

To survive in a heterosexual world, the homosexual plays roles as a child. He turns to his imagination to be himself; that imagination flows easily to the arts. In touch with his sexual persona, the gay artist produces work marked and expanded by its duality—its sensitivity and strength.

Jean Genet. Dual exile. Convict and homosexual. Drag queens and superhung studs. Strength and passivity, violence and tenderness. A stud becomes a queen, a queen a stud—easily in Genet's world.

Michelangelo. The huge, fantastically muscular figures—and the gentle faces. Soulful angels and powerful men.

Proust. The spiraling identities of his male-females and female-males allowed him to convey both the heterosexual and the homosexual experience—in one superb metaphor.

Oscar Wilde. The often flippant wit of his plays coupled with the outlaw courage of his life, especially in his trial.

Djuna Barnes. The somber vision and the lush, narcissistic prose.

Pasolini. The religious communist.

William Burroughs. The passivity of heroin and the frenzy of orgy.

Tennessee Williams. Repression and liberation. Blanche Dubois, whore and poet.

Gertrude Stein. The ostensibly flat, conversational prose disguising the poetic rhythms.

Truman Capote. The "high-drag" style exploring violence.

Shakespeare in the sonnets. The dark lady and the mysterious youngman.

Carson McCullers. The tenderness within the grotesquerie.

Visconti. The obsessions with inner disorder and madness and visual order and composition.

(At least the audience is quiet. Maybe they don't know what I'm talking about. I glance at the knitting woman. Oh, God, her head is cocked, and the needle is poised!)

I continue: Conversely, the avoidance of one aspect of sexuality and the extreme acceptance of the other has kept many artists from their full potential. Ronald Firbank produces a precious literary sundae. Andy Warhol creates lifeless grotesques.

Then there are the screaming heterosexuals— . . .

(Chuckles—thank God. Only from my friends? . . . I glance down. The needle darts!)

. . . —the male impersonators.

(More chuckles. All *right!* This time I don't look at the woman in the front row.)

Hemingway, the hairy godfather of heterosexual writers; his suffocatingly heavy breathing stifling the tender part of himself. Significantly he came close to realizing a fusion in *The Sun Also Rises*—where he deals with a castrated hero.

And take the Tarzan-howling of Norman Mailer.

(Sorry, in a way, that there's a ripple, a very slight ripple, of applause, and some laughter. I like Norman Mailer, despite his bullish fuckups.)

More intelligent than Hemingway—and a far better writer— . . .

(I'm making up with Norman.)

. . . —he faces the possibility of *intellectual* homosexuality. But that can be a greater subterfuge, doubly restricting him from his sensual potential.

And Kerouac. Eternal jock buddy.

No, the artist doesn't have to be homosexual to produce good art; and certainly not all homosexual artists are "good." But the artist who represses either the male or female aspect of his or her being produces unfulfilled work. James Joyce, Shakespeare, Picasso, Flannery O'Connor, D. H. Lawrence, and many, many other finally heterosexual artists have accepted, often joyously, the female and the male sides of themselves.

If only by the nature of the acute sensibility and sensuality he has brought so abundantly to art, the homosexual should be an object of admiration, not reprobation and hatred. Without him, the arts—and humanity—would be vastly diminished.

(Good applause. Not wild, no, but not just polite either. I'm pleased, of course—but I am much more pleased because—Jesus Christ!—Madame DeFarge has set aside her needles and her threads and is clapping spiritedly!)

Now there's to be one of those grim panel discussions "necessary" to make these programs an "educational experience."

But the program has dragged on so long—the man who followed me, quite fully recovering from his snit, talked forever—that there are more panelists than audience. (Hyperbole.) I jump off the stage and split.

Later I wish I'd gone further in my speech, spoken outright about gay dominance in certain arts. Yes. Oh, and narcissism. "The gay sensibility, obsessed with appearance, produces beautiful bodies, people. The result in males ranges widely—from ballet dancers to bodybuilders." Yes, narcissism as art form. And certainly bodybuilding as art form. Not that all bodybuilders are sexually gay, of course not, but the *form* is gay—the pursuit of the idealized grace of the "woman" and the idealized strength of the "man."

And I forgot to mention the silently symphonic, intricate, instinctively choreographed beauty of the promiscuous sexhunt.

1:09 A.M. *The Lots and Alleys Near the Costume Bars.*

JIM PARKS ACROSS the street from the Turf bar—one of several "costume" bars in an area of dark houses and closed commercial buildings. Outside the bars, the lots and alleys become the sexual arena throughout the night. Scouts are already hunting the terrain in preparation for the main bouts immediately before and after the bars' closing, when accumulated sex will flow outside. Now the preliminaries are occurring.

Jim waits in the lot. Grime-veiled streetlights intensify the sense of otherworldness. A car's brights enclose him slowly in a brilliant net. The car stops, the lights blink in signal. Jim moves past the passenger window of the car. The driver is handsome, blond. He leans over and opens the door for Jim.

Inside, the man goes down on Jim. Jim reaches for the other's cock, but the other eases his hand away; it's obvious that he does not want Jim to respond in any way. Jim leans back. Outside, another hunter circles the car slowly. A few feet away a man stands next to a van, another man squats before him. In the car, Jim raises his body, the other's tongue rims him. The man outside watches through the window. The exhibitionistic splendor is exciting Jim, he's close to coming, and he doesn't want to, not yet. He eases his body away. "Sorry, man, I can't come," he lies. The man watching through the window replaces him in the car.

Jim stands within the dark doorway of a building for rent. A man in leather chaps stands before him. Soon each has pulled out his cock. Two warriors, sex weapons pointed at each other. Neither advances. Jim breaks the tie by moving away. Increasingly more outlaws linger in the lot's shadows.

A goodlooking man begins to cruise him. A third appears across the street. The first man crosses. Jim turns away quickly, not wanting to see them if they move toward each other, away from him; the wing of depression touches him again, a constant intrusive presence within his victories.

Guarded by a cluster of trees, a long partition between two darkened impassive buildings at the end of the parking lot provides a cramped place for encounters. A muscular man stands there. He and Jim glance at each other then instantly away. Both too similar, both instantly attracted to each other, that very attraction and similarity causes each to turn away, to show the other that, for him, the other doesn't exist. But both glance back at the same time, and again away. Certain the other has left, Jim returns to that strategic place. Soon, two men flank him. A frozen triangle. Jim is tempted to cross the street, apprehensive they may glide toward each other; but one of the two moves closer to him, and the other moves away. Dodging the low-hanging twigs and branches, Jim moves into the space between the two buildings. Following quickly, the other man licks Jim's nipples. Jim touches the other's hairy chest. The man blows Jim, then stands, Jim sucks him, then stands. They alternate. They separate.

Back to the lot. More outlaws leaving the bars.

At the back of a squat building is a three-walled indention, like an open cell. An overhead light is periodically smashed by the hunters; the jagged bulb looks out blindly as three men buttoning their pants emerge out of the enclosure. Jim moves into the cubicle. Waits. Again, that recurring awareness of strangeness, to stand, just stand waiting in the darkness. Again, the brushing depression—as figures lurk, pause, move on.

The man in leather chaps—who did not advance earlier—is here again. Jim is about to leave, not wanting to extend the waiting game. But the other gropes Jim's cock with one hand, the other guides Jim's hand to his back. Exploring, Jim's fingers discover that the man's pants have been cut out at the buttocks; the open chaps expose his naked ass. As the other sucks him cursorily, Jim's fingers part the buttocks.

The man in chaps pushes his bending body against Jim's erect cock. Instead, Jim shoves his middle finger in. The man jerks—"Oh, yes!" Jim pushes another finger. Both farther. The man whispers: "Oh, yeah, baby, fuck me big!"

Jim withdraws his fingers. The other pushes his ass forcefully against Jim's hard prick. Jim grasps him roughly by the shoulders, pushing him back and forth, allowing his cock to slide into the parted ass, its movements expertly matching the thrusting of Jim's. He feels the tight ass squeezing out his cum.

He pulls away. The man came too.

Across the street. Past other shadows in the lot. To the bathroom left open nightly in the garage at the corner. The sound of splashing water, as he soaps his cock, obscured— until he finished washing—the sexsighs coming from the lone cubicle.

Outside, Jim decides he'll go home—hours before the purgatory of violet dawn.

But as he walks through the thickening area—new hunters cruising, cars driving up and down frenetically—the nerve of his sexuality is re-awakened still again.

Whrrrrrrrrrr! Whrrrrrrrrrr!

The roar of the cop helicopter cuts the night. The wide shaft of its light pounces on the darkness. The outlaws move for cover, into areas sheltered by walls, into partitions between buildings, under trees—but even so, they move slowly, not violating the hypnotic quality of the hunt. Cold light floods the invaded area eerily, a threatened island of light in the dark. In the shadowed fringes, the hunt continues.

Captured momentarily by the helicopter's light, his shadow swirling strangely about him, Jim moves out of the round pool. Beyond the illumined circle, a man waits in a car for him. He's well-built, wearing no shirt. Challenged as always, Jim removes his vest.

The man gets out—he's more muscular than Jim thought at first. The helicopter's shifting light illumines both muscular bodies dramatically. Jim moves beyond the sidewalk, against sheltering trees bunched before a locked building. Following, the other stops within feet of him. The man flexes, clenched fist to forehead, biceps bulging in imitation of magazine poses. Challenged anew, Jim flexes back. Again, the brushing light of the helicopter accents their defined muscles. The man shifts into another pose, leg rigid at an angle, one arm tensed hard. Jim flexes back, but he's becoming increasingly uncomfortable with this scene. Is this all the man wants—the two posing for each other, here? The man keeps shifting from one pose to another, each time waiting for Jim to follow. But now Jim feels silly. Still, identifying narcissistically with the man, he doesn't want to walk away too fast and leave him flexing in the bushes in the middle of the night! But just this, exciting as it was as a short preliminary, is not enough for Jim; he has to break it. Slowly he moves out. He puts on his vest, walks away from the strange charade.

The helicopter is gone. The hunters who fled return, recharged. The bar has closed. Men wander in the dark, lean against vans, walls, stand before open car windows. The odor of amyl nitrite perfumes the night with sex.

Jim moves to a lighted corner. Several men pass by. All ignore each other pointedly, defensively. Two men drive by. "Wanna come to an orgy?" one calls out to Jim.

"Uh—just tell me where."

The man tells him the address. The two drive off, stop before another idling man: "Wanna come to an orgy?"

Jim returns into the misty darkness of the lots.

2:17 A.M. *The Garage on Oak Street.*

In minutes the area outside the costume bars is deserted. Now the hunt will transfer to the sidewalks, the streets, and the garage near a jammed afterhours club. The quiet street is filled with cars—parking, driving. Men cruise the long blocks under tall trees. Stepping over the crushed barbed wire at its sides, figures are moving steadily to the back of the abandoned garage.

FLASHBACK: *The Garage. A Year Ago.*

The inside of the garage was the size of a large living room. Parched, cold cement for a floor. Walls crumbling into dusty patches. Its large sliding tin door was chained. One side door leading in was ripped open. When you entered, you saw nothing, heard only muffled sounds; you smelled amyl. Then your outlaw eyes adjusted; you saw tangled figures throughout. At times the bodies spilled out into the back, fusing outside among the dead brush.

Jim had just walked out of the garage; countless mouths and hands touched, grasped, and licked bodies in the dark. Only minutes later—safe by his car across the street—he looked back and saw the area of the garage ablaze in white lights; he heard even from this distance the chilling words:

"Vice officers! Everybody stay where you are!"

He saw outlaws running—some made it, some didn't, and those who didn't were thrust violently onto the sidewalk, faces pressed hard against the dirt, cops anxious to grope and mount in violence the bodies they dare not touch in sex. "Fucking goddam queers!" the threatened, desperate invaders roared. They lined the bloodied outlaws before the garage. Handcuffs clanged.

Jim felt the mixture of pain and rage.

Minutes later, with one of the escaped outlaws, he made it in his car parked around the corner from the site of the bloody battle.

2:21 A.M.   *Oak Street. The Garage. The Tunnels. The Shed. The Street.*

The outlaws endured—discovering in the area three new major underground sites—two semen-caked tunnels and a shed—and several minor ones—laundry rooms left open, sheltered garages, stairways. Soon the raided garage thrived again, though its entry was tightly blocked. The orgies shifted to the space behind, outside.

Though the night has cooled slightly, Jim removes his vest and walks shirtless along the sidewalk toward the garage. A very handsome makebelieve cowboy—wide hat, boots, western shirt, open—is moving toward him on the block. Cars are parked solidly flanking one side of the sidewalk; on the other, trees arch over it, bordering a long, empty, hilly lot. Immediately the electric signal of daring rashness is sent out between the two men. Jim stands near a street light. The "cowboy" squats before him. Not furtively, not hurriedly, not for only seconds—but slowly, defiantly, ritualistically, openly—the cowboy sucks Jim, while Jim lightly maneuvers the curly, bobbing head, cowboy hat sliding back. Now Jim's hands slide into the other's open shirt, touching the hair-matted chest.

Other hunters freeze watching. Cruising cars pause to stare at the beautifully defiant spectacle. The cowboy comes into his own hand—and in another moment Jim would have come too, gladly. To seal the liberating act between them, they kiss very, very long.

They separate slowly.

Jim walks into the area behind the garage.

Perhaps five men stand there. But nothing is happening. Everyone is waiting. All that is required will be one motion, and the orgy will spring. And it does: Almost simultaneously, a man cupped Jim's groin, and another touched another's. The sexual current flows. Bodies, hands, mouths connect. Soon other shadows are led here by the silent signals. In the clear night, they look like barely moving statues.

Without coming, Jim left the orgy. The interest was too diffuse, too indifferent. Along the block, a man in a van is cruising him. Jim stands by the window of the stopped van. The man reaches over and unlocks the passenger door. Jim walks in—the driver is attractive. He drives the van a few blocks, to another oblivious neighborhood.

In the back of the van, pants pulled down, the two lie on the carpeted floor. The other man wears a cock ring—a current fad, a ring of metal, like his, or of studded leather, around the base of the cock and balls, supposedly insuring harder hard-ons, better orgasms. They lick each other's balls, Jim feeling a curious arousal as he sees the other's ringed cock and balls. Jim doesn't want to come again. He withdraws his cock from the other's mouth and the other's from his—tempted very vaguely to take the cum but pulling away just as a tiny dot, just a dot, of creamy liquid crowned the other's cock.

The man dropped Jim off in the area of the garage. "I think we made it once before," the man tells Jim.

"Uh—maybe." Jim can't remember.

Still long before dawn. The street still thrives. New hunters have left the bar-turned-coffeehouse.

There are too many people by the area of the garage, and so Jim crosses the street to the tunnels.

Two tunnels across the street from each other; stairs rising connect the lower street to the upper thoroughfare. In the muffled light, a man squats on the landing of stairs. Jim walks up. Suddenly he stops, remembers the strange earlier rejection at Greenstone. And the empty infinite hours of terror. Footsteps from the upper-street level! Another hunter? The cops? Jim moves away—to the other tunnel across the street. There, one man is fucking another blowing a third. Jim retreats.

Beyond the cave of the tunnel he passes a forlorn old man, waiting, alone, ignored, wasted; waiting for anybody.

Jim moves toward the shed behind a commercial building. The door to the shed is open. Inside the dark room there's a water tank, a blacker presence in the darkness. Gardening tools. A curled hose. And the odor of amyl nitrite. The sex chemical lurking from earlier encounters? His practiced eyes adjust to the dark beyond the door. There are three men at the back of the shed; as he moves forward slightly, a hand attempts to pull him into the cluster. More than three outlaws are here. Again the dark anonymity sends him away. His body is too special for totally crushed darkness.

He moves up the stairs into the yellow tunnel again. Two men, startled, pull away. Jim retreats, not wanting to break them apart.

On the corner a lightly but definitely muscled young-man stands; perhaps twenty years old. He's obviously proud of his beginning muscles, which he flexes. As Jim passes, the youngman nods. Jim stops a few feet ahead. The youngman joins him. "How long you been working out?" he asks Jim, quickly establishing a bond. The words, so friendly, so easily spoken, challenge the anonymous silence.

Jim answers.

A squad car passes them, backs up threateningly. But the two don't move.

"You got a beautiful body," the youngman says. He clearly waits for Jim to comment on his. But right now Jim can't.

Motor running, the cops still stare at them from across the street.

"You got a place?" the youngman asks.

"Yeah—a few minutes away."

Suddenly the cops flash lights on them.

"Where's your car?" the youngman asks.

Jim points it out.

"I'll follow you," the youngman says.

They separate within the glaring lights, to their cars.

The cops move away, motor growling.

As he drives to his apartment—the youngman following in his car—Jim glances at his watch. Before long, dawn will come in a blue arc. Jim has a sense of— ... Of having *survived* the night.

On the street, the outlaws scattered by the cops wait in their cars. The lone old man still stands anxiously by the tunnel.

VOICE OVER: *The Gay Threat*

"WHAT IS THE REAL GAY THREAT?" I've asked the mixed audience I'm addressing. Earlier, in balking at an overt call for sexual revolution on the streets, I backed off. But I know only too well the commitment, the dangers, the sacrifices. You don't recruit.

I go on:

Since we are not child molesters, nor seducers of the straight—but a stop-gap against overpopulation—and since it is very possible that we are more law-abiding (dismissing sex laws) than the straight population, and since we have abundantly enriched humanity, how then are homosexuals a threat?

Biblical arguments do not hold. Scriptural admonitions are used entirely selectively. That route is clearly subterfuge.

There are, in fact, two very real threats that the gay world poses to straight society. One is of course psychic— the fear of being what religion, laws, doctors have wrongfully branded, condemned, persecuted, prosecuted, punished, forbidden.

The second is that an acceptance of homosexuality— including, importantly, its tendency toward promiscuity— would result in a traumatic questioning of what, in the extreme, becomes oppressive within the heterosexual norm.

Why one wife? One husband? Why not lovers?

Why marriage?

Why sex with only one person?

Why *not* open sex? (Even the mere knowledge of it threatens, since gay promiscuity is invisible to all but the participants and voyeuristic cops.)

Why *only* relationships?

Why, necessarily, children?

The heterosexual would thus be questioning, not heterosexuality itself, no, but the stagnant conformity of much of his tribal society.

4:08 A.M. *The Apartment.*

"You got weights here?" the youngman asks enthusiastically inside Jim's apartment.

"Yeah, this is where I work out." Jim leads him to that room. He draws heavy drapes against the sky which will soon lighten.

They begin tossing the weights about—not in a strict workout but only to heighten their awareness of their own and the other's special bodies. Jim is very proud of his much more muscular body. He pumps his muscles easily, wallowing in the obvious admiration of the youngman. Yet, with an unwelcome stab of hurt, Jim can't help noticing . . . that the other's body . . . though just beginning to sprout muscles . . . has a luminous velvet smoothness . . . that only . . . the very young . . . possess. Jim thinks: He looks like me when I was— . . . Turning away from the youngman, Jim pumps his body frenziedly, fully.

Soon they're both flushed. They stand before each other.

"You really do have a beautiful body," the youngman tells Jim again—and waits again.

This time Jim can say: "So do you."

The youngman smiles, Jim smiles back at him. But neither commits himself to advancing first. For moments Jim thinks it will not happen, that both will be trapped in their rigidity. He touches his own chest, a signal. Now the youngman's hand rests lightly on Jim's bare shoulder. For seconds Jim doesn't touch him back—wanting symbolic acknowledgment of his own muscular superiority. Fearing that Jim will not reciprocate, the youngman withdraws his hand. Now Jim touches him back, on the shoulder. The other's hand returns easily, moves down Jim's stomach, slowly, to make sure Jim's moves down on his—and it does. Bodies inch closer. Lips touch. And now the two men begin a game—the acute attraction tinged with competition: Wherever the youngman touches Jim—tentatively at first— Jim touches the other. The tentative movements firm.

Leaving the weights randomly on the floor, they move into the bedroom. Jim draws heavy drapes there too, looking away from the window and the soon-lightening sky.

Naked, they stand kissing, erect cocks pressed together like extensions of each other. Neither has yet touched the other's cock with his hands. Not yet. But now simultaneously, guardedly simultaneously, their fingers edge there, touching still tentatively for full mutual commitment; assured, both hands grasp the other's cock.

They lie on the bed, limbs entwined. Now they shift, holding each other's cocks close to their mouths but not touching the blood-hardened shafts to their lips. "Let's count to three and go at the same time," the youngman suggests.

"One," Jim says. *He's so much like me,* he thinks.

"Two," the youngman counts.

"Three," they both say.

Heads push forward onto waiting cocks. Sensations indistinguishable—mouth on cock, cock in mouth. Both tongues lick furry balls, return recurrently to cocks.

Heads locked by firm thighs, cocks pushing in and out of each other's mouths, Jim feels a magnificent confusion, as he did earlier this afternoon in the park, his own cock and the other's growing as if one. The other's mouth increases its lunging movements, Jim's matches them.

Now! Jim wants to shoot in the other's mouth, but he's not sure whether, as always before at the crucial moment, he will withdraw his own mouth from the other's pulsing cum. So much like me! he thinks again.

The tightening magic at Jim's groin unknots, and he shoots in the other's eager mouth and feels the other's cum jetting into his and doesn't pull away, doesn't want to, and imagines that his own cum flowing into the other's mouth will course through the body and flow back mixed with the other's into his own mouth filling it with the creamy juice. Swiftly, bodies still thrusting, they kiss, exchanging each other's cum back and forth in open mouths, tongues mixing it together, gluing it with their saliva, cocks still pulsing.

They lie back. Their legs touch lightly.

Now both are slightly embarrassed. Too much was given, which neither has given before to that degree.

But: "My name is Steve; yours?" the youngman asks.

"John," Jim says.

Neither can bring himself to ask what they both want—to spend the night together. Tentatively, slowly, the youngman begins to dress, sits back, resumes dressing. Trying to sound casual, he says: "Hey, I'll give you my phone number."

Jim says quickly: "I'll give you mine too."

They exchange phone numbers—knowing unequivocally, as well as they know their outlaw world, that despite the intense moments—afraid of rejection—neither will ever call the other. That this is all.

"Bye."

"Bye."

Sunday

7:34 A.M. *The Apartment.*

HE WOKE AND LOOKED toward the windows. Dawn has evaporated. He moved from night to morning avoiding the purple limbo.

This memory lodges in his mind: the man at Greenstone turning from him fiercely, spitting angrily. Jim's mind rushes to drown the memory: the muscular man in the park, the long, beautiful orgasm; the fact that he was paid to be desired (but remembers: the bronzed baby shoes, the aged photograph of the woman; Roo). Danny—that memory obtrudes. . . . The youngman named John . . . and Steve; the many, many others who admired him, desired him; and those he desired back. . . . Yet: The memory persists of the strange man at Greenstone—and the eternal vacuum during which nothing happened.

Suddenly he wishes he had got up earlier and joined the first wave of post-dawn hunters in Griffith Park.

FLASHBACK: *Griffith Park. An Early Sunday Morning.*

Those still up after the purple stasis in the broken cycle of sex must push the search forcedly into the next day.

The gates into Griffith Park open early, when foggy mist still clings in shreds. Jim drove up the hill for the intense moments. Within the lingering mist, flagrant exhibitionists stood openly naked by their cars. Other outlaws walked silently along the rustling brush.

That morning—and the world was ice-green—Jim stood shirtless halfway up the road and by his car. A van drove up. The side door slid open, the driver unseen. Jim walked past the door. A goodlooking man lay on the floor naked. His own narcissistic exhibitionism, not nearly as blatant, is affronted by the other's. Jim would have walked away, but the man called out to him. Inside, he took Jim's clothes off. The door left open, they made sex for long minutes.

Moments later, on a rocky trail in the barely clinging haze, Jim leaned against a tree. Two men took turns blowing him. Hostile only in those misty moments, the bright sun stared into his sleepless eyes.

When Jim emerged out of the trail, the sun shone in splendor, preparing for the afternoon shift of hunters.

11:07 A.M. *The Apartment.*

Lying in his bedroom, Jim knew that the early moments in the park had vanished for today. He fell asleep again—and didn't wake till near noon. He showers in cold, cold water. Again he breakfasts on eggs, milk and honey, whole-wheat bread and butter—and coffee. He prepares the thermos of liquid protein which will charge his body through the day. Sundays he does not work out. His muscles ache deliciously—proof of their growing preparation for the onslaught of the next workout. He stands in front of the mirror. Yes, he has managed to challenge sextime.

12:02 P.M. *Griffith Park. The Isolated Hill.*

Preparatory to moving into the heavy Sunday-afternoon arena, he wants to sunbathe. He drives to a secluded place not strictly within gay turf; he walks up a hill. The increasingly warm sun flirts with his body as he climbs. In a place enclosed by rocks, he spreads his beach mat, places a towel on it, removes his cutoffs and climbing boots, drinks from the thermos, and lies facing the sun. He stretches, glancing at his stripped body gleaming. Loved indifferently by the promiscuous sun, he dozes off.

He woke bathed in perspiration. He looks around, hoping for an outlaw. But not here, not now. With the towel he wipes his sweating body. Dressed again in cutoffs and climbing boots, he drives, then walks to a water pipe down a trail. There he splashes his heated body with the cold water, letting the sun dry him sensually. He applies a light coat of oil to his further-darkening body.

As he emerges from the trail, he sees a squad car driving past. Moments later, about to enter his car, he sees another. This is relatively rare in this area, which is usually patrolled by plainclothes vice cops.

Jim gets in his car and drives down the road to join the afternoon tide of hunters.

FLASHBACK: *Griffith Park. Nine Years Ago.*

He had just moved out of a nest-like enclosure of twigs and branches. Moments earlier, inside the inclined nest, he had unbuttoned the top of his pants, just one button, as a signal to the youngman who had followed him there. The youngman's hand advanced toward Jim. But nothing happened because they heard the untypically clumsy crunching of branches along the path. They parted. On the trail, Jim secured the top button of his pants.

Simultaneously, two men rushed toward him down the winding path—a bleached-blond man, and another, hickish in stiff-new, rolled-cuffed jeans. The hickish one glanced wildly at him, and the bleached man intercepted Jim:

"Vice officer!—you're under arrest!"

The hickish cop rushed into the branchy alcove. Jim heard spat words coming from the hollow he had just left, "Fucking queer!"—and the sound of fists on bones. Jim tried to pull instinctively toward the youngman he had been with, the youngman the cop was beating, but the handcuffs and the bleached cop held him back. The hickish cop emerged out of the brush with the handcuffed bleeding youngman doubled over.

They were taken to a gray rectangular cop-fortress of a building. Both were fingerprinted and stripped. In defiance, Jim flexed his naked body. Later, the hickish cop took him into a room alone.

"That guy wanted to give you head, right?"

"No, man," Jim said.

"I saw it."

"Nothing happened."

"Why were you buttoning your pants on the path?"

"Just noticed the top button was open."

"I saw him give you head." The voice was becoming increasingly agitated.

"You couldn't have, it didn't happen."

"It can go better for you if you— . . ."

"Nothing happened," Jim said. Then angrily, "Look, are you getting off on your lie?"

Jim was booked, locked in a barred cell alone with a dirty toilet and two naked cots like iron skeletons.

Only when he was bailed hours later did he learn the cop was charging them with a felony punishable by up to ten years in prison. Of all the times he might have been busted while making it in the park, it had occurred with terrible irony when nothing had happened.

All they could prove to the judge who would hear the case, Jim's attorney decided, was that from the distance the cop had clumsily designated—twenty feet away from the enclosure—he could not possibly have seen what he claimed, Jim's cock inserted in the youngman's mouth, the placement of hands; the pants. . . . In court, they showed movies of the terrain. The judge shifted the trial to the park. There he saw the impossibility of the cop's statements. He also saw the sexhunters lurking.

After eight months of court appearances, Jim and the youngman were convicted of a misdemeanor not requiring sex registration. They were fined six hundred and fifty dollars each.

Nothing happened, Jim's mind kept challenging the reality. And even if it had!

That same afternoon, he returned to the exact area of the park, and made it, over and over and over.

MONTAGE: *The City*

LOS ANGELES IS HAUNTED. By dead people, dead places.

Pershing Square. Tanned derelicts, tanned preachers, tanned malehustlers, tanned innocent sinners, and powdered-white queens—all defied smog and the cops in old Pershing Square. Gone. Gone with the lazy indigent afternoons; banished by parking lots and cleared paths; no protective shadows. And no more sweet angelsisters and their picture of Christ bleeding wax. Oh, and no more Jenny-Lu bumping "Lord-*uh!*" in heavenly orgasm under benign pubic-fringed palmtrees. No more Saint Moses with flowing white hair and admonitions of hell, tomorrow.

Gone with Clifton's Cafeteria, across the street. A phosphorescent Hawaii of fake brooks and plastic neon palmtrees, and lei-ed ladies in Biblical drag, really—and, below, in The Garden, amid moaning organ music, a giant statue of Christ, meditating.

Swept away with Angels' Flight, the motored lift from a low street to a heavenly high one, where ubiquitous palmtrees waited as if to escort you even higher.

Gone. Gone with dead movie stars and the wind.

And ghosts lurk in Venice West.

An exalted madman was going to re-create Venice right here in Southern California. Venice West! he called it. He started. Built the canals, the bridges. A small town square. Quaint benches along the shoreline, wooden shelters from the water's glare. And that was that. They found oil. He stopped. Now giant-beaked machines drill remorselessly into the earth.

The old Jews came here and built their synagogues and delicatessens along the beach. Wearing sunglasses and pasting cold cream on their noses, they sit together, eyes closed, facing the white sun. (Little urchin boys nasty in their sun-bleached blondness pedal with skinny bare legs past them—impossibly ignoring the kewpie-doll woman carrying a Vermeer reproduction, a FOR SALE sign pinned ambiguously to her bursting breasts.)

Then the jazz outcasts came to Venice. Among the imitation-Venetian buildings, the voices roared good and bad poetry, shouting for mad sanity.

While along the fabled Sunset Strip soon after, the insurgents of the legendary sixties—the most remote period in the history of time—proclaimed that flowers in one's hair meant love and peace, and, man, that's all you need. But the rampaging cops said *ugh-uh!* and, to prove it, crushed the flowers because the children had refused to move on, move on.

And then they did move on. To Manson and Altamont.

And to Venice West.

Blood-initiated, the children turned to acid for pretty dreams and got bummers instead. They were zombies on the spent battlefield of love.

They live now hunched like cold birds on the white beaches, rousing themselves occasionally to ask for change, to beat a drum funereally, or to walk stoned for hours along the glaring white beach. Betrayed. Beautiful dim ghosts in skeletal frames. Betrayed.

Junk came. Blacks and whites together shoot up skinny vein-dried arms in dung-heaped alleys.

Surviving.

12:29 P.M. *Griffith Park. The Roads. The Hills.*

As JIM ENTERS the area of the hunt, the road that winds up the hill for several miles past sporadic forests of bushes and hills, he notices red signs posted at irregular intervals on trees. Less than a foot by slightly more than a foot square, they were not in the area he left—only in the sex arena, and they were not here yesterday. Up the road, the signs recur. Motor of his car still running, Jim stops by one:

RESTRICTED
ENTRY

Mountain Fire District

MOTORCYCLES,
MOTORSCOOTERS
& OTHER MOTOR
VEHICLES PROHIBITED!

There's more; unintelligible, jumbled, obscurely legalistic sentences and clauses printed in tiny letters. Probably motorcycles and jeeps have been exploring the steep paths and trails. The hunting outlaws are apparently not affected.

And there will be hundreds of sexhunters in the park this hot, hot Sunday afternoon. Though still not the peak hour, dozens of cars are already driving into the sexual turf. Others will come in shifts throughout the afternoon, from the beaches, bars, early parties.

Up the road, almost every good area is taken. Jim drives farther up, to the water tank. Another cop car races down the road.

Jim returns to the hill where he sunbathed yesterday. Hunters emerge throughout the tall brush. They stand against the clear sky. There are too many on this hill, Jim decides. He descends to the main road, back to his car. Some of the red signs lie on the paths. Intense and ominous, the heat pulses in the stirless air.

At a sandy outpost where Jim stands, dozens of other shirtless men cruise each other, soon moving into the secluded paths across the road. Here too are the ones who come to meet others, invite them home. The tall blond muscleman in strapped sandals is here again with his equally muscular dog. Again he and Jim turn instantly from each other.

A short distance away from an inviting branch-tangled cove, Jim stands later, showing off on an indentation off the road beyond the water tank. A very goodlooking brown-haired youngman has been driving slowly back and forth, glancing at him. Unfortunately, another man stops before he does. Jim doesn't want to hurt this man, but he prefers the other; so he begins to walk away idly from the cove until the man leaves. The brown-haired youngman drives in. "Hi."

Now another car drives in. Two unattractive men eye them slowly. "Got a match?" one asks. No. "Got a lighter?" the man persists. There is something uncomfortable about them. Jim and the brown-haired youngman say no. The car drives off.

Jim and the youngman, also shirtless—body slender and hard—slide down the hill into the cove.

Whrrrrrrrrrrr!

The helicopter!

The two men look up. The cop helicopter is circling the hill where Jim was only minutes earlier. From here, they hear its muffled speakers, electronically amplifying harsh voices.

The youngman and Jim move out of the cove, farther down the path.

"I wonder what's happening," the youngman says.

"I don't know," Jim says.

1:12 P.M.   *Griffith Park. The Beginning of the Invasion.*

As Jim and the youngman move farther down the path, they hear the roar of cars, clearly different from the more flowing sound of outlaws' cruising cars.

"It sounds like an invasion," Jim laughs.

In the distance and above, the helicopter swirls angrily. Undefined electronically magnified voices echo distantly.

"Jesus," the brown-haired youngman says, laughing too, "it *does* sound like an invasion!"

As they continue down the path, they instinctively avoid being in view of the helicopter, now circling widely.

Startled, they hear the distant clap of horses' hooves.

They reach an alcove and move into it.

"I'm on probation," Jim thinks aloud, not knowing why that occurred to him at this moment.

"Me too," the other says.

As far as they are from the main road, they can hear heavy tires. Trucks? The screeching of rushing cars. And now they hear the loud speaker—either from squad cars or the hovering helicopter:

"THIS IS THE POLICE DEPARTMENT. MOVE TO THE MAIN ROAD. PROCEED IMMEDIATELY TO THE MAIN ROAD!"

The incredible reality assaults them. The cops are actually invading the park!

"They can't bust everybody for just being here," the youngman says.

But the sounds of battle along the roads beyond are unequivocal.

"We can't go back to the road now," Jim says. "We could go around the hill and into the straight section—it's safe there for sure."

"What about our cars?"

"Get them later."

"It's a long way around— . . ."

They both know that to get to the straight side of the park without returning to the main road they will have to walk very far along clawing brush, down a steep slippery hill, around, then over another high hill, and down again and across the road.

The helicopter whirs directly over them.

They throw themselves on the matted leaves. Hooves— still distant.

"They're using horses— . . ." the other starts.

"I don't believe it," Jim laughs, to obviate the fact that they are actually in danger for being in the gay section of the park.

The mechanical rumble grows.

1:28 P.M. *Griffith Park. The Invasion.*

"MOVE TO THE MAIN ROAD. PROCEED IMME-DIATELY TO THE MAIN ROAD!"

"They've seen us," the youngman blurts.

"No," Jim says. "The fuckers are just covering the whole park."

"Shit bastards!" the other says.

He turns to face Jim lying beside him on the leaves. Jim faces him. "Fuck them," Jim says. The youngman touches Jim's bare shoulder.

Their bodies connect tightly. Listening to the distant clap of horses, they lie chest to chest.

"They must be busting everybody," the brown-haired youngman says.

"Everybody they can find," Jim says.

Hands nestle in each other's groins.

The dipping helicopter scatters the leaves.

Bodies charged by the atmosphere of danger, they kiss.

The amplified voice demands again: THIS IS THE POLICE! PROCEED TO THE MAIN ROAD! THIS IS—THE POLICE!"

The brown-haired youngman is opening Jim's pants, Jim

opens the other's. They're almost naked on the leaves. Jim's body mounts the other, mouths and cocks kissing.

Whrrrrrrrrrrrrrr! Whrrrrrrrrrrrrrrr!

The sound recurs vengefully.

This time they feel the blade-stirred breeze hot on their bare bodies. Quickly aroused, each takes the other's cock in his mouth.

"EVERYONE PROCEED TO THE MAIN ROAD!"

Hands sliding over beautiful flesh, tongues touching in moist tips, muscle-straining thighs pressed hard together, cocks aroused sliding up and down on sweat-moistened pubic hair . . . they come, their liquid cream smearing each other's stomach, cock, balls. "Oh, God!" And they continue pressing against each other as if to extend the orgasm.

Now they lie quietly side by side in the cove, listening to the sounds of the invasion beyond.

After minutes: "Should we try to go around the hill to the straight side?" Jim asks.

"It's all quieting down—maybe it's cool now. Maybe we should just go up on the road to our cars."

They dress.

"I'm not sure it's over," Jim says.

The other listens. "I don't hear anything. I'll take a chance on the road. Wanna come?"

Jim pauses. "I'll go around the hill," he says.

They kiss again. They laugh—the reality is too difficult to accept. *They are actually in danger—but for what?*

"Good luck."

"Good luck."

Jim weaves along the park's lower rough paths. Branches scratch his bare perspiring shoulders. After long, long minutes the steep descent is over. Now he has to go around, then over, another hill. He pauses. Then he begins to move toward the straight part of the park.

Whrrrr!

Jim can see the helicopter. He lies on the ground. Something pierces his leg. A glass? A broken branch? A branch—not a serious cut. But the blood pours out rich and red. He blocks it with dried leaves. He remains there until the helicopter rises into the sky, whirs away. Jim continues to climb, his body clamped by the unmoving heat. Now he's on a main path connecting bridle trails. He hears hooves. He starts to rush away. But this time it's only a man and a woman on horseback. "Hi!" they call to him.

"Hi," he answers.

"You know what's happening on the other side of the park?" the woman asks him.

Jim looks at her. He shakes his head, no. His world is totally invisible to them.

As he moves now more slowly along the path, he encounters other straight couples hiking. In minutes he has entered a completely different world. Standing on a path, he looks out at the unthreatened straight section of the park. There are no red signs here.

The sound of horses. This time he doesn't even start. Another man and a woman on horseback approach him. The retreating helicopter hovers momentarily overhead. But here there is no sense of danger. The man and the woman don't even look up at it. "Hi," they call to Jim.

This time he doesn't answer.

On the main road in the straight area, Jim hitchhikes down the hill. A man he's been with in the gay section stops. On the car seat is one of the red signs. Jim reaches for it.

"They used those weird signs to bust people in the gay area," the man tells him. "Some kind of fire ordinance. I ran when I saw what was happening."

Jim tries to read the sign, the convoluted vague wording in the tiny letters: ". . . firebreak or fire road . . . motorcycle, motorscooter vehicle within any mountain fire district . . . special permit from the chief . . . obstruct the entrance . . . firebreak. . . ."

He throws the sign on the seat.

Where the straight section of the park and the gay section clash in a "V," Jim gets out. From here, he'll eventually hitchhike back to his car.

3:54 P.M. *Griffith Park. The Detention Compound.*

He sees: At the foot of the hill—deliberately at the

entrance to the gay area—the cops have constructed a temporary detention compound. Giant barred cop buses, jeeps, squad cars, park gates form an enclosed camp. A busload of outlaws is being brought in. Unmarked police cars spew out other men, handcuffed.

Then Jim thinks he sees the brown-haired youngman he was with minutes earlier. No, it's not him in the compound. Yes, it is— . . . No— . . . Jim remembers that the youngman, like him, was on probation; if they caught him emerging out of the brush and busted him, any infraction is a violation; the terms of his probation might have even crazily included staying out of the gay area of the park; they'd take him to jail— . . . Jim convinces himself it wasn't him, no. He tells himself it was almost over at the top of the road when they emerged from the trail. No, it wasn't him.

In the compound, uniformed cops and vice cops in trunks and cutoffs are laughing. They have all returned down the hill. Apparently the invasion is over.

Jim gets a ride up all the way to his car. Anxiously he hopes the car of the brown-haired youngman he was with will be gone—that would mean he got away.

The car is still there.

Jim's stomach knots.

Racing, he drives back to the area of the compound, hoping to see the youngman. Some of the outlaws, booked at the compound, are now being released, walking back to their cars in disbanded squads. But not the brown-haired youngman.

Jim waits across the road from the compound.

The cops are dismantling the battle station.

MIXED MEDIA 3

39 CITED BY POLICE
IN GRIFFITH PARK
TRESPASSING DRIVE

"Thirty-nine persons were taken into custody briefly Sunday at Griffith Park in a sweep of fire hazard areas.

"The 39 were stopped by Los Angeles policemen, firemen, and park rangers and taken to a command post . . . where they were held until their names and addresses were taken. . . .

"Names of those cited will be presented to the city attorney's office for possible prosecution under city ordinances prohibiting trespassing into sections designated as hazardous.

"All those taken into custody were adults, officers said. They could face penalties of up to one year in jail and a $500 fine. . . . Similar sweeps have been made at the park during the last few years, officials said."

—Los Angeles Times,
October 1, 1973

PARK SWEEP 'BURNS' L.A. GAYS

"A Sunday afternoon police sweep of Hollywood's Griffith Park to enforce two fire hazard ordinances resulted in the arrest and detention . . . of several dozen gays.

"By all accounts a full-scale military operation, with a command post, detention buses, jeeps, a helicopter, marked and unmarked cars, uniformed and vice police—and even a contingent of mounted cops—it was seen by . . . the gay community as a new harassment strategy.

"The strike apparently concentrated on one section of the mammoth park—an area . . . known as a stamping ground for cruising and socializing gays. All those who were taken into custody could face penalties of up to one year in jail and a $500 fine. . . .

"In contradiction to the official LAPD explanation for the roundup . . . both the Fire Department and the Recreation and Parks Department denied they had requested the action or 'designated an enforcement area.' . . .

"According to witnesses—some of them detained for two hours in a dusty compound just inside the park's main entrance . . . —the operation began at about 1 P.M.

"All thought it unusual that vice officers took part in a fire hazard action. . . . [Witnesses] saw unmarked cars admitted to the compound and short- and long-haired young men emerge wearing everything from a T-shirt to bathing trunks and collegiate-style dress. . . .

"One [man] said that moments before he and a companion were arrested by uniformed policemen, 'while we were sitting on a rock,' two 'plain-looking guys' came up and asked him for a light. . . . He said he later saw the pair from his seat in one of the detention buses at the compound, 'laughing and talking with uniformed police.'

". . . the spectacular sweep . . . was concentrated along the road where gays often park, socialize, or slip away into the brush. . . .

"Also seen at various locations in the 'enforcement area' were six mounted personnel, three of them . . . cops wearing blue jeans. . . . The other three . . . were park rangers, who, according to a park spokesman, 'took no part in the arrests and were only there to guide policemen on the trails.'

"A jeep with a man riding shotgun was also observed taking off from the compound. . . .

"[Another] witness indicated that the rangers were reluctant participants in the sweep. He said he and two friends were on a climbing expedition. . . . They saw two marked cars with people in the back, 'obviously handcuffed because of the way they were sitting.'

"He said that as he and his companions were making their climb on a steep ridge, they were repeatedly buzzed by a police helicopter. . . . 'The 'copter hovered close, and over a loudspeaker someone told us to return to the main road.' . . . He then said the helicopter . . . instructed them to get into back of [a] ranger's vehicle, 'but one of the rangers kept motioning the helicopter away and shaking his head "no".'

"When at last an unmarked car drove up containing two plainclothes police, the witness continued, 'a ranger got out of the station wagon and in an annoyed voice asked the cops, "Are you going to tell these three persons why they were being held here?" '

"The three hikers were then told they were 'in a restricted area'. . . .

"Taken with his companions to the maintenance area, the hiker observed 'a full-scale field operation,' including 'some sort of camper vehicle where persons who may not have had ID's were being photographed, I think.'

". . . Inside a small shed . . . refreshments were being served to the police and other persons in plain dress. . . . He said three of the detained persons, 'including one older, dignified-looking man who was obviously frightened,' didn't have ID's, and expected to be taken to the Hollywood station to be booked.

"He said two complaints were filed on him and his two companions.

"[A witness] determined from talking to some of them that 'gays were arrested even outside the restricted areas.' He said, 'One guy was picked up who was just sitting by his car reading' and 'another had just been strumming his guitar right out beside the main road when he was handcuffed and taken to the bus. . . .'

". . . The [*Los Angeles*] *Times*, [accepting] without question . . . the official LAPD explanation for the roundup . . . reported only that 39 persons had been held 'until their names and addresses were taken' and made no mention of the 'enforcement area' or . . . of gays . . . detained.

". . . According to the first arrested witness, both buses in the maintenance (compound) area were 'almost packed'. . . . Another witness . . . said he drove 'on every road and I saw no cops anywhere else except in the gay area—not by the zoo, not by the merry-go-round, not anywhere, despite the fact that the last major fire in Griffith was near the zoo.'

"Other observers asserted they had seen 'straight couples . . .' in posted areas who were 'not molested' by police.

". . . [A police captain] said vice officers had been used because of 'a manpower shortage for such an operation'. . . . He also said it was 'ironic' that so many arrested witnesses were reportedly handcuffed 'when . . . I left whether or not a person would be handcuffed to the individual officer's discretion.'

". . . One witness also noted that when the operation apparently disbanded shortly after 4 P.M. 'the remaining cops [at the command post] broke out a couple cases of cold beer and celebrated the end of their successful hunt.' "

—Doug Sarff,
The Advocate,
October 24, 1973

NOTE: The arrested men were charged with misdemeanors and fined. A few days later fire *did* erupt in Griffith Park. In a straight area.

VOICE OVER: *Imaginary Speech to Heterosexuals*

I IMAGINE that I speak to a group of assorted heterosexuals:

Do you know how much we often distrust you? Even at times hate you. Not all of you, nor arbitrarily the way you hate us, if only because among you are our mothers, fathers, sisters, brothers, even sons and daughters.

We have every reason to hate the men who take out on us their terror of facing themselves. Women who try to "save" us. Posturing males measuring each other's cocks by joking about us. The marauders your hatred turns loose in our areas. Your ignorance about us. Every reason to hate your heterosexual fascism. Your television, newspapers, magazines feeding us condescending crumbs. Your cops, the executors of your hatred, a hatred that kills even your own children; do you know that over half of child suicides are because of sexual identity?

We live each moment of our lives with the stupid judgment of your psychiatrists (will they change unhappy heterosexuals to homosexuals?), your judges, lawyers, juries (who in one moment can wreck our lives forever), your priests, rabbis, ministers, preachers (making damn sure we'll experience an aspect of hell).

What they do, you condone. What you condone, you do.

Imagine this: Your heterosexuality is legislated against. Even a proposal of a sex encounter renders you a criminal. Every moment you try to connect sexually, you're threatened with prison. You sit in a bar, you ask a woman who's been smiling at you to make it with you at home. Busted for it, you may be jailed for years. If you're the woman and you accept, you'll be busted too and forced to register as a "sex offender" the rest of your life; you may be pulled out of your home and into a police lineup on the flimsiest reason. Imagine that your bars are raided. Cops pick you out at random, just for being there; they handcuff you, jail you— and you keep wondering, *Why?* Imagine you're at a party and ask someone, or accept someone's invitation, to go home and make it—the other turns out to be a cop infiltrating the party. Busted. Imagine you're making out in a car—and you're sentenced to prison for eight years. Not merely told to move on—but sentenced to prison for eight years. *Will you stop being a heterosexual, or will your defiance flare?*

Imagine that any mad cop can call you sick; imagine that any quivering preacher, priest, rabbi can hound you from childhood for being "damned."

Will you stop being a heterosexual?

Now in my speech to heterosexuals I focus on liberals:

Why don't you support us like you do blacks, Chicanos, farmworkers? Do you know that there are constant mass roundups and beatings of homosexuals? That our civil rights are routinely violated every day? Do you know that one who says "faggot" also says "nigger," "broad," "chink," "kike," "spic"? We are the minority ostracized by both the right and the left.

Not so, says a radical woman in the audience. "The S.L.A. condoned upfront gay relations."

Oh, sure—for women. And that's a male-heterosexual fantasy trip. Did they have one word of revolutionary doctrine about gay men? Were the men being encouraged to make it?

And to the parents in the audience:

One of your children, right at this very moment, may be

struggling to bring himself to tell you that he's gay. You love him—he knows that. But will you still love him when he tells you?—will you turn him into a stranger? Will you, as so many before you, throw him out?

And to the straight blacks and Chicanos in the audience:

Why do so many of you—who should know so well what it's like—oppose us while you wallow in transparent machismo? The evil that pursues us is the same evil that pursues you. It only begins with us. We provide a barometer for tomorrow's general repression. We're first—but you're next.

"What makes a homosexual?" a nice lady or gentleman in the audience asks earnestly, trying-hard-to-understand.

What makes a heterosexual? It's that relevant.

"Does the sexual outlaw you've described oppose heterosexuality?" asks a man, forcing his voice low, low.

If you think so, you've misunderstood entirely. He would not replace one restrictive tyranny for another—homosexual fascism for heterosexual fascism. He opposes only the totalitarian imposition of the heterosexual norm on him.

Is he against love and relationships?

No. He merely upholds the right to have sex with or without love, with one or with many. Within or outside marriage.

I go on, anticipating:

And how can you say that our sexual presence intrudes on your lives? Even when we have sex on the streets, we're invisible to you—you don't know we're there. (Just us and the cops, man.) *Have you ever, once, seen us make out?* And if occasionally we trespass into your garages to fuck (and even then you don't see us), what is that compared to how you've trespassed into our lives, trampled on them? What cops can *we* call to thwart that?

Your hatred has thrust us out of your world and we have formed our own, unseen by you. You allowed us no "security" and now we live to question the props of yours. The impermanence you've pushed on us, we've converted from an aimless hell into, at best, a joyous promiscuity to confront you and question *your* "permanence."

Now I relent in my imaginary speech. Especially because I see in it some of my most beloved friends.

We accept your heterosexuality. Now accept our homosexuality, as equal. It is an acceptance that will enrich and free us all.

4:58 P.M.   *The Movie Theater.*

HE DROVE TO his apartment. He took a shower, changed to fresh jeans, mixed more of the protein liquid. Still drenched in anger at the attack on Griffith Park, he drove to Greenstone Park. No one there. He remembered the strange man who spat, last night, when— . . .

He goes to a gay movie theater where he knows hunters congregate in the afternoons.

He enters a darkness so dense that not even an outline can be seen. But he's aware of presences in the roiling blackness. On the screen, a movie with unsynchronized sound and bleeding unreal colors is flickering; orange bodies grind on a green bed. Jim waits until his eyes adjust. Slowly, outlines emerge. Then forms. Now he sees men leaning against the back wall or idling in the space behind the back row, at least eight hunters in the small area. Perhaps a dozen more sit in the rows farthest back. Now definite bodies and faces emerge like flotsam from a black sea. Throughout the cavernous mouth which almost devours the screen, there is only a scattering of permanently occupied seats, mainly by older men watching the screen raptly. Others shift constantly from row to row. The concentration of hunters is now in the back—those who have come to make it, not to see the cheap movie.

Jim moves a few feet into the aisle, to be seen clearly;
his torso is barely covered by a tight sleeveless T-shirt open
in front. A man sitting at the end of the row near him leans
into the aisle. Moving just slightly back, Jim allows his thigh
to be brushed by the other's straining shoulder. The man
opens Jim's pants and takes out his cock to suck. In the
same row another man's head burrows into the lap of the
man beside him.

Jim retreats to the back. A man tries to grope him
randomly, but he's very unattractive, and Jim moves away,
to the other side of the theater; twin sides flank the squat
projection booth. Fewer people here.

He notices a handsome man a few rows ahead. Another
sits next to him, but the first is clearly not interested in the
second. Jim walks down the aisle, just slightly past the row
the handsome man is in. The man looks at him. Now Jim
stands at the end of that row. The man moves one seat
over—separating himself farther from the other man on that
row—and lowers the seat next to himself, inviting Jim. Jim
sits. The man's hand floats over Jim's groin. Hands inside
each other's flies feel warm growing cocks. Leaning over
the seat, the man sucks Jim's cock. Then he straightens up.
His hand encourages Jim's head downward, to blow him.
Jim wants to, but not here. To move away, he uses the fact
that another man has sat behind them. But he glances back,
hoping the man he sat next to will follow him elsewhere.
But he doesn't.

Toward the front of the theater and to the left, Jim
notices, there is a concentration of forms for these minutes.
That signals activity; the few men who came to see the
movie sit far apart from each other, deliberately isolated.

Propping his feet on the row before him, Jim sits toward
the left-front of the theater in the circle of hunters, but still
enough apart that it is he who will be approached. He
glances cursorily at the movie, where a man leaning over a
motorcycle is getting fucked with a huge dildo. . . . A tall
figure approaches Jim, but instead of sitting next to him, he
sits directly in front so that Jim's boots are virtually on the
man's shoulders.

Turning his head, the tall man licks Jim's boots, hands

drawing them closer to his head. Instantly, Jim feels the powerful rush of wayward excitement triggered disturbingly; the excitement aroused by another's total submission, implied. The man's tongue laps at the boots. Jim removes his feet from the back seat. The man slides down on the floor, and through a break in the rows of seats, like decaying teeth in the dark mouth, he crawls along the floor. His tongue bathes Jim's boots. One of the man's hands tries to raise one of the boots over his own groin. But Jim shifts his body on the seat. Now the man's tongue rises up on denim, to Jim's groin. The unwelcome excitement growing, Jim presses the other's head down—harder, harshly now. The other's teeth gnaw at the belt. Jim pushes the searching mouth roughly against his groin, forcing his cock in the others' throat, holding it there until the man gags; the man's hands grope Jim's boots, fingers sliding under the soles.

Glancing up again at the movie, to look away from the submitting cowering form squeezed before him, Jim sees a man dressed totally in leather flagellating a naked man tied at the wrists and feet. Immediately, Jim breaks this disturbing contact with the groveling man. Stifling the strong excitement, he moves to the back aisle. The handsome man he sat next to earlier is being sucked by another. Jim moves to the other side of the theater. A youngman with the back of his pants slit open is being fucked. On the screen the leathered man is burying his boot into the other's naked groin.

Feeling an aroused agitation, Jim leaves the theater. He takes off his sweaty shirt.

The man who licked his boots has followed him out.

Jim walks hurriedly away from him.

6:06 P.M. *The Afternoon and Early-Evening Bar.*
          Another Bar. The Turf Bar.
A bar in West Hollywood thrives on Sunday afternoons and into early evening. Like Jim, many others here are shirtless, naked torsos, some smooth, some hairy, some

tattooed, muscular or slim, oiled. Proud of his muscular chest, Jim squeezes through pressing bodies. Hands clutch at anyone. Occasionally a form slides down surreptitiously to blow random cocks of indifferent men who continue to drink without looking down. Paired too arbitrarily here by the churning bodies, Jim feels devoured within a mass of flesh. He leaves. The agitation is increasing. He keeps remembering the raid in the park, the youngman he was with. And, suddenly, Danny, the years-ago image destroyed yesterday. And he keeps thinking of the groveling man in the theater.

In another bar: Again the bare torsos. Suddenly Jim sees the bodybuilder he left flexing in the bushes last night. Spotting Jim, he again adopts his favorite pose, face set, clenched fist at his forehead; clearly he expects Jim to answer him with a similar pose. "Oh, fuck," Jim says aloud.

He drives to the Turf Bar, a bar he has often cruised outside of but never been inside, knowing what it's like. Inside now, he regrets immediately that he came. The bar is deliberately meant to suggest a torture dungeon—chains, manacles, boots hang on the walls, ceilings. Most of the men, even in the hot, hot afternoon, are in heavy leather—or military costumes. Many of them are goodlooking; all determined, with varing degrees of success, to be masculine; some are ugly, absurdly wrong in the rigid uniforms. There is too much of charade in the ramrod poses, the forced low voices—an embarrassing veering toward male impersonation, especially among the most heavily leathered or militaristic; a feeling created of male drag—the studded instead of sequined belts; the tight leather pants, instead of tight vinyl skirts, both almost silky in their sheen.

There is an electrified ugliness in this bar, of the rotting of fantasy.

Jim turns to leave. Near the door he's intercepted by a man wearing a full cop uniform—glasses, helmet, even handcuffs. A heavy ring of keys dangles on his right side. A lowered voice out of the fake uniform offers to buy Jim a drink. Jim ignores him, reacting immediately negatively to the costume. "I make a good slave," the cop-costumed figure offers. "Fuck you and your cop uniform," Jim reacts angrily to the man's charade of the enemy. As Jim pushes the door to exit, two men in Nazi brown-shirt uniforms strut in.

Why did I come here? Jim wonders in disgust, knowing he will never enter that bar again. Outside, he remembers Steve and Tony. Not the Steve he exchanged numbers with last night—no, another Steve. A memory which both excites and shames him.

FLASHBACK: *Somewhere in Los Angeles. Last Summer.*

The youngman, wiry, sexy, dark, moodily Italian with a boxer's tight body, had cruised him curiously from a distance all afternoon in Griffith Park. Finally, in the late afternoon, he approached him; would Jim come home with him?—he had a roommate. . . . Jim went.

So began one or two or even three blurred days of drugs and sex and hatred. The dark youngman was Tony; his roommate was Steve, a wild-looking muscular blond man— very handsome—who greeted them at the door in brief shorts. Looking at Jim, "You got us a gorgeous body," he said to Tony.

Electronic sounds and images charged the house. The stereo throbbed. Deliberately distorted, the television flashed colored acid shapes. The radio shot rock sounds. Naked, the three smoked hash, snorted cocaine, inhaled amyl, ate uppers—even downers. Their heads drummed with the amplified sound, flashing images, rushing drugs.

Then the ugly orgies began. Barking, Steve commanded Tony to do whatever he was ordered: to Jim first, then to Steve, often to both. "Suck him, lick his ass!" Steve ordered Tony. "Now mine, fag!"

Drowning in churning waves of warring dope, they floated for hours or days from orgy to orgy, dope to more dope. Steve used Tony's body, tongue, mouth, ass, as they used the dope throughout that miasmic blurred time. Periodically Jim wanted to pull away, yes, but, he tells himself, the dope and the electric excitement forced him to stay. And, yes, the hint of a subtle struggle between him and Steve, a struggle not recognized fully until the whole thing erupted.

Moody silences. Then the sex bouts resumed. The stereo, the TV, the radio—they pounded out smashed sounds and wiped colors. At Steve's command, Tony's tongue crawled over Jim's body, Steve's, and he groveled at their feet. Steve would shove Tony around roughly, even spitting on him, pissing on him.

They both fucked Tony throughout that time. Once they attempted to do it simultaneously. Jim would retreat, despising what he was doing, but, yes, aroused—and, yes (he reminds himself of this constantly when the memory recurs), waiting to—this was the word he conjured—"conquer" Steve. Yes, that—and the dope (he has to rationalize at least partly for his aroused excitement) kept him there.

Into this there flowed at least one more person—sometimes Jim thinks there were two—Steve's sex client or clients. The client, older, would watch; if he joined in, Steve would treat him the way he did Tony—laughing contemptuously. Jim asked for and got half the money, a matter suddenly of major importance to him. They popped dozens of poppers, the sex-triggering odor erupting in the rooms.

Sulkiness again—they would retreat from each other. The sex bouts resumed with Steve's harsh commands at Tony.

Then Steve ordered Tony merely to watch while he made it with Jim. Jim wishes this hadn't happened, but it did: Because physically—and only physically, he emphasizes—Steve turned him on, and he obviously turned Steve on equally—they kissed, licked each other's body, sucked each other before Tony's hurt eyes. Steve wanted to fuck Jim, but Jim wouldn't allow it. Instead, Jim kept fingering Steve's ass—and Steve resisted. Deliberately Jim broke another popper, held the ampule relentlessly to Steve's nose; Steve inhaled anxiously, inhaled longer, inhaled. Suddenly, looking at Tony as if whatever would happen now would be at least in part to torture him further, Steve spread his own legs in a wide V, as if to allow Jim to fuck him. Tony turned away. "Watch, you goddam queer!" Steve demanded. Jim lunged at Steve's asshole. Laughing loudly, Steve pulled away. Then he lay waiting again, his legs still spread, his eyes nailed on Tony. Again Jim pushed his cock at Steve's ass and entered it fully. "Oh, baby, yeah," Steve moaned.

Suddenly Jim pulled his cock out. He glanced at Tony; Tony was crying. Steve's legs still waited open, his hands holding the buttocks apart. Then a strange smile slashed his face as if he knew, already, what would happen—and was perverse enough to enjoy even that: Jim looked down at Steve, and with contempt said:

"I don't want to fuck your goddamn ass!"

Steve laughed hoarsely.

Jim dressed, feeling as if the pulsing room were imploding in his head. He wanted desperately to breathe fresh air. He didn't know if it was day or not, or exactly where in Los Angeles he was.

Steve still lay in bed, snorting what was left of the cocaine. Jim said: "I'm sorry I came here."

"Bullshit," Steve said.

Jim turned to Tony: "How can you stand that sick motherfucker?"

Standing up fiercely, Tony exploded: "Don't you say anything about him! I don't want to hear you say anything about Steve!" Then, through tears: "I love him."

"Bullshit," Steve repeated. He was still laughing when Jim left.

Outside. It was morning. Standing in the white sun of Los Angeles, Jim thought the palmtreed city would explode before he reached his car.

VOICE OVER: *The Ugly Gay World*

AT ITS BEST, the gay experience is liberating, adventurous, righteously daring, revolutionary, and beautiful in its sexual abundance. At its worst it is a stark vision of hell.

Stunning in its choreography, giving in its promiscuity, the hunt can turn brutal and raw. The elegant artistic sensibility can slide into bitchiness and bitter cruelty. The glamor can become grotesque. The beauty a haunted parody. Instant love, instant hate.

Every indictment of the gay world is a stronger indictment of the straight. The heterosexual norm—marriage, children, home, property—is ingrained into homosexuals as the only possible means of happiness. Homosexuals are taught—*by heterosexuals*—to expect and even yearn for what, given societal attitudes, is impossible under a different lifestyle. Warring attempts to fuse heterosexual expectations with homosexual needs and realities create the contradictions in the gay world.

No criticism of the gay world can be made outside that context; that the straight world has shaped the homosexual with threats of hideous "cures," insane laws, and "moral" admonitions—attempting deliberately to transform him into a "sick, criminal sinner."

Beyond that important context—which must constantly

be emphasized—what of the gay world itself? How is the *inner* revolution being waged?

Gay liberation. Yes. But even that may be used as subterfuge for lack of interior awareness. The necessary exploration of self—alone, isolated—may be dissipated by protection within the club; static rhetoric substituted for active individual responsibility.

Increasingly easy on campuses and within other enclosed groups to announce openly that one is gay. The shock is gone. Safe in sympathetic numbers, propped by encounter-type jargon, homosexuals may even put down gays in small towns who "don't come out" (ignoring the vast difference between, say, womb-y glitterbars and dusty, queer-hating hick towns).

It is equally easy to say "gayisbeautiful—gayisproud." Almost one word, meaning obscured. But are homosexuals discovering their particular *and varied* beauty? From that of the transvestite to that of the bodybuilder? The young to the old? The effeminate to the masculine? The athletic to the intellectual? Gay must be allowed variations. It is gay fascism to decree that one *must* perform this sex act, and *must* allow that one, in order to be gay; it is gay fascism to deny *genuine* bisexuality, or to suspect all heterosexuals.

Within the gay world, gays still refer to each other as "she"—a putdown of women and homosexuals. Still say "queer" and "faggot." Still hear without protest brutal "straight" jokes about "fruits." Still contribute to the breathy excitement at the discovery that a celebrity is gay, as if to be gay is to be naughty. Masculine homosexuals still heckle queens, who are true hero-heroines of our time, exhibiting more courage for walking one single block in drag than a straight-looking gay to "come out" on a comfy campus. She—and she prefers "she"—hurts our image, we say. What she may hurt most is our symbolic lack of courage; she might just more easily take on a threatening bully or a vice cop than a black-leathered gay might!

I spoke once to a group of young homosexuals, so unaware, so unconcerned, and so conservative despite their youth, that I have come to think of them as "Nephew Toms." They sipped punch and nibbled crumbly sugar cookies—and expressed a murderous complacency. As long as they could go to dance bars and hold hands on campus, hey, well, ah, everything was okay, they kept repeating.

As in all minorities, there is no uglier figure than that which preys on his own. Publishers of gay books and magazines, owners of gay bars, restaurants, clothes shops— these often raise their prices, exploiting a certain—inevitable—gay-ghetto mentality. Crank gay psychologists and psychiatrists (not to mention crank straight psychologists and psychiatrists dealing with homosexuals) and vulturous gay lawyers—who occasionally own interest in frequently busted bars that provide them clients—drain homosexuals and notoriously put nothing back into gay causes. Those who do commit their time and money—often providing free aid—are left by richer prospective clients to struggle alone financially.

Similarly, powerful gays who could afford to be daring remain in silence. The quiet rich, the closeted politicians, uncommitted gay movie directors, cowardly producers, clowning gay writers. And the often politically reactionary gay middleclass threatened by the prospect of having to see the prosecution of homosexuals in the context of all other minority prosecution; they cringe—these uptight middleclass homosexuals—in stylishly décored, ferned homes— at the thought of street sex (which nevertheless gives them a closet hard-on). Soothed by the now-reactionary soft lisps of the largest-circulation gay newspaper—*The Advocate* (whose editorials seem to be written by a gay William Buckley but whose money-bringing classified advertisements balk at nothing)—they forget, the silent rich, the cozy students, the "quiet" couples—that the outlaw absorbs the hatred that would otherwise swallow *them*.

Complacency and indifference about our own are among the ugliest aspects of the gay world. Two cops invade a gay area to bust two men—and other gays often watch as if at a circus—making no protest. We read deliciously the details of gay busts. And savage, sexually repressed criminals raid gay areas. So what?—*we* weren't there.... Not this time. A sad commentary, that the minority that could be among the most powerful ever has no organization to thwart violence in our sex-hunting areas—we squander our rage in rituals of self-hatred. We reduce "gaypride" to a matter of holding hands in public.

After the cleansing rebellion of the Stonewall riot came a few activist lawyers, small radical groups of proud fighters and daring revolutionaries—and more sexual outlaws—but not enough, not nearly enough. And there came as well too many tacky parades of bickering contingents, "gay leaders" riding like grand marshals on limousines flanked by acolytes. On sweet floats, coy boys posed in loincloths.

It may be that overall—and with marked exceptions—the gay minority cares less for its own, does less for its own, than any other minority.

That may be in large part because what holds other minorities together—ready identification, familial ties—is absent from the gay minority: It is very easy, and tempting, to "pass." (A homosexual psychiatrist claims the "gay problem" would be resolved instantly if overnight *all* homosexuals turned a definite, defining color.) Unlike blacks, say, who have black fathers, black mothers, black sisters, black brothers, the homosexual is gay in total isolation in his family. He is often cast out when he is "discovered." There is this additional factor: Since his is a minority defined by its sexual preference, the gay energy flows into two areas—the revolution of the sexhunt and the revolution against bigotry.

Fear of rejection, at the root of so much of gay isolation, alienates us from each other and often makes us mean. Threatened by rejection by the straight world of parents, friends, teachers, the gay child finds fear of detection a factor in his early life; he hates what creates it, his homosexuality. Even as a "liberated" adult, that nailed fear may fester to infect every contact, wound every possibility. Attracted to each other, we often turn away in fear. We have intimate relations one moment and the next day we'll cross the street to avoid each other, in fear. We often use each other in misdirected anger, even hatred. Fear of threatened taunts on our "masculinity" pushes us to become posturing studs in fascist uniforms. Xeroxed pseudo-"butch" conformity.

We want to marry. We long for one true lover. Wrong? No—if one wants that. But one should not *have* to marry or have *only* one lover.

Adopt children? Well, we might be better parents than some.

Join the army? Become cops! Support the rancid institutions that have slaughtered us?

Join the churches that have crucified us?

Revolutions are thwarted when the threatened established order hands out crumbs. So they may well "allow" us to marry, join their armies, become cops and church members. But they won't let us fuck.

Trying to be straighter than straight in our lifestyles is a form of self-hatred.

Yes, there is much in the gay world that demands critical exploration. But hardly a word of criticism is heard about those tendencies that just may weaken us as surely as outside pressures; not a word from gay newspapers or magazines; not a word—at least not a public word—from ever-ready gay "spokesmen," one under each palmtree in Los Angeles. For a gay person to criticize any aspect of the gay world is to expose himself to howls of wrath and betrayal. Because of that, a "serious" gay newspaper carries an approving cartoon on fistfucking—but refuses to run a news item on the fact that this increasing activity has caused maiming and death. A magazine prints a glossary of "symbols"—colored handkerchiefs, single earrings, keys, all displayed to indicate desired sexual positions and acts—but doesn't point out that these symbols may obviate even the few exploratory words we might otherwise exchange to discover each other, in sex, yes, but also, at least at times, beyond sex; extending rather than limiting possibilities.

Allowing no interior criticism of the gay world, we invite a deceptive lulling that disastrously drains us by assuring us that all is fine, fine. We prefer not to face that when we weaken ourselves through lack of introspection, we strengthen the real enemy. Then the handcuffs snap on our wrists and the sticks bash our skulls.

Straight expectations clash with gay realities, and the result may be a vision of hell. The glorious abundance of the sexhunt becomes the murderous anxiety to feel sexually tested every moment of the search—glorious when you "win," suicidal when you "lose." The obsession with youth and appearance which makes us beautiful can make us desperate. (Old homosexuals wasted—we cast away even the heroic fighters who "came out" when it was *really* courageous; we have no tradition of respect.) The anxiety about being busted at any moment augments our sense of instability in every area of our lives—the profession prepared for for years may be shut away in an instant. Our obsession with fantasy, often our escape in childhood, may render us invisible to each other's reality. The fulfilling freedom of orgies may, in the exclusive extreme, cancel out love, the dark side of cruising freezing all tenderness.

And the most grotesque—heavily rationalized—reflection of the heterosexual world's hatred of the gay, is the proliferation of sadomasochism.

Sadly, it is not true that we homosexuals no longer hate ourselves or each other. Many—and increasingly more and more—do not. Many still do. And most just less.

7:16 P.M. *Hollywood Boulevard. Selma.*

HE ATE IN A restaurant. He sat moodily alone.

Suddenly, he needs to hustle, or merely to be offered sexmoney, whether or not he actually goes. Perhaps he'll just walk those streets, storing admiration, to answer the hideous questioning that erupts in the still times, cold islands of no action; storing remarks and solicitations to be called forth when desolation freezes despite the stunning triumphs. He remembers one night when no connection worked—a desolate night which still wounds him and by which he measures the terror of others. The questioning horror burst when a beautiful youngman who had been cruising him broke the standstill between them by moving off with someone else. Jim was left alone on the street in terror. It was the very next day that, counting rigorously, he made it with 22 people in one afternoon in Griffith Park, not once coming, not once reciprocating, determined to cancel out—which he didn't and still cannot—that arid night.

Hollywood Boulevard. The hot, still night is inviting tribes of hunters to the grimy street.

Past warm, inviting glances, Jim turns off the boulevard, to Selma. He loves this ugly street. Each time he enters it, the awareness that he continues to thrive on it years after others would be through, washes him anew with sensational pleasure. Although when he first returned— . . .

FLASHBACK: *Selma. Ten Years Ago.*

After moody years of seclusion, away from the streets and Los Angeles, experiencing, deliberately alone, the transition from youngman to man, working out compulsively, changing the tightly slender kid he had been to the muscular man he would become, not realizing that he was preparing his return, challenging time, the enemy of his breed of outlaw: his shirt open—and later he would leave it off entirely on warm days, nights—he returned to Selma. Despite his mirror's approval, he felt terror. This was the street where he would pass or fail the exacting test—the selling again of his body. Not quite dark yet, the night lurked within the smog. He saw the others on this street, the very young hustlers, careless in their tacky beautiful youth. . . .

An obvious sexbuyer, a man in a new long car was already cruising him. Yes! Jim felt warmth like a reprieve from execution. The man stopped ahead. Jim could hear his own heart. The driver of the car looked back at him. Slowly, Jim walked toward the stopped car—as he had done years ago on this very street. Years ago. The man leaned over, to lower the passenger-side window, to speak to Jim. And to look at him better? Years ago! . . . *What if he realizes I'm not as young as he may have thought at first? What if he drives away?* The man motioned to him.

Overwhelmed suddenly by terror, Jim ran away, losing himself in the crowded boulevard, time roaring at him.

Midway down the block, he stopped.

"I haven't seen a body like yours in a long time," a man walking up to him told him. "How much do you go for?"

Reprieve. Jim touched his own body, breathing.

7:23 P.M.   *Selma.*

"What's happenin?" The blond hustler is standing on the steps of the Baptist church. A deep tan reveals the tiny wrinkles at his eyes, like scratches.

"Not much—with you?" Jim answers. Pauses.

"Making it, making it." Looking away from each other, even as they stand together on the steps, tanned survivors in a tough world, they glance at the parade of cars. "Hot tonight," the blond hustler says.

"Yeah, it's a hot night," Jim echoes. Silence. This is perhaps the longest they have stood together.

The blond hustler says: "I don't think I've ever seen you with a shirt—always showing off, huh?"

"Got to," Jim says. But he knows the other hustler *has* seen him with a shirt, often.

"Let's see what you look like. Try mine." The blond hustler removes his tanktop, hands it to Jim. The shirt is moist with perspiration. For moments both stand shirtless. They glance at each other, laugh—look along the street. Jim slips on the sweaty shirt, very aware of the other's sensual body odor. The blond hustler looks at Jim. "You really fill it out."

"So do you," Jim hears himself say. They laugh, look away again.

Jim's cock begins to strain. He can see the other's straining too.

His own sweat on the other's shirt, Jim removes it slowly. The blond hustler holds the shirt, flings it over his shoulder, his head turning toward it, as if to touch his mouth to it. Then he slips it on. Silent moments. They look at each other. The smiles freeze. Then they both laugh—and move on.

As Jim walks away, he feels longing clash with anger.

Standing by the telephone booth—and the telephone is ringing—Jim sees a man he's gone with many times before. Seeing Jim, the man begins to make a U-turn. Jim takes a few steps away, around the corner, to avoid the man. But then he waits there. The man drives up to him.

Athletic, like a highschool coach, the man calls out, "Hi."

It's always the same; each time the man pretends—and Jim goes along with the charade—that this is the first time they've met. And each time he goes with him, Jim promises himself he never will again.

"Hi." Jim stands by the open window, but he's preparing an excuse to walk away.

"Hustling?" the man asks.

"Uh— . . ." Jim pauses. He starts to turn away. "Yeah." He faces the man.

"How much?"

"Thirty dollars," Jim answers, higher than usual—to court the man's saying no, he tells himself. Or because he knows the extent of the man's desire.

"Okay," the man agrees.

Jim waits a few seconds before getting into the car.

7:45 P.M. *A House in the Hills.*

As always, the man pays Jim before they enter the airy, comfortable house. Beyond a windowed wall, the city is a smashed jigsaw puzzle.

In the bedroom, the man immediately breaks a popper of amyl nitrite. Jim inhales. Sex implodes. The man holds the crushed ampule urgently to his own nose, as if to smother in the powerful fumes.

The ritual begins, and Jim surrenders to the part of him he hates. The man kneels before him.

"Master!" the man's hoarse voice pleads.

Reeling scenes, spat words, rushing sensations, clashing emotions: The man groveling at Jim's boots, tongue washing them. . . . The man's face pressed down by one boot. . . . Jim lifting the eager head, bringing it harshly against his groin. . . . The man pulling at Jim's belt with his teeth, sucking the tip, which Jim holds as if it were a long, menacing cock. . . . Another ampule of amyl. . . . The man's exhortations: "Piss on me! Spit on me!". . . . Gurgling. . . . Swallowing, pausing to swallow. . . . "Master!" The man's hands pinioned behind. . . . The liquid splashing on the man's face, on his chest. . . . The belt. . . . The boots. . . . Jim's rough hands directing the head. . . .

Jim's cum spurts on the man's protruding tongue. The man's body writhes. Jim rubs his smeared cock over the other's rapt face. Groaning, the man comes into his own hands. "I love you!" he blurts out at Jim.

8:30 P.M. *Selma.*

Never again, Jim tells himself. The sight of a cruising cop car—hating faces staring out the window—and the evoked memory of the cops raiding the park earlier—that, and even more the memory of the brown-haired kid he was with then—all increase his overwhelming rage at himself for having acted—again—in another's nightmare of hatred.

"How much?" a man calls out bluntly to him through the open window of his car.

"Twenty." He's sure the man isn't a cop. "And I don't do anything," he adds.

"What do you mean?" the man asks indignantly. "Oh, hell," he understands; "you mean you expect me to pay you just to lay back and let me suck your prick? Go fuck yourself in front of a mirror!"

Jim laughs, welcoming the laughter, which soothes somewhat the raw memory of the earlier scene.

VOICE OVER: *S & M*

"We too must love."
—Miss Destiny, 1977

THE PROLIFERATION OF sadomasochism is the major internal threat to gay freedom, comparable only in destructiveness to the impact of repressive laws and persecution by cops. The basis of both is the same: self-hatred.

The hard-core of S & M is relatively small—perhaps tiny—in proportion to the vast gay world—and much of S & M is soft-core fantasy. Nevertheless its grip on the gay world—by reverberation, and perhaps more psychically than physically—is fiercely strong.

(It is important to differentiate between consenting gay S & M and the imposed, uninvited S & M of police chiefs, cops, prosecuting attorneys, judges, and "straight" gay-haters stalking sexual arenas. Gay S & M—and this must be emphasized—is a *willing* activity, not to be legislated against. In it, both the "S" and the "M" agree mutually to participate. There is no force to join, there is no outside seduction. Participants generally agree beforehand on how "heavy" the activity will be. Few "S"'s will go any further than actually allowed by the "M," who is therefore still in control. These important considerations totally separate homosexual S & M—without vindicating it—from the legally sanctioned and protected, imposed S & M of cops and other gay-haters. In the area of the latter, a totally unwelcome invasionary force is thrust on unwilling, non-consenting, uncontrolling, arbitrarily chosen victims. Much of gay S & M is strictly playacting. The legally encouraged, official cop-kind—stagnant from sexual repression—always deals in very real, life-crushing brutality.

(It is important, too, to point out that much of what is assumed to be S & M is not. Members of "bike" clubs—among whom there often occurs a definite sense of camaraderie rare in other segments of the gay world—are all arbitrarily linked to the leather world because of similar costumes; here, the props may be more functional than symbolic, even when *also* symbolic. Still others who wear the full leather regalia, often do so merely to provide a lead-in to a certain fantasy of, say, making it with a "tough motorcyclist"—or other "super-*macho*" figure—depending on the costume. The sex then may range from the power-oriented to the loving, even gentle; it is not contingent on pain *or gay-humiliation* and is therefore outside the penumbra of S & M. Indeed, it is the ability to act out fantasies that enriches the gay sexual experience at some of its best.

(One must point out also that gay S & M observes definite boundaries of time and place for its enactment; it does not spill over into unwilling arenas of "reality." Actors, clerks, hairdressers, truckdrivers, teachers, salesmen, even ministers—the whole spectrum of professions—these participants in gay S & M lead lives no different from those of any other segment; like actors in a play, performing only on stage—stepping out of their roles once the play is over. With the exception of the tiny knot of full-time "spokesmen" for S & M—constantly issuing bombastic manifestoes and styleless treatises on the joys of masterhood and slavehood—most participants in gay S & M do not proselytize. The bars catering to this activity are known, the arenas defined.)

The manifestations of the growth and power of S & M in the gay world are many: Gay leather bars are jammed nightly from Los Angeles to New York. Classified columns in gay publications are cluttered with exhortations for "masters" and "slaves"—and for humiliation. ("MOTOR-CYCLE GANG captures a bike thief and gives him the punishment he deserves—whips, chains, the *ultimate* degradation! Wow! One-hour cassette," shouts an advertisement in the politically conservative gay newspaper, *The Advocate.*) A significant part of the content of gay magazines is taken over by advertisements for "toys"—a revealing euphemism, evoking childhood, for implements of "torture": steel clamps, branding irons, whips, straps, even handcuffs. The recurrence of S & M in gay pornography is underscored by a gay filmmaker who points out: "Every porno flick, no matter how lyrically it deals with gay love, has to have at least one S & M scene to make it, even if the only way you can get it in is to have two guys beating each other up in the neighboring room."

Increasingly, gay bathhouses feature at least one room constructed to evoke a dungeon, or a jail cell, replete with chains. The catalogue of one of the most popular gay publishers uses a man in Nazi costume to advertise a film: ". . . the boots, the belts, and the leather!" it screeches. Some gay magazine shops sell handcuffs (this perhaps primary symbol of gay oppression by straights has become the standard prop of S & M!). A layout in a non-S & M magazine features photographs of naked men in stocks (the implements used in even less enlightened times to punish homosexuals are now flaunted in "celebration"). S & M publications relish, in articles, stories, and photographs, the mimed torturing of "slaves" by "masters."

(I am speaking, throughout, about gay S & M. Manifestations of widespread heterosexual S & M—which may have similar dynamics—abound. Indeed, a cursory glance at S & M publications in any pornography shop—or a glance at straight classified columns listing items pleading for "humiliation"—would lead one to conclude that the occurrence of heterosexual S & M far, far exceeds that of gay S & M—although the numbers may be equivalent when proportions are designated.)

The costume of S & M is unindividualistically standard. Stiff, posturing clients in leather bars often resemble mannequins manufactured, with varying degrees of attention, from one iron mold. The costume is total fantasy, having virtually no discernible context in reality; there is nowhere else one would wear it other than to a gay leather gathering—as specialized, say, as a space suit. Black is the dominant color: black leather vest and/or jacket and/or shirt, black chaps, black cap, dark sunglasses, black gloves, black belts crisscrossed at various parts of the body. (In effect, a costume of death—an effect corroborated by an article on necrophilia in an S & M magazine: As if the ultimate celebration of S & M were death.) Chains, straps, and bradded silvery studs on the leather paradoxically evoke the profuse use of necklaces and sequins on satin by transvestites. Keys, one earring, color-print handkerchiefs, worn on this or that side, the latter with this or that degree of exposure, are messages of varying degrees of dominance or passivity. (Confusion often results because these signals change from place to place.)

The appeal of the costume is such that some gay men will go only with another in full regalia, in effect to make it with the costume. (It is possible for an S & M scene to include no real sexual contact, the body surrendered to the fetish, nudity shunned with an almost Victorian prudery.) In a leather bar with its oppressive props and its black-costumed males, there is a collective aesthetic ugliness.

The extremes to which this world appeals are indicated by the emergence of a bar fashioned as a torture dungeon. A heavy prison steel door guards its entrance (a double horror when one considers the real prison sadism of Attica). Inside the dimlit bar are a torture rack, shackles for "slaves," whips, electric prods (another double horror, evocative of Southern sheriffs), handcuffs, a ceiling hung over with military boots. A Halloween party drew leather-bedecked "masters" and their "slaves"—pitiful, ugly, hooded, manacled creatures led on harnesses. Another ugly extreme of S & M is the burgeoning of a "group" calling itself the F.F.A. (Fist Fuckers of America).

Why is S & M so powerful in the gay world? Given the crushing pressures and hatred from the outside world, wouldn't homosexuals move determinedly away from pain and humiliation? To the contrary, it is *precisely* because of the demons of religious, psychological, and legal repression that S & M thrives.

The roots of this ritual are in the humiliation of gay children by heterosexuals. No gay child can totally escape the self-hatred powerfully implanted in his early years. When he reveals gay tendencies, he is humiliated, even physically tortured—called "queer," "faggot," "cocksucker"—choice Christian names with which gay children are baptized. His homosexuality is inevitably branded with guilt. Carried into adulthood, that imposed guilt may easily push him into S & M in punishment and humiliation for his "evil." If he becomes an "S," he will pitifully imitate the very bully who perhaps taunted him. The ritual of S & M embraces the straight world's judgment, debasement, hatred, and contempt of and for the homosexual.

In the gay world—where, as in the world of other minorities, there is a dangerous, but understandable, reticence to criticize anything within it—the very subject of S & M is charged with emotionalism. Some gay groups will not even allow critical discussion of it. In an interview with the editor of a gay-liberation newspaper, my negative remarks about S & M were heavily edited and in instances omitted. A university group recently presented a two-hour symposium on the joys of slavery—during its gay-liberation week!

Even outside homosexual circles, gay S & M is defended by *nouveau chic* heterosexuals. Because, apparently, we have reached a time when it is fashionable to accept anything, no matter how destructive, as long as it qualifies— in the clinging phrase of the prehistoric sixties—as "far out." Reactionary to put down fascism. I hear, increasingly, intellectualized defenses of Manson, even of Hitler. From there the defense of S & M is easy. We are not confounded by the paradox of opposing (correctly) police S & M and government S & M in genocide and yet supporting its charade. We find it difficult even to differentiate between speaking out against what is destructive, though willing, and legislating against it—*no mutual consenting sex act should be outlawed.* But the right must be held to decry what is destructive, in one's own sexual, social, or racial group, or in another's.

Not a subject to be shunned, S & M should be of primary internal concern within the homosexual world; a subject to be explored thoroughly and honestly.

When it is discussed, it is often defended as a lifestyle; even by those who claim too emphatically not to participate in it; even by those who put down "queens" and "sissies" (and most leather gays do so, loudly) for hurting our image. (Ironically, it is a notorious truth that mass arrests of transvestites almost inevitably result in rough, heavy punching out of the cops, whereas a mass raid in a leather bar will result in meek surrender, by both "M" 's and "S" 's.)

Is S & M simply another gay lifestyle?—like hustling, transvestism, promiscuity?

Substitute the homosexual in an S & M relationship with another minority: A black playing white red-neck sheriff uses electric prods on another black and calls him a "dirty nigger." A "lifestyle" to be applauded by blacks overcoming white humiliation? A Jew tortures another in a charade of concentration camp. A "lifestyle" to be supported and endorsed by other Jews decimated by genocide? (Significantly, the language of S & M is often racist—the usage of "nigger"—and it also uses "fag"—is not rare.)

Apologists for and adherents of S & M present three main arguments. The first, now a cliché, is that S & M merely imitates nature. There are always the weak, and there are always the strong. The ritual of S & M imitates, and therefore respects, nature. True enough, of a certain nature—but is it a desirable imitation? It belies man's basic evolutionary struggle—*to overcome nature's destructiveness,* from the exterior manifestation of floods and earthquakes to the interior ones of rape and murder.

The second argument—made by proponents—is that, no, S & M does not involve hatred; "it involves a new dimension of love." No, S & M does not involve pain; "it involves a new sensation of pleasure." No, S & M does not alienate its participants; "it brings two people much closer in a sharing of pain."

In the very necessity to invert terms—to defend pain by saying it isn't pain, to defend hatred by calling it love—is an implicit judgment—that *if* there is pain, *if* there is hatred, then there is destruction, because pain and hatred are negative by definition. So call it love! One supports the inversion in a sophistic argument that acknowledges, more than anything else, the destruction involved.

(It is true that few experiences bring people closer together than shared pain—closer to each other, yes, when the pain is uninvited, but not to the inflictor of the pain.)

An additional—and significant—confusion in terms occurs in that, for most, "S & M" means "sadist and masochist"; whereas for some it means "slave and master"— a "sadist-slave," therefore, and a "masochist-master."

The third argument—and perhaps the most subtle rationalization in support of S & M—is that the fantasy absorbs the potentially destructive reality. This implies that if homosexuals did not indulge in rites of mimed violence with each other, the real violence might be thrust out on unwilling gay, or possibly straight, victims. That is antithetical to gay S & M. It is *consent* that defines it. The slave *must* by gay, and willing, even pleading, to accept "punishment" *for desiring homosexual sex acts.* Thus, the gay "master" "makes" the willing gay "slave" beg for humiliation in order to be allowed a homosexual contact. Here, the enactment of the fantasy *is* the reality, the object in the ritual, not a sublimation for "real" violence. What is being sublimated are the reasons for one homosexual to *want* to play at humiliating another.

S & M adherents claim that theirs is the only faction in the gay world that is not "sexist" or "ageist" since it puts at least as much emphasis on performance as on looks and youth. "Leather" articles and guidebooks—usually written, significantly, by older, perhaps not terribly attractive homosexuals—propound this theory recurrently. Although it is true that performance is important in gay S & M, as important as the fetish-uniform, the theory is far from being strictly true. As in all of the gay world, youth and beauty are badges. Additionally, there are at least as many young "masters" and older "slaves" as there are older "masters" and younger "slaves." Any weekend evening in a leather bar will confirm this. True, idealized stories in magazines often make the "master" slightly older—but not old; and always, always super-masculine, super tough-goodlooking, an extension of the "coach" figure, say. But even assuming, for examination, the vaunted myth, one arrives at the paradoxical conclusion that the relative (and "relative" must be emphasized) exception to the gay world's "ageism" is a negative one, a grotesquerie by S & M of the classic Grecian relationship between the older "teacher" and the younger "pupil," the latter enriched by the former's experience and knowledge. In S & M, the myth of the "older master" and the "younger slave" calls for the re-enacting of a charade—thoroughly ageist against the young—of cruel punishing "father" and guilt-ridden, punished "son"—a sadly real dynamic not uncommon among gay children.

Beyond those dynamics and others discussed later, there is a very real physical danger in S & M. Though most of it is soft core, more fantasy than actuality, involving the charade of pain, even the little that is real is too much. In orgiastic frenzy the acting may catch fire. Ritual whippings, beatings, and kickings, even when "controlled" and consensual may, though very rarely do, draw real blood.

Fist-fucking is more talked about than performed, like so much of S & M. It nevertheless unquestionably does occur, and with increasing frequency. A gay S & M magazine recently gave lovingly detailed instructions on how to perform this act. Near the end of the article the author added, almost parenthetically, the exhortation to "be careful," because: "Rough action can perforate the walls of the rectum and cause death."

Defended stupidly by blind gay apologists who uphold that there is no physical danger because the body is made to "adjust" to such an assault, this activity has already resulted in death and permanent crippling.

Explore the dynamics of gay S & M: Playing "straight," the "S" humiliates and even tortures the "M" for being "queer." But since the "S" is himself a homosexual, too, he is transfering his feelings of self-contempt for his own homosexuality onto the cowering "M," who turns himself willingly into what gay-haters have called him. Now one homosexual uses, and the other begs for, the straight world's words of hatred:

"Queer!"

"Fag!"

"Cocksucker!"

In effect, the "S" says, "*You* are the queer now, not me, and I'll punish *you* for it, just as I was punished for it—and I'll call *you* the names others would call me, and have called me." It is not surprising that numbers of "S" 's will easily play the "M"—"turnabout is fair play" is one of the clichés of the S & M world.

(A paradoxical, sad spectacle often occurs outside leather bars: Two heavily leathered homosexuals walking to their cars to get together later in an orgy of simulated humiliation encounter a carload of gay-hating punks who yell: "Queers!" "Fags!"—the very same terms one of these homosexuals may soon be using on the other.)

Chilling proof of the self-hatred at the core of S & M is the existence of a gay bar—constructed to evoke a police headquarters station—which openly solicits gay patrons to dress in cop uniforms. (A further irony is that it is owned in part by a gay social-psychologist, ubiquitous "spokesman" for gay freedom, and denouncer of cop actions!) Thus the cop—the primary symbol of external hatred of gays, executor of the straight world's repressive laws—is celebrated here in imitation by the victims themselves, wearing their oppressors' uniforms, replete with handcuffs! The ugly story goes that several of the clients of that bar are "real, off-duty cops," coming there to act out, now courted by gays, their very real hatred of homosexuals. Whether there is any substance to that, just its breathless repetition attests to a profound gay self-contempt in that faction.

Here and there, actually begin to appear "brown shirts"—now in imitation of the Nazis, who exterminated homosexuals before they began on Jews. (An S & M publication recently carried—and subsequently deleted—an ad for the National Socialist League—complete with swastika and eagle—though at least one leather club has refused its literature.)

No, I am not a stranger to the world of violent sexual power. I am not speaking from a rarefied distance, but from within. I have worn the leather costume, have felt the surge at humiliating another. Once, I was no stranger to the props of S & M—yes, the belts, thrusting boots, straps for restraint. An admission not easily made, but necessary, so I can speak from experience. And I still feel the great rush when another submits. But I want to explore thoroughly what is really at play; and, knowing that much of what is called S & M is not, to separate and differentiate between the feeling of power implicit in virtually all sex relations, and the substitution of sex for pain, the humiliation of real S & M— to purge myself, because of my very real self-love, of the need for externalized hatred and contempt, thrust onto another.

Yes—and I believe in the freedom to destroy oneself, and to *allow* oneself to be destroyed. I uphold the right of suicide. But I believe in the need for full awareness that one *is* destroying oneself or another, no matter how willingly. I believe in the necessity of exploring the real, not the rationalized, world of S & M.

I believe that the energy produced by this hatred turned inward dissipates the revolutionary energy. Redirected, refunneled, that inward anger would be converted into creative rage against the *real* enemies from without.

The conclusion is inescapable. The motivation of the "M"—*as well as of the* "S"—is self-hatred. There is no "S" in such gay relationships. The whimpering "masochist" and the "tough" posturing "sadist" are, in reality, only two masochists groveling in self-hatred.

Gay S & M is the straight world's most despicable legacy.

8:59 P.M. *The Baths.*

ON THE STREET, he touches his arms, round, full, hard.

His need for the outlaw world fluctuates. Sometimes, like others within it, he stays away for days, even weeks. Sometimes he makes it only once a day, or once every other day, with one or perhaps only two persons, three. Other times he will sexhunt for many contacts, but only from Friday to Saturday, say, or only on Saturday, or only one night, one afternoon. There are times when he will have all his encounters at home, his or another's. Other times, like this swelling weekend, he commits himself entirely to the extreme hunt. He knows these fluctuations, variations, and modifications are so for the other outlaws too because he will see the same ones recurrently in the same shifting arenas, then not at all for long.

He will store memories of this abundant weekend for the dreaded, strange times when the hunt turns indifferently cruel against him.

To get into the gay baths throughout the city, you must be a member. To be a member—and some clubs screen out only the already-rejected old, the very unattractive—you merely pay dues. Jim will go to one of the most popular in the city.

Wordlessly the attendant hands him a towel and a basket for his possessions, a key to a locker. Jim undresses in an empty room, puts his clothes in the assigned locker, and he looks admiringly at his nude body in a full-length mirror.

Towel wrapped around his middle, he passes the television room. Other toweled men, a few, the more subdued, sit pretending to be watching the screen.

Jim walks on. His room—small, with a cot—will be one of many along dim corridors. Nude figures prowl. Bodies lie on cots in the cubicles, doors open. Naked men stand in doorways, playing with their cocks. Someone enters a cubicle. A door closes, another opens. Jim moves on to the orgy room.

Within dim lights, naked bodies toss and squirm in one groaning mass, heads, feet, hands, buttocks bob occasionally out of the sea of flesh. The bodies could be crushing each other soundlessly. Only occasional moans rise out of the amyl-tinged air. Jim has barely entered the room when several hands are pulling him into the twisting flesh. He had not expected this many hunters—perhaps a dozen. The mass of flesh stirs, changing shapes.

Jim leaves the room. The showers are better lighted. He can be special. Four men are here. Jim moves along splashing hot water to the end of the row, alone. An attractive man glides through the misty steam toward him. The man edges his ass closer to Jim's cock. The man Jim really wants has not come over, is merely looking at him through alternately clearing, thickening pools of steam. The man near Jim touches his ass to Jim's rising cock. Now the man Jim wants approaches—reaches for Jim's flushed cock— and guides it into the ass of the other man. Jim pushes it in. The man who guided Jim's prick into the other now turns his own lubricated ass to him. Pulling it out of the one, Jim enters the other. The first man he fucked now presses against Jim's buttocks, attempting to spread them with his fingers, to enter him. But Jim has never been fucked and he pushes the probing fingers and the eager cock away. The man now presses his ass against the cock of the man Jim is fucking. Two others watch the sandwiched bodies. The man being fucked by Jim and fucking the other, turns his mouth to Jim's, which opens. Out of the mist, other hands float from one body to the next, fingers and lips brushing entered orifices; moving from limb to limb.

Abruptly Jim pulls away before coming. At the opposite end of the room, he turns the water on fullblast. Cold. Cold water shreds the steaming clouds.

He returns to the corridors. Naked now, without a towel about his middle. In his cubicle he lies on his cot, the slightly ajar door opens wide. He closes his eyes while a mouth sucks him. His eyes remain closed. Another mouth. Jim pushes two heads away. He opens his eyes.

A handsome man with short-cropped beard stands at the door, motioning with his cock. Jim motions back. This time they close the door. Jim wants the man to blow him first, and the man wants Jim to do it first. They separate quickly.

In the corridor again, Jim sees an obvious bodybuilder. The attraction and the competition are instantly stirred. Jim is prepared to ignore the other. But the other pauses. Jim looks back. With a nod, the other invites Jim into his cubicle. Again the door is closed. Flexed muscles press against flexed muscles. Only that. After minutes, they separate as if they must not allow each other too much time.

Jim goes back to his cubicle. Again he lies on the cot. One, two. A man wants to fuck him. When Jim rejects the advance, the man offers his own ass—but Jim isn't that attracted to him.

Outside in the corridor a man lying on the floor is getting fucked.

In the orgy room, the mass has thinned. Jim surrenders for only moments to the hands, limbs, mouths, bodies. Only for moments. Here, it doesn't seem to matter whose cock, whose ass, whose body.

Back in his cubicle. One, two.

Only when he left the baths did Jim—outside, alone—realize he hadn't come.

10:35 P.M. *Outside the Tool Bar. The City. The Lot Outside the Turf Bar.*

He parks across the street from one of the costume bars. He sees two figures disappear behind a wall. He moves across the street. No other hunters, not yet. A man offers him a ride, but he's unattractive, and Jim doesn't accept.

He returns to his car. One of the two men he saw leans against a van in a lot. Moments later, he's blowing Jim—only for a few strokes, that's all Jim needed to fill this fraction of time. Pretending to hear a noise, he pulls away from the man. "You want to go to my place? I'll be your slave," the man says breathlessly.

His words stir the earlier festering memory of the man he went home with earlier. Jim drives away. Again, the memory of the brown-haired youngman he was with when the cops raided the park pursues him. Is he in jail right now?

Restlessly, he drives from place to place in the vast city, merely moving in his car, not getting out now, as if to feel the energy, all of it, his, the night's, the city's, to grasp it all, as if the city and night themselves are throbbing sexually with him. He feels a giant longing without object.

As he drives up to the lot outside the Turf Bar, he sees two gay men in cop costumes, goggles gleaming, handcuffs dangling, bully sticks protruding. Both men are heavy, slightly drunk. At the corner, one stands stiffly in a military posture and, boots clicking, salutes the other.

VOICE OVER: *S & M vs. "S & M"*

SOME TIME PRIOR to April 10, 1976, a number of Los Angeles police were involved in a secret mission of major priority. They were on their way to Universal Studios. They might even have to stop off at Columbia Studios and the Western Costume Company. Through those facilities they would obtain important crime-fighting equipment, including: "4 bleached Levi's—tight-fitting; 4 bandanas, 2 red, 2 blue"; also, "boots, rough, dirty . . . [a] motorcycle hat; studded Levi's, jacket."

Somewhere else in the cool city of angels, a police officer planning his small—but important—aspect of the operation was doodling nervously on a sheet of paper containing names and telephone numbers of organizations the IRS might have information on and that the suspects might contact as a result of the surveillance involved or of the operation itself. He drew an open-ended parallelogram, another, another, eight such, each straining to become what it finally did only on the ninth doodle: A box!—hesitant, yes, but nonetheless distinctly a box. Now having committed himself, he drew—under the trembling series—an assertive, fully erect version of the same troubling box.

Elsewhere in the city that seems to float on flowers, for four grueling days four officers, specialists in their fields, were being "briefed and schooled ... as necessary" on details including "proper attire to be made with help of Universal Studios."

Still elsewhere in the vast city that stretches palmtreed to the lapping ocean, a surveillance team was trailing the main suspects. The surveying officers had become quite familiar with their quarries, they had been watching them intently for weeks and weeks. They even knew—and recorded—how many pieces of mail were received in a day by one of the suspects, and from whom.

Certainly they must have felt a certain wistfulness, these surveying officers, as they began their final observations before the operation would swing into reality. Is it unfair to imagine that there was no total lack of fondness as they recorded—on videotape and in penciled entries—the last crucial moments of the suspects' activities before it would all end? Is it unfair to assume that they did not resist at least one final look, an emotional tug, a pinprick of regret? How else to account for the loving intimacy of those final entries? At "2030" (8:30 P.M.) one of the suspects "carried [sic] lumber out of location," while another suspect "unlocked van rear door, removed lumber—layed [sic] on fence."

It would all be worth it—the weeks plotting careful strategy, fretting, yes, fretting that something—oh, anything—might go wrong. It would be worth it, who could doubt it? Particularly dear to Los Angeles police (behind it all the way, sir), the operation was one of those that elicit personal commitment and enthusiasm. Chins-up team pride.

Although officially (because how can the public be expected to understand these things?) the police would claim that the operation involved only 60 brave officers, subsequent discoveries would point out that the brave 60 had actually been 103.

But what of it? It was The Mission that counted. No expense to the City of Los Angeles—anywhere from $150,000 to $500,000, it would later be estimated—was too great. There were the salaries of the officers, the expense of setting up several command posts, the cost of deploying

"3 ... cars for quick response" and "7 more ... at CP [Command Post] 2." There would have to be a video van, telephones and radios for flashing communiqués as the battle progressed. There would be "chase units" for those attempting to escape. And buses. There would be a mobile lighting unit to rival those used for filming *Police Story* on location (because goddammit this was the *real* thing), a "small truck for evidence ... cartography for scene diagrams," and police "secret service money." *And helicopters!*

No, no expense must be spared. The operation was of major importance. So much relied on it. So much at stake for the chief.

It is almost Target Hour!

But wait, a tense moment occurs at 2105 hours! "Hi Point reports one body transmitter on operator defective, will attempt repairs before entry," the police log notes nervously. But at 2115: "Scout 1 reports alternate body transmitter available, will switch and test."

And so at 2355 on April 10, 1976, a Saturday, dozens and dozens of police set into operation their Mission Impossible.

They raided a gay bathhouse.

Almost at the exact time, nearby, a murder and a rape occurred.

But on The Front things were dandy. Several officers were already inside the raided bathhouse. Six other cops arrived by the driveway, six others climbed a fence to the rear patio from the east, six more from the south, and sixteen entered through the side entrance. Inside, plainclothesmen were already signaling to arresting cops "who has done what to whom," as the plan worded it; that was their mission—along with, as the same plan phrased it, looking for "exposed genitals."

True, it was not just any gay bathhouse they had raided. It was a strange one. Along with small cubicles there was a make-believe jail dungeon for rent; it had bars, chains on the walls. Also for rent were harnesses, handcuffs, paddles.

For at least two months the cops had known that the so-called "leather fraternity"—a loose, unorganized group of gay men having a common interest in leather and "masculine" costumes—was going to hold a mock slave auction at the well-known bathhouse. Cop surveillance was doubly absurd in view of the fact that the information they spent thousands of dollars and hundreds of manpower hours to gather was accessible to anyone who read the gay magazine sponsoring the affair; an advertisement had appeared in the magazine asking that those who wanted to attend the bizarre function send in $5.00 to receive an "invitation." In its latest issue, the magazine even previewed the affair. Weird as it was, the mock slave auction was not secret—and it was totally consensual.

By most accounts, the auction quickly headed toward becoming a flop. Police logs reveal that by 10:20 P.M. people had begun to leave—at least 18 out of the 135 to 180 there (including how many undercover cops?). For one thing, there simply were not enough "slaves"—perhaps only four. One invited youngman was asked to be a "slave." It was explained to him, as it had been to all the others, that he would "belong" for twenty-four hours to whatever "master" bought him, that he would not be forced to do anything—would not, in fact, have to go with the "master" unless he wanted to—that it would all be largely pretending, and that whatever he was bid for would be given to the gay charity of his choice. (The irony in that was not perceived.) Finally, the organizers had to make do with only seven slaves, kept in a "cell row" until each would be paraded onto the platform in the patio.

After a dance contest dutifully recorded in the police log, the auction began. Despite the carnival hype of two "masters" conducting it, the thing kept pulling toward farce. Too loose, the shackles on a "slave" slipped off and he almost fell, helped solicitously by a "master" or two. Told by his "master" that he would be taken to a cell and chained, one "slave" said testily, "No, I want to stay right here and watch the rest of the auction!" "Okay," said the chastised "master."

Still, they tried to keep it going, the strutting auctioneers puffily vaunting each handcuffed-slave's capacity for pain. One or two of the "slaves" were nude, one wore a leather mask, some wore cockrings. While the "slave" mimed enormous pain and pretended to resist, testicles were squeezed by some of the posturing "masters," buttocks spread, fondled. One "slave" was briefly turned upside down. Nipples and cocks were pinched with plastic clamps.

It was very ugly theater of pain, ugly charade, like most gay S & M.

Then the courtyard lit up angrily, a helicopter washed it in dirty light. "EVERYBODY FREEZE! THIS IS THE LOS ANGELES POLICE!"

Thus, that April 10, 1976, at "2355 hours," two reactionary forces collided in a battle of dizzying ironies and tumbling realities. Los Angeles cops attacked the gay "leather fraternity." A clear vendetta—at the city's groaning expense—it was one of the most wasteful, reckless, needless, silly police raids in a long history of wasteful, reckless, needless, silly police raids.

Why the leather faction?

With its strange paraphernalia and chains, sinister props and costumes, it is clearly the most vulnerable and potentially embarrassing within the gay world. In television closeup, it would be captured in one of its ugliest moments. No matter that the leather faction was a minuscule segment, it would be depicted as representative of the homosexual world. The fantasy auction would be flushed into home screens as real. This would counter gay gains, demands that homosexuals be employed as cops, and pressure that harassment stop. "*These* are the people demanding acceptance!" the bizarre newsclips would proclaim.

Within the lighted circle of the hovering helicopter, cops poured into the bathhouse and arrested 39 men and 1 woman, the latter one of the organizers; an enigmatic presence among all the costumed men. (According to the police log, at least one courageous officer was wounded in the Battle of the Bathhouse: "hit in the mouth by an unknown male who was running past him . . . feels the blow was struck unintentionally . . . lost one tooth.")

The arrested men were paraded before representatives

of the District and City attorneys offices (who had approved the raid beforehand) and—important to the police design, indeed essential—before television cameras alerted carefully in advance to create the desired circus. One of the "slaves" was brought out to be photographed semi-nude—and then returned inside to put his clothes on. The camera eye glared at confiscated "toys," S & M props for make-believe pain. A commercial photographer "just happened" to arrive in time to record the police version of the bust; he was therefore able to sell footage of the event to stations that did not have cameras there.

Headlines and news stories across the country proclaimed the cop-rehearsed version of a real, sinister ring of gay slavemasters. *Newsweek* gloated with photographs and text. (In notable contrast, the *Los Angeles Times*—which has in recent years become exemplary of enlightened coverage concerning gay affairs and problems—treated the matter with unsensational straightforwardness, its letters column underscoring the arrogant waste of funds and manpower in such a police action.)

It was with the arrival of the police at the bathhouse that real S & M began. The arrested men were handcuffed tightly—some complained futilely of blocked circulation. They were pushed contemptuously into buses, they were shoved, some knocked to the ground. They were taunted by the cops: "Goddam fuckin animals." "Bastards." "Queers." The arrested men had been drinking beer heavily, but hours later they were still not allowed to go to the toilet. Some had to urinate in the bus, others at the processing station. Inflamed wrists were ignored by the cops. Despite the fact that no one was forced to attend the auction or participate in any way—and there were no minors—the 40 were booked on the serious felony of "involuntary servitude," a charge unused for years and originally aimed at pimps.

Now in real jail cells, the arrested men felt a closeness that the staged charade of "master" and "slave" had implicitly violated. Experiencing a genuine sense of fraternity, most agreed to stay until all of their number would be released. Some slept together in jail bunks. They embraced, kissed. Their morale rose on learning that at least 100 gays were demonstrating outside on their behalf and that support, even from the straight community, was mounting—but that morale fell crashing when they heard of hysterical media reports being spread across the entire country claiming that the cops had freed gay slaves, that school books had been found on the bathhouse premises— outrageous and untrue lies, all adhering to the police objective of depicting the charade auction as real.

Although every other detail of the bust had been carefully planned for weeks and weeks to culminate in this television "spectacular," a sudden failure in the workings of a police computer was blamed for the fact that the defendants' names were not correctly recorded. Thus, even those who had been quickly bailed out, were forced to remain imprisoned—some until as late as Monday.

The day after the raid, police broke into the homes of the organizers of the auction, leaving upturned laundry and waste baskets, gutted drawers, as their calling cards.

In the following days, the cops cynically claimed they had thought the gay community would thank them for freeing their own slaves. On television a cop held up a pair of confiscated gay handcuffs as if they were objects totally foreign to his own profession—and not one of its main props. Forgetting all the bashed skulls, crushed groins, iron-squeezed wrists, another would claim that the mock slave auction was the most pitiful thing he had ever witnessed. It was all a pose filled with contempt and hypocrisy. In view of their constant harassment of gays and their apathy in responding to calls for help during truly sadistic attacks by gay-haters—the cops' cousins—obviously no concern for homosexual dignity had motivated the massive attack. The cops themselves had encouraged the auction by buying several tickets in advance and even purchasing a slave. (Apparently they quickly got into the swing of it: The police log indicates that undercover police would "attempt to buy another [slave]—first buy bad.")

The public was cynically being asked to believe that the private auction so outraged the cops, aroused such human pity in them, that they carried out into life-smashing reality the fantasy of pain.

274 / john rechy

But the cops miscalculated. The raid backfired. Feeling even more unsafe within their homes and on the jungle streets because of depleted police power, the straight community vented, in letters and loud public utterances, their outrage that so much of their money had been drained on a matter of no concern to them or to the police. The ACLU announced its support of the gay defendants. A California senator sent $600 for their defense. With the backing of councilmen, assemblymen, supervisors, and other legislators, demands were strong for a grand jury investigation into police conduct, their silly priorities at the expense of curbing real crime, the amount of money used in the raid, the number of personnel diverted, the high crime statistics for that night. Feeling the onslaught, the police, the district attorney, and the city attorney began to point accusing fingers at each other.

But no investigation would be conducted into the misuse of funds. Supposedly because of "pending litigation," the key police witness in the matter was instructed by the district attorney not to testify before the Governmental Efficiency Committee.

On the gay front, homosexuals rallied in support of the arrested. No matter, for now, that one objected to the implications of the auction—that was for later important exploration—now was the time for solidarity.

Unfortunately, the most visible support took a dizzy turn. Instead of an elegant rally provoking true gay pride, a new "slave auction"—a parody of the earlier charade—would be held to raise money for the defense of the 40. Before 600 people, gay leaders—several of whom had long fought bravely and with dignity for the cause of gay freedom—posed on a stage as "slaves" and were "sold" to the highest bidder. A well-known minister, auctioned, proceeded coyly to do a mini-strip, removing his jacket, tie, opening his shirt. Another gay reverend offered "absolution when it's all over." Part of the auction was conducted by a woman ridiculous in male leather pants. Further attesting to the interchangeability of roles—that the "master" in gay S & M is a closet "slave"—one man auctioned himself off as a "master"! The second auction unhappily converted other gays into seeming camp followers of the S & M faction.

In a move reminiscent of a scene from Kubrick's *Paths of Glory,* in which an insane general is assuaged in his intent to court-martial and execute 100 men by being offered 3 instead, the District Attorney attempted to placate both cops and homosexuals by dismissing felony charges against 36 of those arrested; but, exhibiting the idiotic "logic" that only the law can tolerate, he charged the two sponsors of the auction and the two who had acted as auctioneers, with the afterthought felony-charge of pandering—the original charge of involuntary servitude being even more clearly indefensible. Against the 36 others, all charges were eventually dropped. And so the City of Los Angeles had been robbed of more than one hundred thousand dollars to bust a gay bathhouse on hoax charges.

As the war went, it was a victory for the gay side. Despite the gay excesses, the police action had been so absurd that it drowned every other consideration. There was no public support for the action; none—not even from the conservative provinces. The cops had aroused citizen indignation. Gays had stuck with gays.

Soon after, during a televised news conference, a visibly unnerved chief of police proclaimed that he would, once and for all, define the difference between homosexuals and heterosexuals. As psychiatrists, sociologists, psychologists, and laymen—homosexual and heterosexual—waited for the ultimate revelation, the chief—converting his arms into "wings" and fluttering his "tail"—did a baffling imitation of a "heterosexual bird" mating in a nest, and then of a "heterosexual (*sic*) bird" mating in the nest but this time saying, "Slam, bam, thank you, sir." The difference still remains blurred.

Of course there were major casualties on the gay front. Despite dismissed charges, some of the defendants lost their jobs; others were alienated disastrously from their families, who had seen their faces captured by the cop-alerted TV cameras. Identification information had been gathered by the police on all the men at the bathhouse, license numbers

had been recorded; for what present and future harassment? Soon after, the token gay "legislative aide" to a
councilwoman who in a heavily gay district had overtly
courted—and received—homosexual votes was dismissed
because he was "too involved" in gay causes, including
criticism of the bathhouse raid.

And—the worst casualties—the four remaining defendants prosecuted on trumped-up charges would become
political scapegoats caught in the barbed wire of courts and
hearings.

"Now I know how Hitler did it," one of the arrested
"slaves" said, with an amount of unconscious irony—the
analogy was apt since Hitler had rehearsed on homosexuals;
but was the speaker aware also of the paradox of the leather
contingent's overtones of fascism, and of its acceptance, at
least tacitly, of "brown-shirt" uniforms in its bars?

"The only real pain inflicted at the bathhouse was by
the cops," said a busted "slave." True enough, if pain is
only physical. But was he ignoring the psychic damage
inflicted by *all* humiliation?

"The raid radicalized me," said an arrested "master."
But had it? And if so, had it others?

Had the experience of real jail and real handcuffs
revealed the dynamite buried in gay S & M? Did a purging
reality invade the posturing "masters" when they were
converted into real slaves by the very cops they often
imitate?—in dreadful "*macho*chism," as one writer recently
put it. Did they recognize the real enemy—the cops, not
ourselves? The gay men dressed as cops at the auction—how
did they feel about the enemy's uniform after being
handcuffed and called queer by real cops? Would the gay
"cop bar" still teem with black-uniformed cop-imitators?
Would the makebelieve prison cell at the bathhouse affront
both charading "masters" and "slaves" now that they had
experienced the real one?

Would the "real prison door" of the popular gay leather
bar (and the owner had been among those arrested) still be
opened and closed by gay men unaffected by the repulsive
symbol—when so many homosexuals are behind actual
prison doors?

Did the contradiction glare of saying, "Give us liberty" while enchaining our own in fantasy humiliation? Did "masters" and "slaves" realize that to want to wear handcuffs is as wounding as to want to enchain another—whether either desire emanates from the cops or from gays?

Was there an awareness that there is too much of real, uninvited pain, too much of hatred, oppression, enslavement, much too much, to add to it even in playacting?

It was a time for asking those questions, at the same time that one underscored emphatically the leather faction's right to hold their ugly willing auctions; a time too to point out that that faction is not representative of the gay world, that one could and should support the bathhouse defendants against police sadism without condoning the paradox of a slave auction even in announced support of gay freedom (any more than one would logically condone the charade of lynching to support a black cause or an imitation concentration camp to assert Jewish pride).

Yes, and it was a time for questioning oneself anew. For facing one's still-lingering fascination with that world. (Because in a period of my life I am not proud of—and no outsider even now to the beckoning "power" within S & M—I acted in an interlude with a man who begged for the humiliation I only too gladly provided, and afterwards he confessed he had found in me a surrogate for the man who had punished him in the concentration camp he had been incarcerated in as a boy. His story real or fantasy? It doesn't matter. The hateful image had scorched.)

And it was a time to emphasize that the true "radicalization" of the leather faction would come—if it came at all—only when the counter-revolutionary energy expended in even fantasy rage against our own and ourselves would be diverted into combating the real oppression, the real oppressors—and seeing that combat in the context of all the hungry evils that devour other minorities.

Were any of those questions being asked by the "masters" and "slaves"? Were any connections being perceived? Perhaps. Perhaps, among some of those arrested. Perhaps, hopefully.

Outwardly nothing changed. The prison door of the

thriving S & M bar constructed to evoke a torture dungeon opened and closed nightly, just as before, as gay patrons entered and exited, unconcerned; and the "costume" bar, owned in part by the ubiquitous gay-liberationist, still saw gay men dressed as cops, posing in ludicrous imitation-authority and threat. The magazine that had spawned the auction still displayed photographs of costumed "torture," its classified ads still pled for "humiliation."

And the cops? Did they see that they had busted a charade of their own very real brutality? Did they face their leering fears? And, assaulted by citizen outrage at the waste, did they alter their priorities to focus on the muggings, robberies, rapes—one every thirty minutes, it was estimated—and murders that pillage this city?

No.

The wasteful vendetta continued. Cops would lurk in bars to entrap homosexuals. Because courts might conceivably determine that a bar is "semi-private"—and therefore beyond the purview of the public-solicitation law—vice cops would solicit inside a bar and then reiterate the proposition outside, thus rendering it "public." Sixty cops would break up a peaceful gay parade on Hollywood Boulevard. Systematically they would wait in gay cruising areas to pursue homosexuals, stop them, and cite them on trumped-up traffic violations. At least a dozen cops would rush absurdly into a small gay bar—and on a ruse that they had received a complaint that two men there were drunk, would arrest one bartender for having no identification (it was in his car outside, but they would not allow him to retrieve it), another bartender for serving the allegedly drunk men, and the two "drunk" men—who were given no sobriety test. A gay newspaper would report that, in a period of four days, 15 gay arrests were made *each day* in one tiny corner of Hollywood. On another street, squad cars would parade up and down the blocks, loudspeakers demanding that certain circling cars leave the area. More squad cars would actually blockade a street cruised by gays after the bars close, stopping everyone walking through or driving, whether or not he lived there. Turned-up squad-car loudspeakers would still be used to insult homosexuals.

Nightly, a small army of cops—up to eight cars jamming and blocking a single block to question as few as four hustlers—would pursue homosexuals on one single street.

And still unfound as of that time, and along with countless other killers, attackers, robbers, and muggers, was the brutal rapist-murderer of at least ten terrified lone old women, within blocks of each other in one small section of the city.

Postscript

Early in December 1976, the city attorney's office requested that all criminal charges be dismissed against the five Los Angeles cops accused of statutory rape with teenage Explorer Scout girls. The motion was granted. No hearing, no witnesses, no bubble-gum wrappers as evidence. A terse statement from an assistant city attorney stated: "Evidence uncovered since the filing of these cases has persuaded us that the defendants' guilt [*sic*] cannot be established beyond a reasonable doubt. Several key witnesses have declined to cooperate with the prosecution." Given the circumstances that had grudgingly been allowed to surface (consent on the part of the girls, no force involved), this was a proper decision.

One would have unqualifiedly hailed the dismissal as a victory for sexual sanity had not, just a few days later, a judge ruled in a preliminary hearing that the four gay-bathhouse-raid defendants *would* stand trial on charges of "pandering" (procuring another person for prostitution). No matter, here, that consent was involved—and among adults in a private gathering; no matter that the "slaves" would not be friendly witnesses either. Parallel situations between the cop defendants and the gay defendants had produced opposite results—and the double standard glared.

With what rage had the prosecuting attorney waged his fight to bind the defendants over for trial: The paraphernalia confiscated at the auction was flaunted in evidence—the manacles, wooden stock, studded collar, riding crop, cat-o'-nine-tails, leather shackles, paddle, rings and clamps for parts of the body, leg chains--all the nasty "toys" of S & M with which some homosexuals play self-hating charades. The objects had no bearing on the charges; but their presence in the courtroom was meant to stir the same bigotry the cops had sought to create in their televised spectacle of the raid.

At first the judge had seemed almost sympathetic to the defendants. He observed that, during three days' testimony, no connection with pimping had been made. He summarily dismissed the testimony of one cloudy cop who kept consulting a police transcript. He defended laughter as salutary. He criticized the prosecution for not providing the defense with copies of the transcript of a crucial tape secretly recorded by the cops at the auction.

As the prosecutor fought ferociously to bring the case to trial, it was obvious that much more was at stake than the four defendants.

Why, think of the police chief for whom this operation had been so dear!—and now he was making noises about running for governor. Think of the one hundred brave men in blue, and the helicopters, the cop whose tooth got knocked out, the cameras, the buses, the command post! And think of those thousands of dollars poured into the daring raid on the gay bathhouse.

Okay, so maybe you were raped, robbed, or mugged on the night of the raid because the cops were out busting homosexuals. *We got the fucking perverts!* So what if each "slave" knew he didn't have to do anything he didn't want to, didn't even have to go with whoever bid for him? Yes, a lot of consent, as the police spokesman had pointed out in the matter of the cops and the underage girls. None of that mattered, here. *We got the fucking queers!* All four of them. (*Sure, we wanted to get a hundred, busted forty, had to settle for four. But we got 'em!*)

The cops, the district and city attorney's offices (hadn't both had representatives at the raid, in effect condoning it?) had looked, at best, ridiculous after the bathhouse bust, and citizens angered by the squander in the jungle-city had let them know it. Now, to vindicate the wasteful homophobia, ran the demented logic, more money must be poured into the trial of four random martyrs. Additional waste would justify waste!

As much as half a million dollars, estimates indicated, might ultimately be spent to bring *three male homosexuals and one woman* to trial on gauzy "sex" charges.

Up to $125,000 per defendant!

To many, that smacked of very, very expensive legal "pandering"—at the expense of non-consenting adult taxpayers.

At one point during the hearing, the prosecutor had raged about "the perverse sexual inclinations of those people."

There it was. No statutory violation was being prosecuted here. No; not S & M—even the charges of "pandering" had come as a strained afterthought. The purpose of the raid, the preliminary hearing, and the upcoming trial was, and would be, the continuing stirring up of hatred against all homosexuals by zeroing in on its most vulnerable faction.

11:26 P.M. *The Parking Lot Outside the Turf Bar.*

THE ALLEY AND THE lot are deserted for now. But Jim gets out.

As he moves into the darkness, he notices that on the street beyond the alley and the lot, the chrome of parked cars reflects cold silver shafts. He stops. He sees distant street lights. Chalky dull halos, they dirty the dark. He notices the shapes of buildings carved into the night. Short and dark rectangles; and he sees the rigid lines of sidewalks connecting with the distant street. Half a block away, in a small building two windows are lit. He looks up at the highest one, on the third story. Its shade is only three-quarters drawn. From the lower quarter, a rectangle of blue-white light glows. A siren's wail funnels into a shrill peak on a street, then uncoils, dissipates, re-forms into fragments of sound from the lighted window. ". . . that's it." Laughter. "Rock-a-bye-baby." Then the light from the window is smothered along with the electronic voices and laughter. On the main street a car won't start. He can't see it, it's parked behind a darkened flowershop, its back exit cluttered with gutted boxes and frayed string. He hears the motor of the stalled car as it grasps for ignited connection. His attention hinges on the gasping sound. The motor starts. He listens for the slide of tires driving away. Nothing.

The car motor stops. He walks along the alley. White, crumbling plaster creates a dirty brown map on the wall of a building. The building cuts a rectangular angle into the edge of the lot and the alley. He touches the plaster, but not the peeling part. The stone feels cold. He takes two steps, pauses again. Unlighted blind windows of houses face the streets. He looks down. Dark parallelograms, shadows, fall on the ground doubling the darkness. In the lot, the dirt—except where a car has spilled a blot of oil—is the color of the concrete sidewalks. With one foot, he shifts a portion of dirt from side to side on the ground. Then he moves on.

Now there are overlapping triangles of hunters throughout the lot.

It is a moment in the hunt when the outlaws are all unmoving, waiting in the night like frozen sentinels. A mute chorus near walls, against cars, trucks; just standing. Soon one among them will stir, then another, and the spell will be broken.

Booming, a total shock in the stirless dark silence, a voice hammers angry words: "I wanna say something to you— . . . Yeah, you, showing off without a shirt!"

Jim faces a drunkenly swaying youngman. Not particularly attractive, the type he would not reciprocate with. Depression crowds the youngman's thin face. Jim doesn't recognize him even vaguely.

"Hey, what the— . . .?" Jim whispers. But even the whispered words assault the rigid silence.

"You make yourself available," the drunken voice goes on tearing at the silence of the paused choreography. The shadows do not move, the spell locked. "You walk around showing off your body. You didn't even touch me, just wanted me to lick *your* body. Well, I have a body too!"

Jim still doesn't remember this man. One of so many he's been with, and forgotten. But he knows himself well enough to say—softly—to the man, "I didn't force you."

"Just lay there, wouldn't even touch me— . . ." the man pours out desolately.

The two, and their words, seem encased in the dark.

"I didn't force you," Jim repeats, even more softly,

trying not to violate further the stagnant quiet. How many rejections have goaded this assault? What surrogate horrors is he embodying for this unattractive youngman?

"Didn't it matter to you that *I* needed to be touched too?" The man's voice is relenting. The commanding quiet powerfully resists the spilling emotion.

"I didn't force you."

"Afterwards I felt— . . ." The voice chokes. "Don't you ever touch anyone back?" The hurt eyes implore.

Jim looks at him. How can he tell him the truth?—yes, with some I reciprocate, those I desire back, but with others, like you, I don't. He knows the answer the man wants, and he forms it: "No, I never reciprocate."

The man sighs.

Jim stares after him as the man staggers into the alley. In an unwelcome moment the ugly carnage of the sexhunt gapes at Jim—his part in it.

Released finally, the shadows stir. An erratic wind rustles the sun-dried leaves of palmtrees beyond the lot.

VOICE OVER: *Contradictions, Ambivalences, and Considerations*

THE JOY OF promiscuity.

And the pain.

Ecstatic freedom and release.

Loneliness, desolation.

A glorious adventure that, always at the brink, stops even time.

Panic, frenzy, fear.

Ambivalences and contradictions. The outlaw faces the saboteur.

The purgatorial moments, the saboteur announces. The stasis at dawn—the entrapping dawn, remember?—the time to be avoided in the cycle of the sexhunt. Why such a purgatory of questions in an experience so liberating?

A hateful obeisance paid—beyond present control—to the powerful straight world that digs its talons deep, deep when we are most vulnerable—and continues to try, every moment, with stupid encyclicals, laws, denunciations. Yes, a hateful obeisance to *imposed* guilt.

What kind of revolution is it that ends when one *looks* old, at least for most? What kind of revolution is it in which some of the revolutionaries must look beautiful? What kind of revolution is it in which the revolutionaries slaughter each other, in the sexual arenas and in the ritual of S & M?

We're fighting on two fronts—one on the streets, the other inside.

And is the abundant sex ever enough?

No. But that is part of the joy: a hunt that goes on endlessly like the infinitely burgeoning sum of a geometric progression.

"Ended" before its summation.

Precisely! *Without* summation.

What of men reduced to shadows, shadows reduced to mouths in alleys and parks? Jim uses many people—like the man who confronted him earlier in the parking lot; Jim doesn't want them, merely wants them to want him.

He needs them as much as they need him, at times. And Jim does reciprocate—with those he desires; and with all, he's honest, he doesn't use subterfuge. The equation is, finally, even.

A mutual using. . . . What of the aspect of contempt you've acknowledged in hustling, and implied in one-way sex? Then why not S & M?

Because hustling and unreciprocated sex do not *by definition* include hatred. The argument is definitely not against sex without love, no, not at all, but against the substitution of hatred, which includes self-hatred, for sex. Even if affection is totally absent from hustling—the act of getting paid or paying does not, like S & M, rely on hatred and "torture." The impact of hustling on the gay world is very limited, its "problems" may have more to do with prostitution than with gay identity; but S & M holds a strong reactionary power over gay freedom.

Souls still hunting in the mist at 4:00 in the morning. Bodies crushed anonymously in garages, on porches.

Revolutionary sex. The profligate sharing. And the beautiful choreography of the hunt. The silent dance.

And the instant alienation after sex.

Inherited attitudes, indoctrinated guilt.

Is it ever enough?

You asked that.

Nothing is enough, the saboteur insists. Depression

when the hunt pauses, just pauses. Your worth in the balance every moment, 100 triumphs wiped out by 1 rejection, stirring a purgatory of doubts, a hell. Sacrificed relationships. Sex always an ending, never a beginning. Times when you long for 1 instead of 20—will they become times when you long for 20 but never for only 1? Orgies that may— . . .

But don't have to!

. . . —cancel the possibility of love, the proliferation of promiscuity becoming a total lifestyle— . . .

Or an additional experience. The joyful high that only an abundance of sex can bring.

And a suicidal low when it fails. . . . Promiscuity alienating us from any other possibility, limiting us to one— . . .

One *and* many. . . . You said "us"!

. . . —sex *only* in groups, only with many, not ever, ever one to one— . . .

But still, at times, one to one.

. . . —and if so, mostly fragile connections. To enact fantasies— . . .

Merely dreamt by others.

. . . —thus to cancel identities. Always the possibility of a soulless reduction of bodies to limbs and orifices—all limbs, any orifice.

Orgies *and* relationships, both. Sex *and* love—one without the other, one with the other. Desire and love. Desire or love. *All* possibilities. That is the goal of the street revolution. . . . And now the outlaw strikes: And to destroy you, the saboteur.

With that, the saboteur attacks: Perhaps it will turn out that what you—we—call righteous revolution will be the straight world's ultimate revenge. Promiscuity as total deadend. A loveless sacrifice of all human contact. The ultimate in non-feeling and alienation.

You're wrong, the outlaw answers softly. Promiscuity is our noble revolt.

Prove it.

Only this way: Remove the outside pressures. Remove the imposed guilt. Then we'll find out. Then we can view our own homosexual world as *we* make it, not as the straight world's hatred *forces* it to be. Let that happen, and then we'll find out.

I resolve the clashing contradictions by joining the sexhunt in the streets.

11:44 P.M. *The Tunnel Near Sutton. Hollywood*
Boulevard. Selma. Santa Monica Boulevard.
Terrace Circle, Bierce Place, Greenstone
Park.

JIM IS ABOUT TO get out of his car to explore the tunnel near
Sutton when he hears a familiar tapping coming from
across the street. In his exposed apartment, the old, old,
emaciated man, naked, is again rapping on the window like
a used phantom. Jim drives away. Standing by the tunnel is
the same man he made it with Friday—or last night.

Upper Hollywood Boulevard. Outlaws line the street as
he walks it. "What's goin on?" "Cooling it, man." "Lot of
pigs out." . . . Often, like now on this street, Jim deliberately summons up memories, ghosts evoked at random from
the sexual mortuary of his mind. Sometimes he remembers
faces. Bodies. Even names. He knows he will remember,
always, the accusing man earlier in the parking lot.

Jim goes back to his car, drives around Selma, to
determine its vibrations before he gets out to walk, perhaps
to hustle. Suddenly, in his rear-view mirror, he sees a car
stop abruptly, motor left running just feet away from a
young hustler standing on a corner. Four doors fly open,
and five men jump out, kicking and punching the lone

hustler. Jim makes a swift U-turn. Two other hustlers on the street rush toward the scene. The five attackers jump laughing into their car and, lights turned off, speed away. Jim and the two others lean over the dazed hustler.

"I'll take you to the hospital," Jim offers.

The kid spits blood, but straightens up. "No, no, I'm okay," he insists, checking himself out. "Besides, the cops might hassle me there."

Jim knows he's right; and despite the savage intentions, the attackers didn't have enough time to hurt him seriously.

"Just—uh—give me a lift to Gardner, okay?" he asks Jim.

In the car, the kid says, "Fucking shits."

Jim experiences the same rage he feels at the marauding cops. He drops the kid off before a run-down apartment house. "Sure you're okay?"

"Yeah, thanks, thanks."

Driving away, Jim glances at the blood on the passenger seat. In all his years on the streets, through all the different phases of his street life—he has never felt more acutely the presence of violence and hate in the sexual arena.

Now he needs to wash away his rage. He drives to Santa Monica Boulevard. Near Andy's Coffee Shop he and a handsome man begin the slow choreography. Finally the two are together around the corner. Yes, Jim will go home with this man, he knows. Yes, and that will end this weekend, yes, and the hunt, he thinks suddenly, and, yes, that's okay.

"What are you into?" the man asks.

Jim feels a hint of disappointment; that question often indicates the search for something specialized. Or the man might be a vice cop.

"Depends. You?" Jim is deliberately evasive.

"Heavy S & M," the man answers.

Jim rejects it.

"Too bad, you look tough." The man crosses the street toward a mean-looking motorcyclist leaning sulkily on his bike. In minutes, the two roar off together.

On the corner, Jim sticks out his thumb, hitchhiking. For long minutes, no one stops. Doubts peck at him. But here's a car now. "You hustling?" the man asks Jim as they drive away.

Jim sizes up the man, attractive; certainly not into paying. "No, I'm not hustling."

"Too bad, I like only hustlers," the man says.

Jim gets out at Fairfax. He feels an increasingly empty aching. He hitchhikes back to Highland. Gets another ride back to Fairfax. Nothing. Back on Highland, he returns to his car and drives to the area of the costume bars.

No one in the alleys now.

Terrace Circle. A few cars cruise the blocks of pretty houses and new condominiums. Jim wants a close connection beyond what he's experienced all day today. He sees no one here he really wants.

Moments later he's standing on upper Santa Monica Boulevard near a strip of gaybars. Just standing. Not hitchhiking. A man stops his car; he's not especially attractive—ordinary. But Jim gets in, to push time.

"God, you've got a beautiful body! How old are you?"

Jim's heart freezes.

The man guesses—way below Jim's actual age.

The warmth flows.

Jim let the man blow him in the car for moments.

On Santa Monica Boulevard he walks back to his car. The restiveness grows. He drives back to Selma. Tonight this beloved street is being raided by ugliness: Two cops are frisking three hustlers, the spectacle framed harshly by the icy lights of the squad car.

Motherfuckers. Jim drives along Sunset Boulevard.

The hunt. Sunday night's hunt different from Saturday's, but almost as heavy, with the fresher waves of hunters who will be off tomorrow instead of Saturday. And Monday's hunt is different from Sunday's. Tuesday's, subdued. Wednesday's different from Thursday's, and Thursday's different from Friday's. The varying but unstopping cycle of sex in the city of lost angels, paused only once each day—vengefully—at dawn.

The Bierce Place garages. Two hunters draped in the darkness under a stairway. As Jim walks along the deserted alley, a car drives along the intersecting street. It stops. Jim waits. He hears a door open, close. The memory of the violent scene on Selma alerts his body for quick motion. Footsteps. He sees a shirtless man.

The same muscleman he left flexing in the bushes and then again earlier in the bar! And there he is posing again in the dark, expecting Jim to "reciprocate" in kind. Jesus, Jim thinks, we're practically lovers! ... For a moment, he considers pulling out his cock in overt invitation of sex; the other will then approach, and then they'll make it, yes, at home. But, no, that's clearly not the other's trip.

Driving to another dark alley. No one here, but within minutes the soundless dark may explode with moaning shadows.

Near Sutton, the man still guards his tunnel. Parking on another street, to avoid the old man rapping on the window, Jim walks into the gray cavity of the tunnel. But there is another man there too, and Jim moves away.

At Greenstone, several cars are parked in the concrete arc. Many hunters in the arena.

As Jim crosses the street toward the stone grotto, he sees the kid he made it with last night—Steve; they exchanged phone numbers, came so close. They both stop suddenly, facing each other. For a moment they seem about to smile, even to speak. They move slightly closer. Then simultaneously they turn from each other, walking away quickly in opposite directions.

VOICE OVER: *Attack!*

I SIT PARKED in my car in Greenstone Park. It's past midnight. I'm alone, these moments. The tide of hunters has flowed elsewhere for now. Soon, cars will drive up, and the hunt will resume as always.

I feel the presence of the night. So strange to be alone here now. When the hunt is raging, the darkness doesn't hang ominously on the trees, and you don't wonder how many shouts of loneliness the quiet stifles. You don't notice— . . .

A car is driving up the curve of the road, its lights carve sliding shadows out of the darkness before I see it. It passes mine slowly—two men in it—and then parks parallel to mine a few feet away in the concrete arc. Both men look at me and smile. Instinctively I start my car and begin to back up; I'm not sure why, because it isn't rare for hunters to cruise in pairs. The two look wrong, like plainclothes cops, relentlessly drab despite mustaches. If they are cops, they'll hassle me, ask me for I.D.; what are you doing here?—don't you know this is a queer park? I back my car up farther. Smiling even more broadly at me, the driver opens the door to get out. He's out of the car, a burly man in a sweater. Now they'll flash a light, badges, nag me with questions, knowing all along why I'm here.

Suddenly reality alters. The burly man is running at me with a bully club! His hateful face is frozen in a smile. I hear crazy broken laughter. The man on the passenger side has rushed out with his own raised menacing club. And he too is laughing loudly, the sound insane and roaring.

In a moment of thundering comprehension, I realize that I may be murdered by gay-haters who periodically raid sex areas. It has happened in this very park.

I continue backing up my car as quickly as I can on the one-way circle. But I can't maneuver fast enough in reverse in the declining arc. The two strange laughing forms, clubs poised to shatter windows and me, advance closer. In the cold flood of my headlights, they look like giant puppets raging out of control. The bodies thrust murderously toward me in striding gaits, elongated shadows askew and ugly. My car almost cascades down the side of the hill. I brake abruptly.

The evil dancing forms are almost on me. Smashed windows, bones— . . . !

The decision is made without thought. Only these moments, focused tightly in threatening closeup of them and me, exist. I shift the gears into forward, gun the engine, and plunge toward the bounding puppet forms. Will they try to jump my car? I dash forward. Don't let me run them down!—let them jump aside! No, not the crush of bones and spattering flesh!

I force myself to look straight ahead. I hear—feel— metal-tipped sticks crash savagely on the rear of my car.

Breathing again, but with a vision of gaping violence branded on my mind, I rush out of the park. But what of the other sexhunters who will soon be cruising this invaded area?

In a phone booth on the boulevard, I call the cops. Where did this happen? Silence when I answer; the cop knows it's a gay park. As soon as available, he'll send someone to talk to me where I am. No, not to me—to the park; that's where the threat is. The steely voice insists that I wait at the booth. Half an hour. Nothing. I realize he's not going to send anyone. I drive back to the park; maybe he sent the squad car there. No. I call again from the same booth. Okay, he'll send someone to where I am.

Fifteen minutes later a squad car arrives. Where did this happen? I tell them. They look hostilely at me. I insist they go there. Okay, follow them there and show them where the attack occurred. I return to my car, make a U-turn. When I reach the park—a familiar area suddenly turned ugly—the cops are flashing lights cursorily. I park where I was earlier, to wait for them to take my report, get a description, see the deep dents on my car.

Instead, reality is again challenged—as it will be still again in a few moments: The cop car makes a sharp U-turn into the wrong way of the one-way road and drives out of the park. I'm alone again in the menaced area.

I drive down the road, and—impossible!—at the bottom I'm intercepted by the car of the same two laughing men. Both spring out again with their raised clubs. I reverse, swerve around, and thrust my car dangerously into the boulevard. I drive to Western, where for weeks cops in twenty-four-hour shifts have been patrolling massage parlors in order to close them down. Can't leave their posts, a cop tells me. Besides, no crime actually happened!

I call the watch commander at police headquarters. Busy, a cop tells me; what's wrong? I tell him about the dual attack. I tell him that the maniacal men are still prowling the area.

A cold voice accuses from the telephone: "What were you doing in a queer park at midnight?"

1:06 A.M.   *Outside the Tool Bar.*

THE ABRUPT, SEVERED encounter with the youngman he was
with last night, even "worked out" with, sent Jim moodily
out of the park; he drove to the area of the costume bars.

Outside the Tool Bar, a man is standing by a motorcycle. Jim is attracted to him, despite the hint of a leather
costume; he knows that does not necessarily mean the
person is into S & M. Jim moves into a narrow corridor
between a locked office building and an unfinished house.
The motorcyclist follows him. "You wanna get fucked?" he
asks him in a low voice.

"No." Jim begins to move away.

"I do—by you."

"I would," Jim says, "but not out here." Not an overt
invitation, this is his way of suggesting an encounter at
home, without committing himself.

"No, let's do it here," the man insists. He begins to
unbuckle his pants. Now he reaches over and squeezes Jim's
nipples, tightly.

Suddenly turned off by the gesture, Jim pushes the man
away.

Back on the main street, Jim sees a car about to park on
a perpendicular side. But, seeing Jim, the driver makes a U-
turn to intercept him as he crosses the street. Pausing at the

intersection, motor running, he lets his hand dangle over the side of the car. Jim walks up to the window. In the back of the car another man, drunk or stoned, lies sleeping. The driver blows Jim briefly through the car window.

Jim resumes walking. Across the street an attractive man pauses. Jim waits, the man waits. Neither crosses to the other's side. Stalemate. Not even looking back, each walks away from the other.

Jim moves to a side street. In a darkened lot a man squats, mouth open ready to take a cock, any cock; an old desperate ugly man. Jim retreats from the huddled shadow.

Jim is in the yard of the unfinished house. A man is groping him clumsily. Now the man grabs Jim's hand and tries to force it on his cock, to have Jim play with him. But Jim is not attracted to him and he pulls his hand forcefully away. "You don't do anything back, huh?—well, fuck it! You're not that goddam good!" Instant enemies, they split.

Abandoned in the shadows, Jim remembers the angry man in the lot earlier. Then he thinks of Steve—the young bodybuilder he saw again minutes earlier in Greenstone. Yes, he would have gone with him again. If they had talked— . . .

1:23 A.M.   *Outside the Turf Bar. A Parking Lot. The Alley.*
   Still "Sunday night."
The bar at the corner will soon close, like the others. Already it's spilling outlaws into the night. The hot, hot spell may be about to break, there is the hint of a breeze. Dead palmtree leaves rustle. Mist is rising.

Shirtless, Jim goes to the cubicle in back of the locked building on the dark lot. Under the smashed lightbulb like a gaping mouth of shattered teeth, a cluster of men are pressed grayly. Jim walks on.

He sees a man leaning against a van. Pants down around his knees, shirtless, he's playing with himself. Jim walks through the thickening haze. The man calls to him in a whispery voice. Inside the van, both men lie on the floor. The man is goodlooking, tall. He removes Jim's clothes and his own.

Occasionally a passing shadow cuts the light entering through the van's window from the street. Footsteps prowl, alerted instinctively to the scene inside.

The man licks Jim's body, takes his cock in his mouth. Jim reaches for the other's cock. But the man rejects Jim's motion. "Just let me do everything," he tells Jim. Jim leans back, hands under his head. He hardly moves, an adored statue which the man is licking all over from fingers to feet. A face stares in through the van's window. Inside, the man jerks off.

Jim dresses. He walks out into the night. Once again, there is a momentary stasis in the hunt—like when the angry drunken youngman accosted him here earlier. The shadowy outlines stand unmoving against a gray sky.

Seconds later—the recurring spell again crushed by movement—the shadows search through the gathering mist.

2:08 A.M.   *A Deserted Part of the Beach.*

Impulsively Jim drove to the beach, speeding urgently along the almost empty freeway.

Despite the fog invading the city, at the beach the night is paradoxically starlit, a childhood-remembered night. The foggy cloud is moving inland from the darkness. Jim walks beyond the parking lot, cars cruising—parking, moving, stopping; walks beyond the craggy rocks; past dark sex-hunting ghosts standing along the sandy rim of the ocean; like the traumatized birds that stare daily at the coming night. Slowly, male forms emerge in sexual outlines, others lie on the moist beach. But this time Jim walks on, farther, until he's reached a deserted part of the beach. He stands at the very edge of the ocean. The breeze is cool on his bare chest. He's aware of the mystery concealed within night and ocean. The breeze is even cooler on his chest, but he continues standing here.

What secrets?

He walks back to his car without joining the shadowy hunt here.

VOICE OVER: *The Sexual Outlaw*

THEREFORE:

Promiscuous homosexuals (outlaws with dual identities—tomorrow they will go to offices and athletic fields, classrooms and construction sites) are the shock troops of the sexual revolution. The streets are the battleground, the revolution is the sexhunt, a radical statement is made each time a man has sex with another on a street.

What is it to be a sexual outlaw?

Archetypal outsider, he is a symbol of survival, living fully at the very edge, triumphant over the threats, repression, persecution, prosecution, attacks, denunciations, hatred that have tried powerfully to crush him from the beginning of "civilization": Each night after the hunt, the outlaw knows he's won an ancestral battle—just because he's still alive and free.

Only a tiny segment of the vast homosexual world, the outlaw world—secretly admired and envied but publicly put down by the majority of safe homosexuals cozy in heterosexual imitation—is not one easily chosen nor lived in, beautiful yet drenched in recurrent despair. Like the monastic life, it requires total commitment. It's a world one doesn't recruit for, must even warn against because of the dangers, risks, sacrifices the outlaw faces, takes, makes for his outlaw joy. One single encounter may bind him inextricably to the chain of insane repression—handcuffs, beatings, trials, jail. Daily, nightly, he confronts cops and maniacs.

But once chosen, it's a world that carries him to the pinnacle of sexual freedom—the high that only outlaw sex can bring—as well as to the abyss of suicide.

Because within the hunt is the core of the mystery. The search for what is *not* to be found. The search is the end. Not the answer—the riddle. The ultimate life-hunt, without object. Everything is found in nothing.

In the sex moments pressurized into high intensity by life-crushing strictures challenged, the sexual outlaw experiences to the utmost the rush of soul, blood, cum through every channel of his being into the physical and psychical discharge of the fully awakened, living, *defiant* body.

The greater the repression, the greater the defiance. Each time a mass sweep of outlaws occurs, promiscuous revolution increases across the very street raided. Board one place, we'll find two more. Block park roads into sexual arenas, and we'll discover better ones below. And we'll do it in Los Angeles, New York, Atlanta, El Paso, Dallas, New Orleans, St. Louis, San Francisco, Denver, Chicago—and Brownsville, MacAllen, Prairie Ridge, Waukegan, Morganfield, Twenty-Nine Palms.

Why is the amassing of money acceptable and not the amassing of sex experiences?—the first is hoarded, the latter shared.

Why may semi-nude men attack each other's bodies to the approving roar of spectators but not press them together in sex?

Why is the naked body forbidden?

Why may one touch a hand, openly touch lips—but not genitals?

Sex in the streets.

Reality or shock proposal?

On Hollywood Boulevard, Times Square, in the French Quarter, San Jacinto Plaza, Newberry Square, Market Street, throughout the country, throughout the world, at an appointed sun-bright time—let it be high noon—mass orgies! Televise it all, the kissing, the fucking, masturbating, sucking, rubbing, rimming, touching, licking, loving. Thousands of bodies stripped naked joined in a massive, *loving* orgy—and in Los Angeles, let it be on *our* boulevard, Hollywood Boulevard. Yes, and let it happen before the cops, right in front of them that we would fuck, with *joy*. Would the cops break ranks? Flee? Join?

Not an outrageous suggestion—we have seen filmed orgies before. Dachau. My Lai. Others.

Cum instead of blood. Satisfied bodies instead of dead ones. Death versus orgasm. Would they bust everyone? With cum-smeared tanks would they crush all?

Release the heterosexual pressures on our world—convert the rage—and you release a creative energy to enrich two worlds. Pressurize the homosexual world further, and it may yet set your straight world on fire.

And when the sexual revolution is won—*if it is ever won*—what of the fighters of that war? Doesn't a won revolution end the life of the revolutionary? What of the sexual outlaw?

One will mourn his passing.

2:42 A.M. *The Orgy Room.*

A FILTHY HALO of murky light hangs over the entrance room. Beyond the smoky scrim and into other rooms, masses of shadows churn, breathing.

Shirtless, Jim moves farther into the entrails of this one-story house—a "private club": At the door you show a membership card to one of the gay baths, pay "dues," sign another card, show I.D.

The darkness of the converted house parts as Jim moves into it. Against one wall a row of men stand, some shirtless, some almost naked, others totally naked, some fully clothed, several in leather costume. Huddled before them are other bunched figures, moving hungrily from cock to cock. The odor of amyl nitrite bursts recurrently.

Avoiding arbitrary hands inviting him into clustered bodies, Jim moves into another room. Figures float back and forth like somnambulists.

In a smaller room, three men, pants to their knees, stand before a bending man, naked from the waist down. His mouth arcs from cock to cock, his head directed roughly by a hand, another, another. Glued to him from behind—hands clutching him by the waist pulling the exposed buttocks back and forth—a dark man pushes his cock in and out. To the side, other men, cocks in hands, wait to replace the thrusting cock, just as other cocks replace those lined before the man's frenziedly moving face. Still others watch coldly as if at a movie, cocks in their own or in others' hands, cocks in others' mouths.

Tongues and hands surround Jim, who stands against another wall. He's not sure whether there are four or only three mouths shifting on his cock, balls, chest, under his arms, on his thighs, ass. Another mouth now. Even so, his cock will not harden. Has he come at all tonight? he wonders.

He looks across the dirty dimness and sees another cluster almost identical to his. At its center is another muscular man, also shirtless, standing surrounded by groping hands and licking mouths. The two look at each other. For a moment it seems to Jim that that man, standing like him and staring at him, is being devoured in ritual sacrifice and is seeing him, Jim, the same.

Jim pulls away. Bodies and mouths turn to others. Almost at the same time, the other man broke away too from the devouring cluster about him. His and Jim's eyes continue locked. The two men drift toward each other—but bodies flow between them, forming new groups about each.

Standing figures, kneeling figures. Entangled limbs. And the thick wordless silence. Jim swims through pools of flesh. Sucked. Rimmed. Sucked. Licked. The acts mechanical and cold, the sounds of frenzy almost forced, like sobs, not moans. He can no longer see the muscular man. A black-leathered man, no pants under his chaps, which are open in a circle in back, pushes his ass against Jim's cock; it's still soft. Instead of attempting to enter the ass, Jim directs the man's mouth to his groin. Blowing him, the man holds a vial of amyl for Jim to inhale. Not even the gathered rush of blood hardens his cock. He directs his soft cock into another mouth.

Jim moves into a smaller room. Red lights transform the shadows into fiery outlines—but within a cold, cold fire. In quick succession, several mouths take his cock, take others'. Now one mouth sucks his cock and another's simultaneously. But both cocks, pressed together in the hot mouth, are soft.

Leaving that room, moving back into one not as crowded, Jim sees the shirtless muscular man again. Again their eyes meet across the sexual battlefield. Again the two men move toward each other, are almost together—and again dark forms crouch before each—as if taking sides. Looking at each other, Jim and the other muscular man reach out slowly and touch hands. Jim feels his cock begin to harden. Their hands lock more firmly over the bobbing heads, the sucking mouths, the licking tongues.

Slowly, Jim breaks away, wanting the man to do so too, to follow him outside. Yes, he wants to leave, to go home— but not alone. Instantly Jim realizes he miscalculated; the man he wanted and who clearly wanted him has misinterpreted the severed contact as rejection. Not looking back, he moved away abruptly into another room. Jim is tempted to go to the same room—no, not to follow, no, but just to indicate that he didn't leave. But he knows the contact has been irrevocably cut.

Jim stands amid the churning, moaning, carnivorous mass. In an open restroom, a man—head leaning back on a toilet seat, mouth stretched widely—receives the piss of two men straddling him.

On the table in the main room, a skinny man lies totally naked with an inhaler of amyl glued to his nose. His thin legs are being held spread out widely by two leathered men; a third man, an ugly pock-faced figure in black gleaming leather, and wearing dark goggles and a vizored black cap, is methodically pushing his fist into the naked-man's ass. The straining arm pushes. Farther in. A portion of the wrist slides into the stretching hole. Farther. A portion of the lower forearm. The naked man is wet with sweat. Rapt, intent, others watch silently as if around an operating table. The wrist disappears. The naked man on the table lets out a howl of ecstatic pain.

Jim feels a sweeping disgust.

Outside, totally alone, he breathes the air purified by the earlier breeze. Recurring, the breeze rustles the palmtrees.

3:44 A.M. *Selma. Greenstone Park. Montana Street. Hanson Avenue.*

Selma. In the cooling night, still shirtless, Jim walked away from a man who thought he was hustling. He's not here to hustle; he's here because he knows that very late after the night's long hunt this street is cruised by those looking for only one person.

A goodlooking youngman in a sports car keeps circling the block and looking back at Jim; but the car only pauses, as if the driver is reticent to stop, afraid of the cops who just drove by, perhaps, or perhaps thinking that Jim is hustling. Impatient, Jim gets in his car and leaves this street. At Highland Avenue transvestites lean toward passing cars.

Jim goes to the area of Greenstone. A few cars circle the block. As he drives into the park, he notices that the youngman who cruised him earlier on Selma is driving in too. Jim continues into the park—he doesn't stop on the concrete arc, where other cars are. He drives instead around the circle and parks below the playground. He gets out. The sports car parks near him. Jim can see the driver more clearly now. Yes, he'll go home with him.

The youngman reaches out, groping Jim through the rolled-down window. "Not here," Jim offers his vague invitation to go elsewhere. Home. "Yeah," the other insists. "Let's do it here." He blows Jim through the window.

Pulling away after a few moments, Jim stands by his car, alone. He looks up at the skeletal playground on the sloping hill across the road.

A car approaches, lights bathing Jim momentarily. The car moves on. Now another. It too drives on. The tip of the questioning terror brushes Jim. But the first car returns, stops.

"You hustling?" a goodlooking man wearing a cowboy hat asks Jim.

"No—there's no hustling in this park!" There's a growing note of urgency in Jim's voice. He wants to end the night.

"Wanna make it at home?"

"Yes," Jim says. "I live nearby, follow me." His tense body relaxes.

"Just one thing," the "cowboy" calls out, "you don't mind a four-way, do you? I'm with a couple of friends down the road. We'll all make it."

"No, not into that now," Jim says. He doesn't want an orgy, not now. The man drives away. Jim walks across the road and up the hill to the playground. The skeletal merry-go-round looks dead.

Back on the road, he gets into his car and leaves the park. In the area below, cars are circling the blocks.

Jim is stopped at an intersection. Then he sees him: a strange, almost-hallucinatory figure in the darkness: an old, bent man—with dark sunglasses, color-tipped white cane tap-tap-tapping on the dry sidewalk. Is he really blind? If so, what is he doing outside at this hour? Tap, tap, tap, tap. The cane on the sidewalk begins to beat angrily. Tap! *Tap!* Suddenly Jim realizes that the strange night creature is advancing toward his car with the cane flailing fiercely.

Jim puts his car in reverse, U-turns, and drives away.

4:15 A.M.   *The Garage on Oak Street. The Tunnels. The*
            Garage. Greenstone Park. Montana Street.
            Hanson Avenue. The Garage.

There are several cars parked near the abandoned garage. Jim's headlights illuminate one of the stirring figures behind it. Not that. Not now.

Jim drives to the tunnels. A few men—leaving the after-hours bar nearby—are walking into the deserted street. Jim waits for long minutes in his car for the drifting attention to settle. Now he walks past the dark-yellow maw of one of the tunnels. He hears someone whisper to him, a hissing sound. He moves away. He returns to his car, drives back to Greenstone Park. Shadows linger along the trail. He doesn't want to join them. He drives out of the park, circles the block. No one. He returns to the area of the garage on Oak Street. He gets out. A goodlooking man stops his car a few feet away. As Jim approaches, the man opens the car door. Jim gets in. He looks at his watch—then at the driver of the car. Yes.

Jim says hurriedly: "I'm on my way home, I live just a few minutes away." Again he looks at his watch.

"You want some company?"

"Sure." The tension releases Jim's body. "My car's across the street."

"I'll follow you," the man says.

Jim breathes easily. And so the night will end softly.

Jim is opening the door to go to his car when the man says: "Can you get into heavy stuff?"

"Like what?"

The man's voice quavers. "Real heavy. You can get as rough as you like. You can— ..."

Jim gets out of the car. "Sorry," he says, "I'm not into that." For the first time ever, he notices the sound a car door makes as it closes.

He looks at the sky. The darkness barely lingers. He drives back to the garage. Even the stirring figures behind it are gone. Two cars are driving away. Another. Now another. Jim gets out. The street is deserted.

He stands before the garage.

A vague arc of light is illuminating the horizon. Now dawn lifts the night's shadows. All the hunters are gone, the streets are empty. He's alone. The dawning light increases. Sounds of traffic grow on the main boulevard two blocks away. The sun wipes away the dawn. Palmtree leaves lie yellow on the sidewalk. In the neighborhood across the street a door opens. A car starts. Voices.

Jim sees a truck stop along the block. An old man gets out. He gathers the fallen palmtree leaves and puts them in his truck.

Daylight bathes the garage behind Jim. Beyond, the roar of morning traffic increases. The sun is fully out.

Still shirtless from the night's hunt, Jim stares at the garage. At the crumbling walls, the peeling boards, the discarded cans, the broken bottles, the cluttered dry weeds, the tangled barbed wire.